LICENSE TO WED

License to Wed

What Legal Marriage Means to Same-Sex Couples

Kimberly D. Richman

NEW YORK UNIVERSITY PRESS

New York and London

NEW YORK UNIVERSITY PRESS
New York and London
www.nyupress.org

References to Internet websites (URLs) were accurate at the time of writing.
Neither the author nor New York University Press is responsible for URLs that
may have expired or changed since the manuscript was prepared.

LIBRARY OF CONGRESS CATALOGING-IN-PUBLICATION DATA
Richman, Kimberly D.
License to wed : what legal marriage means to same-sex couples / Kimberly D. Richman.
p. cm.
Includes bibliographical references and index.
ISBN 978-0-8147-2546-7 (hardback)
1. Same-sex marriage—Law and legislation—California. 2. Same-sex marriage—Law and
legislation—Massachusetts. I. Title.
KF539.R53 2013
346.74401'68—dc23
                          2013027470

New York University Press books are printed on acid-free paper,
and their binding materials are chosen for strength and durability.
We strive to use environmentally responsible suppliers and materials
to the greatest extent possible in publishing our books.

Manufactured in the United States of America

Also available as an ebook

For Richard

CONTENTS

At the core of any work of social science are the people whose story it tells. This one was inspired by a few groups of particularly brave individuals: the advocates and attorneys at GLAD, NCLR, Lambda Legal, Marriage Equality USA, Mass Equality, and elsewhere who have fought tirelessly for the rights of LGBT citizens; the public officials in local and state government who made same-sex marriage a reality, balancing efficiency and passion, bureaucracy and care, to make these marriages not only possible but memorable; and most importantly, the couples who followed their hearts, braving the elements, political backlash, and long lines to marry one another. I am particularly grateful to and inspired by the former mayor of San Francisco Gavin Newsom, the San Francisco deputy city attorney Therese Stewart, the former Cambridge city clerk Margaret Drury, the former Marriage Equality USA media director Molly McKay, the NCLR executive director Kate Kendall and its legal director Shannon Minter, Phyllis Lyon and the late Del Martin, the 1,467 couples who returned completed surveys, and the one hundred couples who agreed to be interviewed for this book, for their time, generosity, and bravery.

The data collection for this project was a multiyear venture, which would not have been possible without the support of the National Science Foundation Law and Social Science Program (Grant Award# SES-0453080), the University of San Francisco School of Arts and Sciences and (then) Dean Jennifer Turpin, Molly McKay and Geoff Kors of Equality California, the Cambridge County clerk's office, other anonymous individuals in both California and Massachusetts, and a bevy of diligent research assistants over the years: Eric Asmar, Leila Block, Ambar Collins, Christina Fernandes, Christina Hebets, Janice Jentz,

Kelsey Moskitis, Matt Olsman, Cristina Sinclaire, Sarah Takahama, Nicole Torres, and Erin Vuksich. I am very grateful as well for the assistance of Shona Doyle and Amy Joseph of the USF Sociology Department. I am also incredibly grateful to the USF Sociology Department chair Cecilia Santos and to Dean Marcelo Camperi for granting the leave that allowed this book to get written.

Several esteemed colleagues provided valuable feedback during the conceptualization and writing process, from the initial grant proposal through the completed manuscript. Among them, in no particular order, are Josh Gamson, Dan Pinello, Kitty Calavita, Kathleen Hull, Shannon Minter, Cliff Rosky, Jon Gould, Nancy Polikoff, R. M. Harris, K. T. Albiston, Joan Hollinger, Melissa Murray, Russell Robinson, Michael Musheno, Lauren Edelman, and Richard Leo. The writing process was nurtured by several supportive communities, most importantly the UC Berkeley School of Law Center for the Study of Law and Society, which hosted me as a visiting scholar during the 2011–2012 academic year; the USF writing warriors; and the entire staff at Samovar Tea Lounge in the Castro in San Francisco, whose warm welcomes, friendly conversation, and delicious offerings sustained me for months on end. I have been working with Deborah Gershenowitz and New York University Press since 2006 and could not possibly ask for a more supportive, professional, and likeable editor and publishing team. Debbie has provided me not only with invaluable advice on my writing but also the textbook model of what an ideal editor-author relationship should look like, and in the process has most likely spoiled me for life. I thank her for her insight, skill, encouragement, and friendship. I also thank Clara Platter for stepping in midway through the publishing process to see it to completion.

Finally, a moment of disclosure: A funny thing happened on the way to creating this book: I got married. While the two events were independent in that would both have happened without the other, getting married during the process of researching this book helped me to both appreciate the depth of what was at stake for the couples included in this project, and at the same time helped me understand and appreciate more intimately the unearned privilege I enjoy as someone who could marry the person of my choice at the moment of my choice. And indeed, it is my privilege to be married to a wonderfully supportive, generous, and patient scholar, collaborator, confidant, father, and husband, Richard Leo. I thank him and our two miraculous, adorably sweet, and hysterically funny daughters, Emily and Layla, for giving my life balance, meaning, and love.

It was Valentines' Day weekend 2004 when forty-eight-year-old San Diego resident Wes heard the news that they were letting same-sex couples get married in San Francisco.[1] His partner of twelve years, Craig, was out of town—but when he returned a few days later, Wes had an urgent proposal for him—he wanted to go to San Francisco to get married. Craig protested that they didn't have enough money—neither was working, and Wes, who was HIV positive and suffered painful blood clots and sores in his legs, had not yet gotten his Social Security check that month. Between them they had a hundred dollars to their name—driving in their old van, gas alone would cost more than that. But Wes was determined—this was a once-in-a-lifetime opportunity, a moment in history. So the two borrowed $100 each against their next month's Social Security and SSI checks, resolved to sleep in the van if need be, and headed north.

When they arrived, early on the morning of February 19, they found a line wrapped around City Hall. Wes and Craig waited in that line for eight hours, Wes's legs throbbing in pain, before being told that they would not be able to get married that day but to come back on Monday to make an appointment for a wedding sometime in March. This was not an option—even if Wes's health could withstand another trip, their finances could not. So the two parked their van at a rest stop at the end of the Golden Gate Bridge, got what little rest they could, and resumed waiting in line Sunday night—determined to make their case to the powers that be on Monday morning to let them marry on Tuesday. When their turn finally came to plead their case to the county clerk, Wes removed his bandages to reveal the sores on his leg—by this point they were infected and oozing—and explained that they could not afford to come back. The worker from the clerk's office retreated into his office to confer with his boss and emerged a few minutes later. "I have good news and bad news," he announced. "The bad news is, we cannot marry you tomorrow—we just have too many couples getting married tomorrow. The good news is, we're going to marry you today." "And we almost all just started crying," Wes said, "You know, it was kind of like a dream come true. I don't think any of us had felt that we would see a time in our lives when we were actually, you know, going to be legally, legitimately recognized just like all the other people there."

San Franciscans Pat and Terry, who met while working at a newspaper together, had also never seriously contemplated marriage as a reality in the course of their twenty-three-year relationship. Unlike Wes and Craig, however, they had never desired it either. In fact, they had never given much thought to formalizing their relationship in any form, but especially through the state, until Terry was diagnosed with breast cancer. By 2004, when Terry was in the throes of advanced stage cancer, the only protection they had in place was a legal order allowing Pat to see Terry in the hospital and make medical decisions for her. They did not consider themselves marriage equality "activists"—or activists of any sort—although in the past they had participated in San Francisco Pride's Dyke March. Terry had been a member of Daughters of Bilitis (the first lesbian organization in the United States), and they had lived up the street from its founders and lesbian-rights pioneers Del Martin and Phyllis Lyon. As Terry relates, "When I first came here from Ohio, it was a totally different experience. That was like 1970, I think, and you had to hide the fact that you were gay. You just did. If you didn't, you were in terrible trouble. There were police—I think they had stopped raids, but it still wasn't considered good form to be gay and you were looked on as funny-acting." Visibility and safety for gays and lesbians were important, then, to Terry and Pat, but not so much marriage. As Terry put it, "I've actually never really cared about it [marriage]. I mean, the public thing is sort of—in fact, I don't like to go to weddings except for the cake."

But something changed in February 2004. As Pat put it, "Well, we—I used to, sort of, half-seriously propose to Terry every year, and Terry sort of, very seriously, said no, because we both didn't want to do a public ceremony. I didn't believe in a marriage ceremony for us, and then, suddenly, this great mayor, who neither of us voted for, opens up the door." Even as the news coverage emerged of the first marriage ceremonies in San Francisco in February 2004, it did not initially occur to Pat and Terry to make their way to City Hall. Finally, something hit them, and Terry—the self-professed marriage critic—made the call. As Pat related, "It's San Francisco at its best . . . it was a happenin' place, so, of all people, it was Terry who said, 'Why aren't we down there?'" Pat described the scene as something between a protest demonstration and a celebration of unity: "And, you know, here we are in the grand rotunda of City Hall, and this wonderful man was our officiator, our deputy, whatever it was, with a couple friends with us, and surrounded by all these flowers from all over the world, people who just sent them to be in support of all of us, and then you walked out, and everyone would walk out, and everybody's cheering, so that, I think—I was terribly moved by it." Later she added, "We had no idea it would be spectacular. How historic it would be—and the warmth. That was the thing. In the middle of all the wonderful San Francisco celebration, it was terribly moving." Terry and Pat were under no illusion that the marriage license they were granted by the City and County of San Francisco in that winter of 2004 would be upheld in court—and they were not at all surprised when it was later invalidated by the California Supreme Court. But that did not change the personal and historical significance for them.

On the other side of the country, in Massachusetts, Garrett, who held a chief administrative position at Cambridge City Hall, was busy debating how and when the municipality would begin to implement the *Goodridge v. Massachusetts* Supreme Court decision, which had been issued the previous November, making Massachusetts the first in the United States to legalize same-sex marriage. Because of his professional duties and the practical civic implications of the decision,

Garrett didn't have much time initially to consider how it might touch his own life:

> I would say that my perspective was much more political in that being in the position I was in with the city of Cambridge, that the decision immediately for Cambridge has some political implications. . . . For me, I would say that that was more the case that I wasn't necessarily thinking about the personal implication. I mean I knew that it was a very important implication for our life.

Garrett, thirty-one, had met his partner Dean, thirty-two, eight years before over the Internet. They dated cross-country for awhile before moving in together when Garrett decided to move to Massachusetts to attend graduate school. Largely surrounded by progressive colleagues and communities, both Dean and Garrett had come out in college. Because of their knowledge of the law and Garrett's position, they soon became information points on *Goodridge* and its potential impact for their friends and acquaintances. As Dean recounted:

> Garrett would come home and share with me what had gone at the office, so to speak, which was also then going on in the national news, which was also going on in the state and local news. . . . So it was a very emotional time, and it was a time where we were seen as the experts amongst our peer and family group and so we were providing a lot of information to people and trying to correct which seemed to be an endless amount of misconception about what LGBT people did and did not have available to them prior to any decision and what it might mean in a best—or worst-case scenario as things move forward into different paths potentially.

Cambridge made the decision to begin issuing licenses to same-sex couples at midnight on May 17, and as the date drew near Garrett finally began to let the implications for himself and Dean sink in: "[I]n the weeks prior to opening City Hall at 12:00—the light moment for me I of their wedding ended up being a far more emotional moment than they had anticipated. Yet the couples varied significantly in their orientation to marriage: going into it, their expectations, life experiences, and goals. Pat and Terry came from the second-wave feminist lesbian tradition of resisting marriage not only as a vestige of heteronormativity but as an unnecessary intrusion of the state into private lives. Their formative years were ones in which they could be physically endangered by their status as lesbians, were it to become public. Only when the need for end-of-life protections arose in the context of Terry's illness did they take steps to formalize their relationship. Still, they did not marry for legal or medical benefits, as they had no expectation that these benefits would accrue to them after their City Hall marriage. Dean and Garrett, of a younger generation and a social climate that allowed them each to come out comfortably at a relatively young age, never questioned the value of marriage or whether it was something they felt they were entitled to. As residents of a state that did not already offer comprehensive domestic partnership benefits, they sought the protection of law, in light of their plans to soon adopt children. But they also attributed great emotional and civic meaning to their experience. Wes and Craig—who went to great financial and physical lengths to marry—never questioned the desirability of marriage, but they also never believed it would happen in their lifetime. Like more than half of the same-sex couples surveyed for this book, they had already had a wedding ceremony of their own years before, and like all same-sex couples in California, they had the state's relatively comprehensive domestic partnership law at their disposal.

So why were Wes and Craig willing to risk their finances and health to drive eight hours, then wait another eight hours on line on two separate occasions just to get married at San Francisco's City Hall? And why did they, Pat and Terry, and four thousand other couples from all over the country—and some from other countries—flock to San Francisco to do the same during what has now been called the "Winter of Love"? What is it about state-sanctioned marriage that sets it apart, both from other analogous legal institutions (such as domestic partnership) and from personal wedding rituals without the state's sanction? Finally, how does access to the legal institution of marriage—and, conversely, *lack* of access to it—affect same-sex couples like Wes and Craig, or Pat and Terry, or Dean and Garrett, and what effect does it have on their view of marriage and the law, and their sense of civic engagement and belonging?

These are some of the key questions raised—and answered—in this book. Clearly, as is the case in heterosexual communities, not all same-sex couples get married for the same reasons—and its effects on them are not uniform. But until relatively recently, almost all of the litigation and political maneuvering to gain the right to same-sex marriage was framed as an issue of equal rights, and included a refrain about the hundreds upon hundreds of legal and financial benefits and responsibilities denied to couples who are not allowed to marry. This suggested that access to these rights was the main motivation behind both the movement and the individuals seeking marriage. Indeed, few people would choose to dispense with those rights, which include anything from filing a joint tax return to hospital visitation to inheritance rights and child custody. However, as one attorney who was centrally involved in litigating the marriage cases in California confided, "We initially relied heavily on rights-based arguments, but realized fairly early on that very few people, gay or straight, view marriage primarily as a way to get rights and benefits." Indeed, the hundred interviews and more than fourteen hundred surveys analyzed for this book reveal that this is only one of many—and indeed *not* the primary—reason couples from coast to coast and around the world have sought legally sanctioned marriage.

In this book I share the stories of these couples, their reasons for marrying, their perceptions of marriage and law, and the effects of marriage on their lives, through the lens of the concept of legal consciousness, and, to a lesser extent, the newly emerging literature on law and emotions. Although the temptation is to neatly list the top two or three reasons why the right to marriage is important to those who seek it, as one is forced to do in litigation, I found that such a temptation belies the complexity of both the meaning of marriage and the legal consciousness of those seeking it.

Like most other San Franciscans, I woke to the shocking news on February 12, 2004, that our newly elected mayor Gavin Newsom—the conservative candidate by San Francisco measures—had taken the extraordinary step of directing the county clerk to revise the marriage license form to be gender neutral and had invited, at the suggestion of National Center for Lesbian Rights Director Kate Kendall and others, lesbian-rights pioneers Del Martin and Phyllis Lyon to be the first same-sex couple to file an official marriage license in the City and County of San Francisco. Soon thereafter, there were throngs of expectant and exuberant couples forming lines in and around City Hall, often in the pouring rain, to do the same. Although I was writing about other aspects of LGBT family law at the time, I quickly donned my researcher hat, grabbed my two research assistants, a clipboard with paper, and a digital camera, and headed down to City Hall. I started methodically making my way through the line, casually observing and talking with couples as they waited their turn. What occurred to me was that despite a relative lack of racial diversity—a large majority of couples married in San Francisco were Caucasian—there was extraordinary diversity in the way couples talked about marriage and why they were there.

Almost immediately I was reminded of Patricia Ewick and Susan Silbey's landmark study of legal consciousness, *The Common Place of Law*. This 1998 study exposed and examined the multitude of forms of legal consciousness among average citizens and how they are implicated in an individual's actions, attitudes, problem-solving mechanisms, and ultimately their vision of legality and legal institutions. Clearly, in my chats with waiting soon-to-be-married couples, I heard a refrain about the validating power of law and their sense of full inclusion as a result of being allowed to marry. But I also heard from people who already felt married in their hearts and simply wanted the same rights that straight married couples have, as well as from those who had no expectation of either legitimation or legal rights but felt it was an important form of visibility and protest to be there. And of course, there were couples who were there for nothing more or less than the romance of a "cold, wet, sleepless, date," as one couple put it, which also happened to be a moment in history.

The position of these couples was complicated considerably when the California Supreme Court invalidated their marriages later that year—a course of legal developments to be discussed in more detail in chapter 2. But it soon became clear that because the experience in San Francisco was bound to not be "typical"—if that word could be applied to any same-sex marriages in the mid-2000s when this study began—it would be necessary to examine the experience and attitudes of same-sex couples married elsewhere. And, at that moment in U.S. history, "elsewhere" meant Massachusetts. Thus began the several year-long research project that would form the basis for this book—ultimately encompassing the viewpoints of over three thousand individuals—1,467 couples surveyed and one hundred couples interviewed. What follows does not do justice to the life experience or even current depth of opinion of each one of those individuals; nor does it tell us anything conclusive about the LGBT community as a whole, since those who do not seek to be married for one reason or another are necessarily excluded. But I believe that it does get us closer to understanding the social meaning of legal rights for LGBT citizens and what is at stake for the thousands of same-sex couples who have sought legal marriage across the United States.

1

Introduction

Situating the Meanings of Marriage

In a small, little-known museum amid the storefronts on a side street of one of the United States' most famous "gay-borhoods," stands an odd display: among the political signs, photos, handbills, and other histori- cal paraphernalia are two women's pantsuits, one a vibrant turquoise blue and the other a deep shade of lilac. The outfits are unremarkable in most ways and would be equally at home in the aisles of JC Penney. But here in the Castro district of San Francisco, in the GLBT (Gay, Les- bian, Bisexual, and Transgender) History Museum, these pantsuits are instantly recognizable: they are relics of history, having been donned by two octogenarians and captured in photographs instantly beamed around the world. These pantsuits are the wedding attire of Phyllis Lyon and Del Martin, founders of the lesbian rights movement and, later, emblems of marriage equality in the United States, as the first same- sex couple to be married in San Francisco City Hall in February 2004, and again in June 2008. Although their 2004 marriage, performed at the invitation of then-mayor Gavin Newsom and under the watchful eye of a close coterie of City Hall officials and lesbian, gay, bisexual, and transgender (hereafter, LGBT) rights figures, would eventually be annulled along with the other 4,036 licenses obtained that winter, the image of their first putative moment as spouses—heads leaned together and a knowing, contented gaze into each other's eyes—became synonymous with the movement that it helped to propel. It is no accident that when they did become legal spouses in 2008—after more than a half-century together and a successful litigation process—they did so in the very same building, wearing the very same pantsuits, by now having cemented their place in history.

That the image of marriage equality embedded in many people's minds would be a couple who did quite well as life partners before marriage came along—in part because of their own and others' activism on behalf of LGBT individuals everywhere—is striking in a few ways. Phyllis Lyon and the late Del Martin, by this point in their lives—having survived decades of societal ignorance and anti-gay bias, and inspiring countless others to activism—lived comfortably in San Francisco's idyllic Noe Valley neighborhood. They were long since established as a couple to those who knew them, and they had never sought to be married. Their only child, Del's daughter from a prior marriage, was a grown woman with children of her own. As Lyon commented at the time, "We were happy to be able to do it, to show that it was do-able. But it's not going to make a lot of difference in our lifetime."[1] This couple differed in many ways from the namesakes of the Massachusetts case legalizing same-sex marriage just months before in November 2003, Hilary and Julie Goodridge. They had a young child together and had no other secure and comprehensive way to legally bind themselves to one another under state law. All four women no doubt benefitted in very real, tangible ways when they were finally recognized as legal spouses. But none took the plunge—a far steeper and more closely scrutinized one than the average couple getting married—for *only* that reason.

In this book I examine the significance of legal same-sex marriage for those couples seeking it in Massachusetts and San Francisco—the first two jurisdictions to offer it. The two settings, though alike demographically in some ways as coastal, historically Roman Catholic, and traditionally liberal enclaves, provide an important set of contrasts for the study of same-sex marriage and the impact of new rights on historically marginalized citizens. Most obvious of these was the process to obtain these rights and their legal longevity. While the 2004 San Francisco marriages were the result of an act of defiance on the part of a local government and its officials, never gained the authorization of the state, and were ultimately successfully challenged in court, the Massachusetts marriages were solidly legal from the start—having been authorized by the highest law of the land in that state, the Massachusetts Supreme Judicial Court. Although attempts were made subsequently to ban same-sex marriage by constitutional amendment, this effort never gained enough traction to change the legal landscape in Massachusetts. The couples in San Francisco, having been through the roller coaster of receiving marriage licenses from their county only to have them annulled six months later, were again given the opportunity to marry—this time fully legally—in 2008. And again, six months later, they watched as the voters banned any future same-sex marriages in their home state. This time, at least, after additional litigation, couples were allowed to keep their marriage licenses. So tortuous was the path that a major California newspaper ran an ad, featuring a set of male newlyweds, with the caption: "Married. Unmarried. Married. Everything Changes, Every Day." An additional aspect of the legal landscape, which bears repeating here, is the existence of a statewide Domestic Partnership law in California. This law carried many of the state-level rights of marriage in 2004 during the initial weddings, and nearly all of those rights by 2005 when the couples were interviewed. No such law existed in Massachusetts. This distinction in legal status between the two populations—not to mention the experience the San Francisco couples had of being given a right only to have it rescinded—are important points of contrast that help to broaden the scope of inquiry and illustrate the multifaceted significance and impact of legal rights, and their absence, on these citizens.

What is it about same-sex marriage that proves so compelling that partisans on either side are willing to stake millions of dollars on

advancing their positions on it? Why are couples who have no particular desire or need for the protections it offers—an incomplete set of
protections since they were not recognized at the federal level—willing to go to great time investment, legal, and even geographical lengths
to pursue it? And what is it about same-sex marriage that its approximation in both ritual form (through commitment ceremonies) and
legal form (through civil unions) is for many couples somehow not the
same? These questions strike at the heart of one of the most enduring
themes of law and society scholarship—the relationship between legal
institutions and social relations as well as personal consciousness—in
the context of what is perhaps the most hotly contested social and political issue of the early twenty-first century.

I wrote this book during a particularly eventful period in the evolution of legal same-sex marriage in the United States. Only weeks before
its completion, President Barack Obama, after three years of avoidance,
became the first sitting president to publicly state his support for the
right to same-sex marriage. The reasons he cited for his shift, mainly
conversations with his family and interaction with his daughters'
friends' same-sex parents, were notably *personal* rather than exclusively
legal or political. At the same time, it was a decidedly political move in
its way and had the potential to indirectly shift the legal landscape—
and indeed, the landscape did shift dramatically just over a year later,
when the U.S. Supreme Court invalidated both Prop 8 and the Defense
of Marriage Act. The multiple dimensions of these events foreshad-
owed an important element of the focus of this book. *License to Wed* is
not the first to document the legal consequences of same-sex marriage
(or its denial), the politics of the debate, nor the social or emotional
dimensions of such a ritual of commitment for same-sex couples. By
examining both the motivations and the reactions of couples who married in two distinct locales in the early years of legal same-sex marriage
in the United States, however, it takes as its subject the intersection of
these various elements: the legal, the social, the political, and the personal. In analyzing same-sex couples' reasons for seeking legal marriage
(as opposed to another form of legal relationship recognition, such as

domestic partnership, or a non-legal wedding ritual, such as a commitment ceremony), we gain a window onto the couples' legal consciousness—in other words, how they orient to, understand, and use the law. Combining these narratives of motive and orientations to law with a look at the perceived changes couples and individuals report as a result of legal marriage tells a compelling story about the effects of inclusion in—and exclusion from—the institution of marriage. Taken together, these insights offer a unique perspective on both the newest twist to an old institution, and the social significance of legality and rights more broadly.

Description of the Study

Rather than relying on secondhand accounts or briefs filed by legal advocacy organizations on either side of the debate, the explicit aim is to engage the words of the couples themselves in discovering and clarifying the personal, symbolic, material, and legal relevance of marriage for them, the meanings it evokes for them, and its effects on their lives. With that in mind, the analysis here is based on two forms of original data: (1) a database of 1,467 surveys (including both quantitative and open-ended qualitative questions) of same-sex couples married at San Francisco City Hall during the Winter of Love in February and March 2004; and (2) one hundred semistructured, in-depth interviews with same-sex couples married in San Francisco and Massachusetts (fifty in each locale) between 2004 and 2007.[2] The surveys were mailed in early 2005 to every same-sex couple who registered a marriage license at San Francisco City Hall from February 12 to March 11, 2004, based on a list of public marriage licenses available through the San Francisco assessor-recorder's office, obtained via the advocacy group Marriage Equality California. Approximately 40 percent of the more than four thousand surveys were returned at least partially completed, although some of these were excluded due to excessive missing data. These anonymous surveys included demographic data (such as gender, age, race, religion, residency, profession, income, and family size) as well as attitudinal data (such as the couples' political orientations, reasons for wanting to get married, and reactions to the annulment of their licenses). The raw data from the survey were coded and entered both in qualitative and quantitative form in a comprehensive database, with particular attention paid to include verbatim any comment or qualification a participant might have added to his or her answers. Although the unit of analysis was the couple, space was provided on each survey for both members to include their own demographic information and feedback. Therefore, in the relatively rare cases that couples had vastly differing motivations for marrying, they were able to indicate this in their comments on the survey, which were in turn recorded in the database. Those questions I deemed the most analytically important, such as couples' motivations for marrying, were asked in multiple ways—both as closed-ended Likert-type ratings on a one-to-five scale, and in open-ended qualitative questions—in order to triangulate the results and increase reliability. Once all of the information was gathered, entered, and coded, the survey data were analyzed statistically, primarily descriptively but also in some cases with simple correlational tests.

A brief descriptive snapshot of the surveyed couples, based on this data, reveals a population that was not dissimilar demographically from what we know about the overall population of those who married in San Francisco in 2004—and along several dimensions, with what we know about the overall same-sex married population in California.[3] These demographics depict a stable, professional, older set of people, largely female, with long-standing relationships. Of the more than 2,900 respondents included in the 1,467 surveys returned, ages ranged from twenty to eighty-two, with the average age being forty-four. This is significantly older than the average age of heterosexual couples at the time of marriage (twenty-seven for women, twenty-nine for men). Couples had been together anywhere from three months to forty-seven years (with an average of eleven years)—much longer than the average heterosexual couple before they marry (for obvious reasons, due to their previous lack of access to the institution).[4] Household income ranged from $10,000 per year to $1.8 million per year, with an average combined income of $140,000 per year. Forty percent of these couples were male, 59.5 percent were female, and 0.5 percent identified as "other" or transgender.[5] Thirty-six percent of the couples had children (anywhere from one to eleven per family).

These marriages were largely a Caucasian phenomenon, with 88 percent of respondents identifying as such (the second largest racial identification was Latin@ or Chican@ at 4 percent, followed by mixed race, at 3.5 percent).[6] The range of their educational attainment was from eighth grade to postgraduate and higher (e.g., a PhD and JD or other advanced degree), with an average educational attainment of seventeen years of schooling—equivalent to a four-year bachelor's degree. Although the majority of married people lived in northern California (nearly 73 percent), couples also came from twenty-seven states as well as one foreign country (Nicaragua), mainly from urban areas. Perhaps predictably, a little under half (43 percent) identified as agnostic or atheist, while the largest single religious affiliation was Christianity or Unitarian at 22 percent (this included all Protestant denominations and such gay-inclusive churches as the Metropolitan Community Church ("MCC"), as well as Unitarian/Universalists). Significantly, 70 percent were already registered domestic partners either in the state of California or their home state, and 55 percent had already had (non-legal) wedding or commitment ceremonies on their own.[7] This meant that most of the couples seeking legal marriage already had access to the *rights* associated with marriage (at least at the state level), and many had already experienced the *ceremonial* aspect of marriage.

For the second phase of the research, interviewees were recruited in a number of ways. In San Francisco, they were primarily recruited via the survey; in an optional last page of the otherwise anonymous survey, they were given the opportunity to fill in their name and contact information for consent to be contacted for an interview. A few remaining couples in San Francisco or in the Bay Area were recruited via word of mouth. In Massachusetts, interviewees were initially recruited through advertisements in a major LGBT newspaper in Massachusetts as well as through references from San Francisco couples. Subsequent couples were recruited by a combination of snowball sampling and mailings, with the assistance of one of the major same-sex marriage advocacy organizations in the state as well as some of the county clerks in heavily LGBT areas of Massachusetts. The demographic characteristics of the interviewees were slightly more evenly distributed than in the survey but were still skewed toward a largely middle-class female, Caucasian population: 55 percent were female, 75 percent were white, 23 percent were interracial, one couple Latina and one Asian American.

The one hundred interviews occurred after the original 2004 San Francisco marriages were invalidated by the California Supreme Court and before the same court's later decision to legalize same-sex marriage in 2008.[8] This allowed the respondents from San Francisco to reflect on not only the experience of having received a marriage license but also having had it rescinded. Admittedly, it may have also led them to color their reflections on their initial marriage in light of subsequent events. However, most couples, when pressed in the interview, were able to parse out what had been their thoughts and motivations at the time and how their thoughts had evolved in the time since. The elapsed time also had the benefit of ensuring that these couples—interviewed in the comfort of their own homes, away from television reporters—did not feel pressure from the advocacy community or anyone else to bias their responses in ways meant to benefit the cause or "greater good." I also did brief follow-up interviews with those couples in the summer and fall of 2008 in order to find out whether they had subsequently gotten married once it was legalized, and whether their attitudes had changed in the intervening time.[9] The initial interviews ranged in length from thirty minutes to two hours and fifty-three minutes, with an average of just under one-and-a-half hours. Whenever possible, the interviews were done in person, with both spouses present. All but twenty-seven of the one hundred interviews were conducted in person (with equal numbers from each state occurring in person versus over the phone), and all but nineteen were interviewed as a couple.[10]

In an effort to make the Massachusetts interviews as comparable as possible to those in California, I asked the interviewees there for the same demographic and attitudinal information that had been included in the surveys of San Francisco couples, including Likert ratings on a scale of one to five for the various motivations for marrying about which I questioned both sets of couples. In addition, I asked all of the couples about their respective coming-out experiences and about their history as a couple, including how they met, when they moved in together, whether they had ever had a marriage-like ritual of any sort (or even exchanged rings), and about their family configurations. These interviews were then transcribed and searched systematically for analytical themes, especially those relating to the couples' reasons for getting married, the types of legal consciousness they suggested, and the perceived changes in their relationship—or any other changes—as a result of marriage.[11] Some interviewees also provided me with additional materials, including wedding photos, newspaper and magazine articles, their own reflections written at the time of the wedding, and vows, readings, or other portions from their ceremony.

Taken together, these multiple sources of data provide us with a compelling portrait of those same-sex couples seeking marriage—whatever their reason—in the earliest years of its legal existence in the United States. Admittedly, it does not tell us much about the many same-sex couples who choose *not* to seek marriage, except to the extent that some of the individuals surveyed and interviewed for this study had never expressed a desire to marry before presented with the opportunity and, in fact, had been somewhat hostile to the notion of marriage. Nonetheless, the task of this book is to examine the myriad ways and reasons those who do seek marriage conceive of it, why they choose to pursue it, what it means to them and in their lives, and how varying conceptions of legality are reflected (or not reflected) therein.

Legal Consciousness and the Constitutive Perspective

This book is theoretically grounded in the sociolegal concept of legal consciousness and constitutive studies of the meaning and role of law in social life. Legal consciousness has many definitions, but here it is defined as the way that people understand, experience, engage, use, avoid, or resist law and its manifestations, whether in particular moments or on a regular basis in their everyday lives. This tradition of sociolegal scholarship builds on the foundations of both empirical studies of the legal needs of the poor in the 1960s and 1970s, and the school of Critical Legal Studies, which in the 1970s and 1980s sought to expose and explore the oft-present gap between the "law in the books" and the "law in action." These "gap studies" revealed that the workings of "law on the ground"—that is, in day-to-day settings, in courtrooms, in workplaces, and in local disputes—were much different in practice from the idealized image of law as it is written formally. Specifically, formal civil rights conferred by the U.S. Constitution, in legislation, or in case law did not necessarily translate into equality in the day-to-day lives of citizens. This led law and society researchers to question the doctrinal study of law and rights, and to instead focus on the would-be rights-bearers themselves, their experiences in the legal context, how they viewed the place of law in their lives, and how or when they tended to invoke it. In the words of one of its founders, Susan Silbey, the project of this generation of law and society scholarship was to

> show how the lived experiences of ordinary people produced simultaneously open yet stable systems of practice and signification; to demonstrate how the law remained rife with variation and possibility; and to explore how we the people might simultaneously be both authors and victims of our collectively constructed history.

This understanding of "law in action" or "law on the ground" served as the basis for a growing body of research in the field of law and society that advanced the view that legality—in particular, legality involving civil rights—is constructed in interaction between the social world and the legal world. This perspective has been named the "constitutive" perspective because it takes the theoretical position that law and society are mutually constituted in interaction, when citizens act on and react to law (whether expressly or subtly, knowingly or unknowingly), and vice versa. Most studies adopting this framework have, true to their roots, aimed to draw attention to the *social* end of this equation—noting that the law "in the books" is not always the way law is lived or experienced socially in the everyday lives of citizens. Sociolegal scholar Michael McCann, for instance, shows how even when workers' rights are not formally implemented in ways that better the lives of citizens, the value that people attach to rights in their day-to-day lives, thoughts, and conversations is significant in itself, helping to constitute those rights by imbuing them with symbolic currency.[12]

Subsequent sociolegal scholarship has shown that legal consciousness can be diverse, fluid, situation-specific, and even contradictory. That is, one may believe that the courts and legislatures are responsible for providing everyone with equal access to marriage but also simultaneously believe these institutions are not responsible for providing equal access to health care, for instance. Because "[l]egality is among the rules and interpretive frameworks 'that operate to define and pattern social life,'" legal consciousness may even influence how people think of social institutions such as marriage—and vice versa—in their own lives, and how they conceive of social change.[13] Furthermore, as McCann notes, legal consciousness is "necessarily heterogeneous in character"—since every actor brings a different social position, history, and set of beliefs and experiences, different people may come to experience and understand the law in a multitude of ways—or, as he puts it, "to speak law in multiple dialects."[14] Therefore, "[w]hile legal consciousness structures the efforts of citizens to make sense of social relations, it thus dictates no particular course of action."[15] The study of legal consciousness may help to understand not only support for but also resistance to changing concepts of marriage, or domestic relational rights in general, by both citizens and lawmakers. It may also help to understand why some people will choose to invoke their right to marriage (or other institutions), and others will not.

Rather than emphasizing the difference between "rights-giver" and "rights-bearer," the constitutive perspective aims to disrupt this binary by conceiving of rights and legality as constructs that are given meaning in the back-and-forth processes of enacting law and acting upon it (or resisting it). In this case, the act of marrying is one-half of the constitutive process that gives meaning to the state's decision to extend—or revoke—marriage rights. This book takes as its primary focus people's reasons for seeking legal marriage and what they hoped it would bring to them. These reasons help to elucidate LGBT citizens' legal consciousness—as defined previously, how people understand or relate to law and legal constructs (or don't)—and how they rationalize their actions vis-à-vis the law. Because the study of any type of rights or legal mobilization is incomplete without an understanding of why, how, and when people act on law or resist it, a focus on the legal consciousness of citizens is of central theoretical importance. Because such an understanding tells us how, when, and why marginalized groups will act on or use the legal rights available to them—or, conversely, react against or try to change those laws they view as unfair—it is of practical importance as well. As political scientist Kristin Bumiller notes in *The Civil Rights Society*, "rationalizations are important because people act on them."[16] Thus, changes in legal consciousness based on particular experiences greatly impact citizens' sense of civic inclusion, confidence, and their personal and social interactions.

This analysis of legal consciousness, as illustrated in the narratives of couples seeking the new right to marry, draws on the insights of Patricia Ewick and Susan Silbey, who, in their book *The Common Place of Law*, give a detailed account and analysis of the range of legal consciousness among regular citizens in their day-to-day lives. Based on their findings in a variety of settings, they offer a series of "stories" that form a template of types of orientations vis-à-vis the law: (1) *Before the law*—meaning that the citizen orients to the law as a subject would to a sovereign, detached from it but subservient to it; (2) *With the law*—meaning a citizen sees oneself as an active participant who can "play the game" of law, manipulating it to serve his/her instrumental needs; and (3) *Against the law*—where the citizen sees the law as an opposing force against which he or she engages in struggle and resistance or avoids altogether. Although my aim here is not to replicate their findings, this set of schemas provided a useful framework for initially thinking about how the couples I spoke to orient to the law and its role in their lives. Indeed, I heard quite clearly voices of resistance, utilitarianism, and reverence, which allowed me to begin to sort and group couples' reasons for seeking legal marriage according to the type of legal consciousness that their narratives seemed to demonstrate. Inevitably, there is some degree of difference in how these modes of legality were conceived and described, in part because the "troubles" that Ewick and Silbey asked their participants about were far more diffuse and process-based than the relatively life-changing and distinct experience of getting married— not only a process but a change in *status*. But significant parallels can be made regardless. In the context of same-sex marriage, very similar to a "before the law" orientation, one set of narratives implied a deference to the law and often a search for validation or legitimation (these might be called "symbolic" or "civic" reasons for seeking marriage). Another, closely paralleled with the "with the law" schema, evinced a hope to use the law to achieve certain practical or material ends, such as legal or financial rights and responsibilities (what might be called instrumental motivations). While an "against the law" orientation might more intuitively assume *resisting* legal marriage itself or otherwise eschewing it, in this case a third schema viewed the use of marriage as a protest, gay rights statement, or tapped into some other political or oppositional motivation.

After an initial piloting of the survey and through discussion with the couples to be interviewed, I found that some of the narratives voiced by the couples displayed none of these orientations. There was, in addition to these other voices and stories, an unmistakable voice of romance, which did not quite fit with the tripartite model of legality, but rather expressed motives that were seemingly external to the law and legality—they were neither strategic, nor reverent, nor resistant. They were instead aimed at purely emotional, personal, or romantic drives. While it is not surprising that marriage would be a mechanism for attaining these things, it is not entirely intuitive why *legal* marriage, even without ceremony, was a necessary component to satisfying these drives or produce these benefits. This can only be understood by first taking seriously—as Silbey has urged—the hegemonic power of law, and the way that it infuses human relations, even in barely perceptible ways.

Although hugely influential, the tripartite model of legal consciousness offered by Ewick and Silbey—and applications of it since—have also been the subject of critique, even by the authors themselves. Some, such as the observation that the schemas were not distinct enough to separate into a tripartite model, were addressed by the authors themselves, who noted the importance of understanding these differing modes of legality as intertwined, and the legal actors who invoke them as polyvocal. Other critiques, that the three schemas they use are not universal but rather may vary in not only presence but intensity according to substantive domain and social positioning, have since been addressed by scholars in the next wave of legal consciousness scholarship. Multiple authors since have shown how legal consciousness varies—or does not vary—according to race, class, gender, occupation, political affiliation, and setting. The most devastating critique, however, was leveled by Susan Silbey herself, who in 2005 declared that legal consciousness, in more recent studies, had lost "the concept's critical edge and theoretical utility."[17] She argued that this was due to differing definitions of legal consciousness, an overemphasis on individuals and particular groups rather than the broader cultural production of legality and resistance, and a tendency of studies to be "empiricist to a fault"— missing the forest for the trees. The result was a loss of focus on law's sustained power and hegemony, whose explanation were ostensibly the goal of the conceptual turn to begin with.

In response to this sweeping critique, sociologist Kathleen Hull offered a path for resuscitating the field of legal consciousness and pointed specifically to studies of legal consciousness among the lesbian, gay, bisexual, and transgender population to demonstrate how this might be accomplished.[18] Using a sort of meta-analysis of the small field of empirical studies of LGBT individuals' sociolegal subjectivities employing the concept of legal consciousness, she demonstrated how the paradigm still retains utility in examining the experience of marginalization in this population and potentially in others. Responding to Silbey's call for greater attention to institutional factors and political environments, for example, Hull points to a convergence in her previous work and my own on same-sex marriage and marriage rituals, which suggest that changes in the political context (for example the considerable shift in the legal landscape that occurred between Hull's pre-*Goodridge* study and this book) significantly affect same-sex couples' experiences, goals, and visions of legality. She also notes the importance of continuing to look at gender and sexual minorities who, despite variation within the LGBT population and across states, "continue to experience significant differential treatment in the law on the books, for example by lacking access to legal partnership recognition." This is a noteworthy departure from the foundational "gap" studies, which ostensibly took as their subject instances of formal equality on the books but continued marginalization in practice. Finally, continued interrogation of Ewick and Silbey's tripartite model of types of legal consciousness, particularly as it relates to ways to achieve a more nuanced understanding of resistance and how it is variably enacted, may help us to understand how ideas and experiences of legality vary not only between but *within* marginalized social groups, and how this model may be inhibiting further theoretical advances in legal consciousness—as both Silbey and Hull suggest may be the case. The chapters herein do not follow in strict linear fashion the before/with/against the law schemas, even if they are loosely informed by this model; they also demonstrate quite explicitly the degree to which different orientations to law overlap and intersect, both among same-sex couples and within them.

A Look at Things to Come

In the chapters that follow, I begin by legally and historically situating the unique contexts in which the couples whose stories are told in this book found themselves in the position to get married, starting in 2004. Chapter 2 relates, in brief, the history of the LGBT rights movement's quest for marriage equality—the social and cultural forces, as well as legal developments, which led to the emphasis on marriage as a goal and eventually its reality in the United States. By tracing legal and political developments over the length of this movement and particularly since the 1990s, this chapter explains the confusing patchwork of laws governing same-sex partnerships across the fifty states as well as the convoluted path that led to them. This includes a description of the different sorts of legal partnership statuses that exist—including marriage—and how they differ from one another. The chapter then parses out the significant elements of the debate—the arguments for and against same-sex marriage both from a legal perspective and a social perspective, summarizing and evaluating the growing body of doctrinal and social scientific evidence.

The next four chapters are devoted to the voices of the same-sex couples who were among the first to marry in the United States. This includes couples married in San Francisco in the ill-fated City Hall ceremonies of 2004, many of whom *thought* they had been legally married and who oriented to them as such, only to later have their licenses invalidated. Chapters 3 through 6 represent the analytical heart of the book and are arranged thematically according to the various orientations to law, or schemas of legal consciousness. Chapter 3 examines narratives of utility—perhaps the most basic and intuitive of reasons to seek a set of legal rights. In fact, one need only be without the rights attendant to marriage to appreciate how fundamental and all-encompassing they are. However, marriage is very rarely conceived of as solely a locus of material rights and responsibilities. As important as access to these rights is for those lacking them, particularly in the family context, the data here suggest that the concerns raised by the inability to link legally to one's partner are often inextricably entwined with broader ideological or deeply personal concerns that may begin with these rights, but extend far beyond them. In this sense, although a strategic or utilitarian orientation to law certainly exists among the tropes of legal consciousness found here, it is rarely unattached or unaffected by other modes of consciousness.

Chapter 4 takes up a set of motivations that is far less intuitive as a reason to marry: the desire to make a political statement, to commit civil disobedience, or to advance lesbian and gay rights. Particularly for those not party to or present at the time of the 2004 marriages at San Francisco City Hall, marriage as protest seems very nearly like a contradiction in terms. In fact, there was a distinct, if not necessarily ubiquitous, thread of political narrative woven through not only the experience of many of those married in San Francisco, but also (perhaps unexpectedly) in Massachusetts during the first year or two of same-sex marriage there as well. This strain of oppositional legal consciousness—a less expected mode of resistance than most acts of "protest" or even avoidance—took many forms but rarely stood alone. Rather, the data in this chapter reveal an evolution of sorts at work, whereby a resistant or political orientation to marriage is sometimes intersected or supplanted by significantly more reverent modes of legal consciousness that are often quite unexpected, even by the couples themselves.

The shifts in consciousness noted in chapters 3 and 4 are explained significantly in the two chapters that follow them, examining the law as a source of validation and of emotion. Chapter 5 explores perhaps one of the most well-studied functions of law and foci of studies of legal consciousness: the power of legitimation. From early studies of dispute resolution and "naming, blaming, and claiming" to later work on workplace rights, civil rights violations, and street harassment, the vision of law as a source of validation is one that looms large, particularly when examining the claims of marginalized actors. The evidence in this chapter suggests, true to both this extant literature and among some of the key judicial decisions supporting same-sex marriage, that indeed, marriage—or at least the ability to marry—acts as a proxy for full citizenship, and certainly to those excluded from it, a harbinger of broader acceptance. As the narratives in chapter 5 indicate, even when this acceptance is *not* the primary motivator of a couple to marry (though it often was), the symbolic currency of legal marriage sends powerful ripples through their thoughts and experiences in its wake and, as in San Francisco, in its disruption.

Chapter 6 concludes where the story of modern marriage begins: love. At one time a heretical position to take in legal studies, the schema of emotion is one that is at once expected and surprising in a study of newly gained legal rights such as this. On the one hand, marriage—whether same-sex or heterosexual—might be one of the few areas of law that is actually predicated on an assumption of love and emotion. Consider, after all, the consequences that might result in immigration law if a cross-national couple admitted marrying for practical purposes rather than love. On the other hand, it is not entirely intuitive why the legal, rather than ritual or religious, elements of a wedding would be necessary to achieve the emotional ends sought by those who marry. As might be predicted by the study of law as a conduit or cultivator of emotion, the newly emerging right of marriage for same-sex couples is one that is not confined to the instrumental, political, or even symbolic realm. Here again, the data show us that the personal or affective impact of law is often unsought or unexpected, but nevertheless profoundly felt.

*   *   *

Taken together, these chapters present an eclectic, diverse, and perhaps seemingly contradictory set of answers to the question "Why do traditionally excluded people seek legal marriage?" Read separately (and to foreshadow a bit), they seem to suggest that the dramatic legal and financial consequences of not being able to marry are an obvious and driving force; or that gay and lesbian couples at San Francisco or Cambridge City Hall were well aware, conscious political actors fighting for gay rights; or that couples were driven by the desire for validation and, of course, by their love for one another—the ultimate trump card. All of these things are true, to greater or lesser degrees, in ways that are often more contingent than consistent or independent. In the chapters that follow there are stories of strategy, of political action, of validation, and of romance. These stories are not mutually exclusive. Often they are contained within the same series of events, lead to one another or are even coexistent in the very same moment. Just how they interweave with one another, with some becoming more dominant while others recede into the background, is at the heart of this book. But to understand how marriage—and legality—have become so many things to so many people, we must first take a look at the long, convoluted road to legal same-sex marriage in the United States, and the bevy of legal, political, and social issues it has raised and continues to raise.

2

The Road to Same-Sex Marriage

The Beginning

The first decade of the twentieth century witnessed profound changes in the social and legal position of gay and lesbian couples. The U.S. Supreme Court's decision in *Lawrence v. Texas* in June 2003 struck down sodomy laws in those thirteen states where they remained.[1] Five months later the Massachusetts Supreme Judicial Court rendered its ruling in *Goodridge v. Department of Public Health*, making Massachusetts the first state in the U.S. to fully legalize same-sex marriage.[2] Before this ruling went into effect in May 2004, the City and County of San Francisco, in an unprecedented move, began issuing marriage licenses to same-sex couples.[3] Several other local jurisdictions followed suit: Multnomah County in Oregon and Sandoval County in New Mexico, as well as the cities of New Paltz, New York, and Asbury Park, New Jersey.[4] The California Supreme Court ruled on August 12, 2004, that San Francisco overstepped its authority and denied the validity of these licenses.[5] Despite the ruling, these developments sparked a national debate and a renewed consciousness about the institution of marriage, the ramifications of state-sanctioned relationships, and the impact of law on the private and daily lives of same-sex couples.

Same-Sex Marriage in the United States

The history of the debate began decades before the state of Massachusetts and the City and County of San Francisco entered the legal fray and issued the first marriage licenses en masse to same-sex couples. A gay couple, Jack Baker and Michael McConnell, made history in 1970 by entering the county clerk's office in Minneapolis, Minnesota, and requesting a marriage license. Shortly thereafter, a lesbian couple, Marjorie Jones and Tracy Knight, followed suit in Louisville, Kentucky. When they were denied, each couple filed suit and, in McConnell and Baker's case, pursued the case to the United States Supreme Court, which dismissed the appeal "for want of a substantial federal question." Their claim was framed largely in the same legal terms that have been employed in multiple cases in the forty years since—that marriage is a fundamental right, and denial of this right on the basis of gender (or in some cases, sexual orientation) is a violation of the First and Fourteenth Amendments, and the unenumerated right to privacy. Others followed in Washington State, Pennsylvania, the District of Columbia, and in federal immigration court, with similar results. The courts essentially dismissed the claims out of hand, finding preposterous the contention that marriage might be defined as anything other than one man and one woman. The most striking difference between then and now, though, was the extent to which Baker and McConnell's challenge departed from the prevailing ethic and expectation of the gay community, which largely saw this, and in some circles derided it, as an attempt to "enter the most conventional core of the heterosexual mainstream."[6]

In his book *Why Marriage*, historian George Chauncey examines how marriage became the focus of the modern gay and lesbian rights movement. A combination of demographic and political changes, the emergence and trajectory of the American gay rights movement (including its response to the AIDS epidemic), as well as the evolving nature and purpose of marriage itself converged to alter the landscape for same-sex couples seeking formal relationship recognition. Nancy Cott, Stephanie Coontz, and other historians have described in great detail the evolution of the institution of marriage, from a largely impersonal means of regulating labor and transmission of property—in some cases involving polygamous relationships—to a means of regulating social relationships, a contract between consenting parties, and eventually, an expression of love and fundamental right. This evolution initially had little to do with—and actually preceded in large part—the modern gay and lesbian civil rights movement. In the post–Civil War era, former slaves—who had been prohibited from marrying prior to Emancipation due to their lack of standing as legal actors, and were often forcibly removed from their mates and children—focused on marriage as a vital form of freedom and emblem of full citizenship.

It was not until the 1960s and '70s that two fundamental shifts in law and policy altered marriage in a way that helped pave the way for the legal possibility of same-sex marriage. First, in 1967, the Supreme Court ruled in *Loving v. Virginia* that bans on interracial marriage were unconstitutional, helping to cement in U.S. law a trend toward viewing marriage to the partner of one's choice as a fundamental right. Equally importantly, though through a more gradual and diffuse process, the extent to which marriage was characterized by and served to enunciate sharply distinct gender roles began to diminish considerably around the same time. While gender roles have certainly not disappeared from heterosexual marriage in the present era, most laws governing marriage and families have become at least facially gender neutral.

Shifts in the character of the gay and lesbian rights movement in the United States also offer clues as to how marriage became a focus. The post-Stonewall era of radical politics, confrontational strategies, and cultural upheaval had emphasized a rejection of the conventional heterosexual dictates of monogamy and marriage. Although many gay men and lesbians lived in long-time monogamous partnerships, several others, particularly in urban centers such as San Francisco and New York, echoed the creed of the burgeoning sexual revolution and eschewed the constraints of monogamy as having been imposed by an overly restrictive heterosexual culture. This all changed abruptly, however, with the onset of the AIDS epidemic in the 1980s. First, the knowledge that the disease was sexually transmitted dramatically altered opinions about sexual promiscuity; in its brutal way, the disease preached the virtues of monogamy. Second, as gay men saw and stood by members of their "chosen families" falling ill and dying in astonishing numbers, the lack of legal protections and ties to one another became glaringly and cruelly apparent.

Finally, as marriage became the primary site and mechanism for the allocation of financial and medical benefits in the twentieth century, it became an increasingly attractive goal for those traditionally excluded from it. This was especially the case for not only the partners of AIDS afflicted men but also for lesbian and gay parents (in particular lesbian co-parents starting planned families via reproductive technology) at the dawn of what has been called the "gayby boom." The nexus of decreased formal gender distinction and increased articulation of marriage as a fundamental right, coupled with the burgeoning gay and lesbian liberation movement in the United States in the post-Stonewall era and the onset of both AIDS and LGBT parenthood, made the emergence of a defined social movement for same-sex marriage rights not only possible, but for some, inevitable and necessary.

This is not to say that the LGBT rights movement has been unified in its pursuit of legal marriage. From early on there has been a vocal contingent who very much oppose civil (or religious) marriage as a goal for the movement. Often grounded in feminist (and later queer) theory, this group asserts that the goal of legalized same-sex marriage is a regressive rather than a progressive one. They see marriage as a historically and "inherently flawed, oppressive institution" rather than a "path to liberation."[7] As Nancy Cott observed presciently in the opening of her history of marriage, "marriage regulations have drawn lines among the citizenry and defined what kinds of sexual relations and which families will be legitimate."[8] Ironically, this is precisely the concern of those who critique it, as well as many of those who seek it.

This debate within the LGBT community took place in microcosm in a now-famous written exchange between then-executive director of Lambda Legal, the late Tom Stoddard, and Lambda's legal director at the time, the late Paula Ettelbrick. Intended to elucidate and expand the debate, the pieces were published side by side in *Out/Look* magazine in 1989. Stoddard took the position that same-sex marriage should be a top priority for the LGBT rights movement, based on the material and legal rewards of marriage and on the symbolic victory it would represent for inclusion of lesbians and gays in civil society. He further argued that allowing same-sex couples to wed would help to unmoor marriage from its sexist and heterosexist foundation. Ettelbrick, on the other hand, argued that an outcome that resulted only in the extension of marriage to same-sex couples who chose it would ultimately fall short of the goal of justice. It would, she asserted, "undermine the transformative potential of queerness and perpetuate the notion that married couples have the highest form of relationship."[9] This would ultimately imperil the long-time goal of valuing difference and diversity in the family form and the larger LGBT community.

In some respects, the contours of the debate follow closely the more general distinction between radical and assimilationist political strategies: Should the goal for gays and lesbians be to be treated "just like everyone else" or should the movement, as radicals would have it, instead celebrate and maintain its differentness? Queer marriage critics also argue that the pursuit of same-sex marriage constricts rather than expands the palate of available legal options for regulating family ties and distribution of benefits. LGBT legal scholar Nancy Polikoff contends in her book *Beyond (Straight and Gay) Marriage: Valuing All Families under the Law*, that making marriage—whether open to same-sex couples or not—the most important unit of family and hub of benefits not only discourages but does actual harm to family diversity.[10] She argues persuasively that the decision to link benefits and responsibilities to marriage made sense only in the context of what it was a hundred years ago: a deeply gendered, patriarchal institution. Now decoupled (at least formally) from distinct gender roles, the relationship between marriage and benefits is no longer a functionally optimal one. Citing example after example of relationships where children, unmarried couples, or individual adults were harmed because the law did not recognize them as family, Polikoff calls for an alternative approach which values all families—whether involving a romantic partnership or not—and makes marriage optional, rather than necessary for the accrual of protections and benefits.

Increasingly, however, as the mainstream LGBT movement gravitated to the center in the late twentieth and early twenty-first centuries, these voices of dissent were left behind as same-sex couples began to visualize marriage as an option for them, particularly since the Hawaii case of *Baehr v. Lewin* (later *Baehr v. Miike*) in the mid-1990s.[11] In this case, Ninia Baehr and Genora Dancel sued the state of Hawaii, with the help of local attorney Dan Foley but virtually no assistance from the national LGBT rights organizations. The couple lost their case at the trial court, but appealed the decision to the Hawaii Supreme Court. In May 1993, in a ruling that sent shock waves through the gay and lesbian community and the entire country, the court became the first in the country to legally recognize the right to same-sex marriage under the principle of equal protection. It reasoned that the rationale of prior decisions—essentially stating that marriage had to be between a man and a woman because it had always been so—were tautological and unpersuasive. But rather than mandating that a marriage license be granted to the plaintiffs (and others), the Supreme Court sent the case back to the trial court for further argumentation on whether the state could prove it had a "compelling interest" in denying marriage to same-sex couples. Although the trial court subsequently found that there was no such compelling interest, the ruling was stayed pending appeal, which gave lawmakers both in Hawaii and elsewhere a chance to summon the opposition to invalidate the ruling. Indeed, not a single marriage license was ever issued in Hawaii: before this contested ruling could go into effect, both the federal government and the voters of Hawaii approved legislation effectively trumping the court's decision.

Simultaneously, the decision sent the rest of the nation into a panic about the specter of same-sex marriage, which culminated in the passage of what Yale law professor William Eskridge has called "the most sweeping antigay law in the nation's history": the federal Defense of Marriage Act ("DOMA"). Passed quickly and by an overwhelming majority in Congress, DOMA was signed into law by President Clinton in 1996.[12] It banned federal recognition of same-sex marriage and held that the states need not recognize such unions if they are granted by another state. While the latter was the primary motivation for passing the law, its effect was virtually nil, since no state at that time was legally marrying same-sex couples. Still, as Eskridge and many other critics have pointed out since, this law was a notable and, from a constitutional law perspective, somewhat shocking exception to the U.S. Constitution's Full Faith and Credit Clause, which would otherwise mandate that the marriage laws of one state be recognized in other states as part of their "public Acts, Records, and judicial Proceedings" (in other words, the clause ensures that if a heterosexual couple is legally married in Las Vegas, for example, their marriage will still be recognized as valid when they return to their home in California).[13]

The former provision, however, titled Section 3 of the law, had a profound impact on same-sex couples across the nation. The non-recognition of same-sex relationships at the federal level had far-reaching consequences for the filing of federal taxes, social security and other federal benefit programs, immigration law, and spousal benefits for those employed by the federal government among others. It is estimated, for example, that an individual in a same-sex marriage or domestic partnership, recognized in his or her home state, still paid on average $1,069 more per year in federal income taxes than did a heterosexual counterpart for health benefits, which, were the gay couple recognized as married, would be tax-free. This and other provisions of the tax code meant that same-sex couples paid on average 11 percent more than heterosexual married couples in federal taxes every year.[14] Likewise, same-sex surviving partners were subjected to inheritance taxes that heterosexual married couples were not, adding as much as $4 million in additional tax burden to some of these couples. They also did not receive the social security benefits that their heterosexual counterparts did, which translated into a loss of approximately $5,700 per year. In addition to these losses, same-sex couples could not use the Family and Medical Leave Act to take time off from work to care for a same-sex partner or dependent, nor could they sponsor an immigrant partner for a Green Card. Thus, DOMA's material results were extensive, even for couples whose home states did offer relationship recognition.

At around the same time and since the passage of DOMA in 1996, thirty-nine states passed their own versions of the law, sometimes called "mini DOMAs," either as constitutional amendments or statutes, declaring that marriage consists only of a man and a woman.[15] A whopping fourteen states passed these non-recognition laws during the 2004 presidential election year, some commentators positing that support for these measures galvanized conservative voters to a degree that influenced the election of President George W. Bush to a second term.[16] Some of these mini-DOMAs go so far as to bar recognition of any other form of union (for example, domestic partnerships), or even suggest that a legal arrangement such as a will or other private contract drawn up by members of a same-sex couple to attempt to protect their relationship to each other may be considered invalid under state law.

It was well over a decade before DOMA and most of its state equivalents were successfully challenged or experienced any significant political momentum for overturning them. However, in 1999 the Vermont Supreme Court made history by ruling in *Baker v. Vermont* (no relationship to Jack Baker of the earlier *Baker v. Nelson*) that same-sex couples must be afforded the same rights and responsibilities as married heterosexual couples.[17] The case arose from suits filed by three couples who went to their local county clerk's office in 1997 and were denied marriage licenses. Although Vermont did not have a specific state statute that defined marriage in heterosexual terms, the clerks took their cue from a 1975 opinion of the state attorney general that did so. The couples seized upon the seemingly gender-neutral wording of the actual marriage statute and argued that if the statute was indeed construed to ban same-sex marriage, it violated their rights under the state constitution's "common benefits" clause. The trial judge quickly dismissed the lawsuit, and the couples appealed to the Vermont Supreme Court, which rendered its unanimous verdict in support of the couples on December 20, 1999. Significantly, however, the Court did not specify a remedy—it did not demand that the county clerks begin issuing marriage licenses to same-sex couples. Instead, it directed the legislature to come up with and implement a policy that would achieve the result of equal rights for same-sex couples, whether it be in the form of marriage or something else.

The Vermont legislature responded in 2000 by creating civil unions for same-sex couples, which carry all the privileges and responsibilities of marriage at the state level—though without the label of marriage.[18] This was not the first law in the nation to offer a formalized status to same-sex couples, but it was far more expansive than the partnership registries existing in some jurisdictions at that time, with privileges and responsibilities including rights related to inheritance, child custody, hospital visitation, employee benefits, and state taxes.[19] By 2012, seven states had laws that provide registered same-sex couples with rights equivalent to marriage (not inclusive of those, such as Vermont and Connecticut, which at first legalized civil unions but now have legal same-sex marriage), while an additional state, Wisconsin, had relationship recognition laws that provide a limited number of rights to these couples.

For some, the advent of civil unions and comprehensive domestic partnership laws represented a significant advance in gay and lesbian family rights; before long, however, marriage advocates began pointing to their deficiencies. While these statuses overcome many of the legal barriers same-sex partners face in solidifying their relationships and protecting their families, they are unlike marriage in three different but crucial ways. First, they are not actually marriages according to state (or, for that matter popular) definition; second, they do not include the federal benefits associated with marriage; and third, they are generally not recognized across state lines.[20] While the latter two differences have obvious material and legal ramifications, the first is largely seen as a symbolic matter, prompting many liberal critics, and couples themselves, to compare these partnerships to the "separate but equal" doctrine that defined racial segregation until the 1954 case of *Brown v. Board of Education*.[21]

It was this enduring critique, in large part, that led the Massachusetts Supreme Judicial Court—also bolstered significantly by the landmark *Lawrence v. Texas* decision five months prior, which overruled all criminal sodomy statues on the grounds that they impermissibly discriminated against gays and lesbians and violated their rights to privacy—to indicate in its decision in the 2003 *Goodridge* case that anything less than full and equal marriage rights for same-sex partners is unconstitutional. The justices in *Goodridge* held that, according to the Massachusetts State Constitution and the U.S. Supreme Court's ruling in *Lawrence v. Texas*, the state could not deny same-sex couples the right to marry, and that the legislature and county governments were required to make the necessary changes to allow same-sex marriages to begin to take place within six months. Significantly, the court specified that a Vermont-style solution offering an equivalent but distinct form of relationship recognition would not suffice. This represented a marked shift in the debate, as it was no longer just about those several hundred individual legal and financial rights associated with marriage; it was also about the unique cultural status of marriage and the rationale for creating a parallel institution for a defined minority. In other words, the justices in *Goodridge* (and later, in the subsequent California case of *In re Marriage Cases*) were poised to address not only the material consequences of exclusion from marriage but the symbolic ones as well.

In May 2004, after significant debate and many attempts by the then-governor of Massachusetts, Mitt Romney, to sidestep the ruling, the first entirely legal gay and lesbian marriages in U.S. history began. Cambridge City Hall was the first to open its door to same-sex couples, at one minute after midnight on May 17. Many of the couples interviewed in this book were among those who received their marriage licenses that first night in Cambridge—227 applications were issued in Cambridge alone, and more than a thousand on the first day statewide.

If there were any clouds hanging over the heads of marriage equality supporters at this time, they were that there was still a possibility that a constitutional ban could overturn the decision, and because of an obscure early twentieth century law still on the books in Massachusetts—meant to avoid recognition of interracial couples—the right to marry under *Goodridge* was confined to only Massachusetts residents or those who intended to reside there. It would take a subsequent piece of legislation four years later to allow couples from out of state to marry in Massachusetts.

Meanwhile, the same-sex marriages in San Francisco, which began on February 12, 2004, at the bidding of Gavin Newsom, were brought to a halt by the California Supreme Court that March, after 4,037 marriage licenses had been issued. Almost immediately upon hearing of these marriages, conservative and religious organizations such as the Alliance Defense Fund and the Campaign for California Families had filed suit to put a stop to them and overturn those licenses that had been issued. Several attempts were unsuccessful, until finally, on March 11, the California Supreme Court agreed with these parties and California's attorney general Bill Lockyer that a stay should be granted pending consideration of whether the marriages were actually legal. Upon word of this decision reaching San Francisco, the marriage license lines at City Hall were literally cut off—couples who had made a mad rush to the alter in hopes of beating the courts' decision were left stunned and saddened when they were told there would be no more marriage licenses. Those 4,037 couples who had succeeded in getting their marriage licenses were held in a state of legal limbo while the high court considered the question of whether their marriages were valid.

On August 12, 2004, the other shoe landed: the California Supreme Court issued its decision, ruling that the mayor was not acting within his authority in directing the county clerk to issue the licenses and, consequently, invalidated those 4,037 marriages.[22] Although this was a blow to the same-sex marriage movement and clearly to the couples themselves, the decision notably did not foreclose the possibility of legalized same-sex marriage in California. Rather, it limited its rationale to the power of a local authority to trump state law (in this case, California's Marriage and Family Code, as well as Proposition 22, passed by voters in 2000, which limited marriage to one man and one woman). The decision was quite explicit in stating that the court was *not* deciding the legal merits of same-sex marriage per se; it was responding only to the fashion in which they had been done. It seemed to some to be inviting a challenge to the law through the "proper channels," in order to decide the broader issue of whether same-sex couples should be allowed to marry.

As it turned out, the process was already underway by this point. Even before the ruling was issued a handful of same-sex couples (including some of those who were left in line on the day the court ended the marriages), several gay rights advocacy organizations, and the city and county of San Francisco all filed lawsuits challenging the constitutionality of California's Proposition 22 and corresponding family code limiting marriage to heterosexuals. These challenges—six in all—were eventually joined into one case by the courts and commenced proceedings in the San Francisco Superior Court. In March 2005, seven months after the original 4,037 marriage licenses from San Francisco were invalidated, Superior Court Judge Richard Kramer ruled that Prop 22 was indeed unconstitutional on the basis of gender discrimination. Although supporters predicted that it was a careful, conservative opinion by a Republican appointee, and one that would withstand review at the California District Court of Appeals, the appeals court overturned Judge Kramer's decision, in a 2 to 1 ruling, setting up a showdown at the state's court of last resort.

In re Marriage Cases eventually reached the California Supreme Court, who agreed to review the decision in December 2006 and heard oral arguments in March 2008. On May 15, 2008, the court issued its decision: it overturned the state's ban on same-sex marriage and declared marriage a fundamental right, regardless of sexual orientation, based on the California constitution. Writing for the court's majority, California Supreme Court Chief Justice Ronald George wrote in a much broader opinion than even supporters had predicted that strict scrutiny—the highest legal standard for scrutinizing a law that treats one group differently from others (for example, based on race)—should be applied to laws that purposefully exclude people on the basis of their sexual orientation. This was a first not only in California law but also in the nation. Up to this point, "strict scrutiny" had never been applied to sexual orientation in any context, let alone same-sex marriage.[23] However, Justice George went even further. He held that even if one were to apply a *less* stringent basis of review (for which there *is* preexisting legal precedent in the context of anti-discrimination laws that include gays and lesbians, based on the landmark 1996 U.S. Supreme Court decision in *Romer v. Evans*), California lacked a rational basis for restricting marriage to heterosexuals. Again, as in *Goodridge*, the court was clear that a parallel institution such as domestic partnership (which in any case California already had) would not do to remedy the wrong of excluding gays and lesbians. It instructed the state to begin issuing marriage licenses to same-sex couples thirty days later, and on June 16, jurisdictions around the state began doing just that. In San Francisco, the epicenter of California's marriage equality movement four years earlier, City Hall returned to celebration mode. And just as in 2004, Mayor Newsom invited Del Martin and Phyllis Lyon to be the first legally married lesbian couple in the city's history, and one of the first in California's history. Between the time this decision went into effect in June and election day in November 2008, approximately eighteen thousand same-sex couples were married in California.

Concurrently during this six month period, opponents campaigned heavily for the state ballot measure that became Proposition 8, called the California Marriage Protection Act by its proponents and entitled "Eliminates Rights of Same-Sex Couples to Marry" on the official state ballot, which would amend California's state constitution to once again ban same-sex marriage.[24] After intense and extraordinarily expensive campaigning efforts on both sides, Prop 8 was passed by California voters on November 4 by a margin of 52 percent to 48 percent, effectively nullifying the Supreme Court's ruling in *In re Marriage Cases*. In a subsequent court challenge the following year, *Strauss v. Horton*, the

California Supreme Court—the very court that had six months earlier legalized same-sex marriage in California—upheld the new marriage exclusion on the basis that Prop 8 had altered the constitutional land-scape on which their prior decision rested. Nonetheless, the justices held that those eighteen thousand marriage licenses issued before elec-tion day remained valid, effectively and awkwardly creating an isolated and anomalous status for the couples who had married during this time.[25]

This was not the end of the story in California, though. Two years later, in the first successful federal district court challenge of a state ban on same-sex marriage, U.S. District Court Judge Vaughn Walker ruled that Prop 8 was a violation of the U.S. Constitution and enjoined the state from enforcing the ban.[26] Although Judge Walker called for an immediate end to the enforcement of Prop 8, the Ninth Circuit Court of Appeals then issued a stay on this ruling, which in effect kept the ban in place and barred any additional marriages from occurring dur-ing the long appeals process. On February 7, 2012, the court handed down its decision, declaring in an eighty-page majority opinion that Prop 8 violated the equal protection clause of the Fourteenth Amend-ment and was thereby impermissible.[27] This decision was immediately appealed to the U.S. Supreme Court, which heard oral arguments in the case in March 2013, and rendered its decision in on June 26, 2013: a slim 5–4 majority ruled that in fact the sponsors of Prop 8 had no stand-ing to bring the case (as California's governor and attorney general had declined to defend the law), effectively vacating the Ninth Circuit's decision and reinstating Judge Walker's decision invalidating the law. Within days, the Ninth Circuit lifted its injunction on Judge Walker's ruling and legal same-sex marriages began, once again, in California.

During this entire period and in the wake of California's about-face on same-sex marriage, the legal momentum in other states began to mount. In 2008, Connecticut became the third state to legalize same-sex marriage (and the second state to offer it permanently) when its Supreme Court issued its decision in *Kerrigan v. Connecticut*.[28] Shortly after, in a state Supreme Court decision that surprised even supporters,

Iowa became the first non-coastal state to abandon exclusionary marriage laws with the ruling in *Varnum v. Brien*, bringing same-sex marriage to the heartland.[29] By mid-2013, thirteen states plus the District of Columbia had legalized same-sex marriage in the United States, lending an air of inevitability to those in other states who continued to push for the right.[30]

These developments inevitably led to renewed efforts to address DOMA and resolve the federal questions attendant to marital statuses varying by state. In addition to the *Perry* case challenging California's Prop 8, four other federal cases dealing with federal recognition of same-sex marriages legal under state law began to make their way through the litigation process in 2009.[31] In 2010 in a landmark ruling, federal district judge Joseph Tauro, a Nixon appointee, rendered a summary judgment in *Gill v. Office of Personnel Management* declaring DOMA's Section 3 unconstitutional under federal law. This was the first time that any jurisdiction had found any provision of DOMA unconstitutional, but the decision was stayed pending appeal, so DOMA remained in effect. Then in February 2011, the Obama administration dropped a bombshell: Attorney General Eric Holder announced that the Department of Justice determined that Section 3 of DOMA was indeed unconstitutional, and the federal government would no longer defend it. Subsequently, in May 2012, the First Circuit Court of Appeals in Boston upheld the earlier *Gill* decision, stopping short of demanding strict scrutiny for same-sex marriage bans but nevertheless finding DOMA unconstitutional, thereby setting up an inevitable appeal to the U.S. Supreme Court.

In the meantime, on the West Coast, Karen Golinksi, a staff attorney for the Ninth Circuit Court of Appeals in San Francisco, filed for employee's dependent health benefits for her female spouse. When she was denied, she took the matter to the Ninth Circuit's Employment Dispute Resolution process. Chief Justice Alex Kozinski ruled in her favor, but the Office of Personnel Management, an independent federal agency, refused to implement his decision. The judge dismissed the case as it was worded in trial court, but invited Golinski's attorneys to resubmit the case as a direct challenge to DOMA's Section 3, which they did. With the Obama administration refusing to defend the law in court, the Republican-controlled House of Representatives took up the cause by appointing former solicitor general Paul Clement to defend the law in both this and the East Coast DOMA challenges (which now also included two cases from the Second Circuit: *Pedersen v. Office of Personnel Management* and *U.S. v. Windsor*). On February 22, 2012, U.S. District Court Judge Jeffrey White followed Judge Tauro's lead, declaring DOMA Section 3 unconstitutional as applied to Karen Golinksi and other similarly situated married couples. At the same time, in the legislative branch, Representative Jerrold Nadler (D-NY) introduced the Respect for Marriage Act in the House of Representatives, which would repeal DOMA entirely. The bill did not advance beyond committee when first introduced in 2009 but was subsequently reintroduced in 2011 with a corresponding bill in the Senate introduced by Senator Diane Feinstein (D-CA). It garnered 127 co-sponsors in the House, including one Republican, as well as the support of President Obama, former president Clinton (who signed the original law), and former representative Bob Barr (R-GA), who authored the original DOMA law. Proponents of the repeal noted a promising harbinger in the repeal of the military's anti-gay Don't Ask Don't Tell policy earlier that year. On December 7, 2012, the U.S. Supreme Court granted certiorari in the first of the DOMA challenges to reach it: *Windsor v. U.S.* The court heard oral arguments in March 2013, and issued its ruling on June 26, 2013, in favor of the plaintiff, Edith Windsor: by a bare 5–4 majority, the court declared Section 3 of DOMA unconstitutional on due process grounds, giving legally married same-sex couples access to federal rights and responsibilities for the first time.

Debating Marriage

In the time that Americans have actively debated the legalization of same-sex marriage, relatively little about the content of the debate has changed. When the issue first surfaced in the 1970s with Jack Baker and Michael McConnell, the debate was short: marriage had always been defined as a man and a woman, and same-sex marriage is therefore not possible. If forced to articulate a reason why, the courts, government officials, or other opponents quickly turned to either moral justifications or claims that allowing same-sex marriage would lead to a breakdown of civil society and government.[32] In the gay rights community, marriage was either considered a retrograde, heteronormative, sexist anathema or it was not a priority in an era when gays and lesbians could be arrested, fired from their jobs, or even considered insane due to their sexual orientation. It would be several more years before the idea of domestic partnership would even surface.

The 1990s and the *Baehr* case in Hawaii changed that, as did the U.S. Supreme Court precedent in *Romer v. Evans* in 1996. The *Romer* case dealt with a law passed by voters in Colorado, Amendment 2, which outlawed the inclusion of sexual orientation as a status for protection in anti-discrimination laws. In singling out one particular group— gays/lesbians and bisexuals—to be excluded from the same protections offered to other minority groups on the basis of race or religion, for example, the Court found that the law unfairly targeted gay men and lesbians for no rational purpose other than expressing animosity toward them as a group. *Romer* was the first Supreme Court decision to protect gay and lesbian civil rights as a class, and served as an important foundation for *Lawrence* and the same-sex marriage cases to follow.

With a gay rights foothold in Supreme Court precedent and the potential reality of same-sex marriage in Hawaii, opponents were forced to further articulate and sharpen their arguments against same-sex marriage.[33] To be sure, the definitional and biblical or moral arguments remained, but different legal scholars have different ideas of what became the dominant argument at this point. Eskridge has argued that attention shifted from moral or definitional arguments to the consequences of approval of same-sex marriage. These purported consequences include a loss of meaning and respect for "traditional" (read: heterosexual) marriage, a concern about what message it will send for the government to condone same-sex relationships in this way (what Eskridge and Spedale call the "stamp-of-approval" argument and has alternatively been called the "no-promo-homo" argument), and the "slippery slope"—that opening the door to two people of the same-sex may evolve into allowing polygamy, incest, bestiality, and other widely disapproved sexual taboos. Others, such as law professor Julie Nice, have found that the definitional arguments, which revolved around the assumed purpose of marriage, remain most trenchant. Each of these pieces of the debate deserves more detailed examination.

The stamp-of-approval, or no-promo-homo, argument is appealing to moderate conservatives it allows them to express tolerance for the *existence* of gays and lesbians while still making the point that it is not the government's business to affirmatively *promote* homosexuality by offering them rights such as marriage. It allows them to say, in effect, "do what you want behind closed doors, but don't make me have to know about it or recognize it." This was the argument implicit in the Supreme Court's 2003 *Lawrence v. Texas* decision. While recognizing the right of gays and lesbians to be free from criminal prosecution for engaging in private consensual sex acts, it was explicit in stating that this decision should not be construed as mandating a right to government-recognized same-sex marriage. The rationale has proved persistent.

Likewise, the slippery-slope argument is one that persists in popular discourse if not in official legal language: If the state could so distort the concept of marriage that it applies to same-sex couples, then what would be next? Could a man marry his sister, or a horse, or three wives (or husbands) at once?[34] This line of thought has been the butt of many jokes—comedian Ellen DeGeneres (who later legally married her spouse, actress Portia De Rossi, in California) famously quipped in her stand-up act that those who made the immediate leap from same-sex marriage to marriage to a *goat* were indeed the ones with the problem. But the theory exists in legal and policy discourse, and it has been quite effective in limiting such consensual practices as marijuana usage and euthanasia. In particular, the relationship between legal proscriptions against same-sex marriage and those against polygamy has been, for some, the "rhetorical elephant in the room of the modern marriage equality movement."[35]

It is also necessary to examine the law's treatment of gender and sexual orientation for the arguments for and against same-sex marriage. The erosion of legally imposed gender-role distinctions in marriage had much to do with the emergence of the modern marriage equality movement. But are same-sex marriage exclusions really gender discrimination? The issue has been dealt with repeatedly in marriage litigation, as part of the necessary process of constructing a constitutionally legitimate argument. Because gender differences generally enjoy broader protections than sexual orientation differences in existing legal precedent, it is an attractive argument to make. For example, in some state constitutions, including California's, gender is treated as a suspect status (like race), meaning that it enjoys the highest form of legal protection: that of strict scrutiny. In federal constitutional law, gender is the subject of "intermediate scrutiny"—not as high a level of scrutiny as laws dealing with race or religion but higher than the "rational basis" standard applied to sexual orientation as a result of *Romer v. Evans*. Sexual orientation—particularly before 2008 and the *In re Marriage Cases* case—is held to the lower rational basis standard in most state law as well, if it is protected at all. In applying the gender-based standard, then, to same-sex marriage, the argument goes something like this: Hypothetical lesbian A—we'll call her Mary—would be allowed to marry her partner, whom we'll call Jean—if she were a man. However, since Mary is a woman, she is not allowed to marry Jean. Ergo, restrictions on same-sex marriage constitute gender discrimination. This approach has not been particularly successful traditionally.[36] In most cases, judges (and opponents) reason that since Mary—and every other woman—is perfectly entitled under the law to marry (as long as the person is a man), there is no gender discrimination. However, in the trial phase of *Perry v. Schwarzenegger* (later renamed *Hollingsworth v. Perry*), Judge Walker made an important contribution to this argument: he articulated the nexus between the two forms of discrimination and found that the two are inextricably linked. This was a long-awaited judicial affirmation of the intersectionalist argument existent in the scholarly community for many years, and that homophobia is a "weapon of sexism" and, implicitly, the reverse as well.[37]

The controversy remains, however, whether sexual orientation should be subject to strict scrutiny. The traditional legal test for deciding whether a group is a "suspect status" and therefore subject to strict scrutiny involves four questions: (1) Is the group a disadvantaged class that has suffered a history of discrimination? (2) Can the political process (outside of the courts) be relied on to protect them from discrimination? (3) Is the trait "immutable" (is it a born trait and therefore unchangeable) or is it a choice? (4) Is it reasonably related to the ability of the person to perform the task in question? The first and the last of these are relatively easy to answer when it comes to homosexuality. The second and third are less so. In particular, the question of whether homosexuality is "immutable" invites a host of questions about sexuality and essentialism that many queer theorists and sociologists do not relish answering. If one says sexual orientation is a "born" status, it implies that it is genetically determined, which not only contradicts a large body of sociological literature about the fluidity of sexuality but also invites frightening prospects for eugenics. However, admitting that sexuality may be mutable means that not only does it not enjoy heightened legal protection but suggests sexual orientation is a "choice" and gives unwarranted credence to bogus "therapies" designed to eradicate homosexuality. In response to some of these issues, some legal scholars, and even judges, have called for a "new immutability," which does not hinge so much on whether homosexuality can be changed as whether one should *have* to try to change something so central to his or her identity.[38]

Those arguments that focus on an anticipated loss of respect or meaning for the institution of heterosexual marriage at first seem the vaguest of the "consequential" arguments: How would one measure a loss of "meaning"? They are also most closely connected to the earlier (and current) definitional arguments. Again, these arguments appeal to moderates who are not quite comfortable expressing direct animus against gay and lesbian individuals per se. One does not need to hate gay people, after all, to feel that changing the marriage gender requirements means changing the meaning of the word or institution of "marriage." One need only admit that marriage as it stands is an institution worth protecting; thus the wording and purported intention of the federal Defense of Marriage Act. What may be more measurable is the contention that changing the composition of marriage affects the populace's respect for the institution of marriage. Whether the "distortion" of the meaning of marriage constitutes societal damages to the degree that the state has a legitimate interest in protecting against those damages by limiting marriage is a separate question, but one that has already been taken up in courts across the country, often successfully. It was perhaps most relevant in the *Perry* case in California, where the question of who had "standing" to appeal the case necessarily implicated questions of whether Prop 8's sponsors could claim they—or anyone—was harmed by the marriage of same-sex couples.

This is related to a broader political question of democracy and the role of the majority in deciding issues that impinge on the rights of a minority. The argument has been made, for example, that despite California's state officials' refusing to defend Prop 8, for the courts to overturn it and (re-) institute same-sex marriage would abrogate the will of the people—who, after all, did vote for Prop 8—and would thereby undercut the foundations of our democracy. Supporting this is the California Supreme Court's decision in *Strauss v. Horton*, which held that Prop 8's rescinding of same-sex marriage rights was a "permissible exercise of the majority's voting power," as well as the U.S. Supreme Court dissent in *Hollingsworth v. Perry*.[39] However, as legal director of the National Center for Lesbian Rights (NCLR) Shannon Minter has argued, democracy is fundamentally undermined when equality is sacrificed: "democracy embodies a normative recognition that all persons are entitled to participate equally in the process of self-government."[40] As Minter argues, "judicial decisions enforcing the right of same-sex couples to marry are democracy-enhancing, even when they require the invalidation of popularly enacted laws, because they help to counteract the social stigma and invidious stereotypes that prevent gay men and lesbians from participating in democratic self-governance on equal terms."[41] The issue in some respects turns on whether one views marriage as a fundamental component of citizenship. Minter, along with Nancy Cott, asserts that it is. Those who join in the feminist-queer critique of marriage, including Martha Fineman and Nancy Polikoff, maintain that it does not need to be. Those whose arguments against same-sex marriage rely on marriage being placed on a pedestal, such as Maggie Gallagher of the National Organization for Marriage, are caught in a difficult bind, as they would neither concede that marriage is not that important to citizenship nor admit access to gays and lesbians. Often this difficulty is resolved by returning to moral evaluations of the behavior and character of same-sex couples.

Religious and moral arguments against same-sex marriage are perhaps the most difficult to rebut because they are nearly by definition non-falsifiable. The religious Christian Right has interpreted certain passages the Bible to mean that homosexuality is a chosen behavior—a sin—and that the purpose of marriage is to unite man and woman to procreate. Any sexual union outside of that is not only unnatural but immoral. Similar proscriptions are inferred by some more orthodox sects of Judaism and Islam. These objections are not confined to the church, synagogue, or mosque: they have also made their way into legal discourse. As Eskridge writes, many natural law scholars—including judges—see the common law as having derived from Judeo-Christian law and (appropriately) importing these inferred proscriptions. One might appropriately respond in two different ways—appealing to the Constitution's anti-establishment clause to argue that religion has no place in law or, on the other hand, engaging the religious debate by pointing to the relatively minimal and less-than-clear language in the Bible being used to make the argument against same-sex marriage and homosexuality more broadly. Some religious scholars assert, for example, that the story of Sodom and Gomorrah is not so much an admonition against homosexuality as it is against inhospitability and general immorality. Others point to the hypocrisy of interpreting this one passage so literally while others, which condemn adultery, profaning the Sabbath, or disobeying one's parents in the same manner, are ignored. To be willing to engage these arguments, though, one must first concede that biblical discussion is appropriate in a debate about legal marriage. Increasingly, this seems like an inappropriate and slender reed on which to rest a legal and public policy debate such as this; even same-sex marriage opponents and legal decision makers recognize this as a fringe argument, which will not win the day in a courtroom in the post-*Lawrence* era.

One argument that has emerged in great frequency in courts across the United States is the "responsible procreation" argument, which states that the purpose of marriage, both historically and presently, is to regulate the behavior of heterosexuals who have unprotected sex and therefore might beget children irresponsibly. If the only rationale for an institution is to rein in wayward heterosexual fornicating by legally binding these libidinous men to the (potential) mother of their children, then by definition it has no place among homosexuals, who after all cannot accidentally procreate with one another. Some judges have gone so far as to emphasize, ironically, the great investment, expense, and care taken by same-sex couples in their efforts to become parents. As Julie Nice points out, this contention is either self-contradictory or disingenuous (or both), given that the same parties have also argued that gays and lesbians do not deserve to be married because they are by nature promiscuous and uninterested in families or children. Nevertheless, the responsible procreation argument has gained currency in American jurisprudence, where it has been cited in several high-profile decisions denying the right to marriage for same-sex couples, including state supreme court cases in Washington state, New York, and Maryland, as well as appeals courts in Indiana and Arizona.[42] Professor Nice argues that the responsible procreation argument owes its tenacity to a residual effect—that is, it is the only arrow left in the legal quiver of the anti–same-sex marriage movement, which at this point has seen many prior arguments picked apart and discarded either by the "regular process of sorting, sifting, and weighing potential justifications" in constitutional law, or by evolving public opinion.[43] This is likely true, but its use may be most directly related to the waning empirical support for the set of justifications having to do with the raising of children. Two associated arguments are relevant here. The first is also of the definitional sort: marriage is solely for procreation, and since gay and lesbian couples don't ("naturally") have children, they do not need marriage. It did not take long to point out the logical and factual flaws in this argument since many married (heterosexual) people have no children and do not have any intention of having children, and many gay men and lesbians *do* have children (about one-quarter of all same-sex couples, according to recent statistics).[44] In an era of transnational adoption and increasingly sophisticated assisted reproductive technology (or "ART"), it seems quaint and even foolish to assume that any public policy could rest on the assumption that gay men and lesbians can't have children.

In response to this demographic and technological reality, opponents have made a slight revision to the claim: same-sex couples are not *ideally suited* to be parents. That is, they may *become* parents through adoption or ART, but that doesn't mean they *should* be having children. Thus, the courts and the anti-gay agenda have touted the married, heterosexual, biologically related family as the optimal environment in which to raise children. It follows, they claim, that the state should be in the business of promoting only these so-called optimal conditions, even if other arrangements exist in practice. Opponents claim that bringing children into these families means "deliberately" creating "single parent households"; Lynn Wardle, a law professor at Brigham Young University, calls the children of LGBT families "orphans or half-orphans, deliberately conceived to be raised in a unisex parenting environment," which Wardle considers to be a grave threat to the children's welfare.[45] The claim, both explicit and implicit, is that even if gay men and lesbians do choose to have children, they are unfit parents. The perceived legitimacy of this claim in the mainstream was short-lived, largely because it is—again—an empirical question that can indeed be answered. Study after study by developmental psychologists have shown us that the claim is simply false—the sexual orientation or gender makeup of parenting units has nothing to do with their suitability as parents or the well-being of their children. Faced with increasing doubt about the legitimacy of any claim implicating the existence or suitability of

Denmark, and Sweden throughout the 1990s. He claims that similar patterns can be found in other countries that have moved to recognize same-sex partnerships, including not only the rest of Scandinavia but also France, the Netherlands, Great Britain, and Belgium. In mapping these trends across Europe, Kurtz relies largely on a framework proposed by demographer Kathleen Kiernan, which maps the progress of an increasing norm of cohabitation rather than marriage by dividing the Continent into different stages according to their rates of cohabitation. Kurtz finds that those countries in the most advanced stage of this progression were—not coincidentally—the first to offer recognition of same-sex partnerships.[47]

Kurtz and others who sound the death knell of traditional marriage in anticipation of same-sex marriage in the United States assume that individuals, society, and children in particular will be harmed as a result. Researchers on the other side of the debate, like Lee Badgett, William Eskridge, and his coauthor Darren Spedale—not to mention activists in the national gay rights social movement organizations—are forced to counter the claim that same-sex marriage has any effects at all other than on those couples whom it allows the right to marry, or that children are harmed by parental arrangements other than heterosexual marriage.

There are two compelling arguments against the grain of this normative contention, which sometimes seems taken as a given in the debate over the broader effects of same-sex marriage. The first takes up the question, raised earlier, of whether children experience harm if raised by same-sex parents (or any parental configuration outside of heterosexual marriage). For many years, a body of developmental psychology literature accumulated, which sharply rejected the idea that there were *any* differences in children raised by gay/lesbian parents in comparison to those raised by heterosexual parents.[48] This body of empirical work was important in building a foundation for rebutting claims of unfitness used in court to deny gay and lesbian parents custody of their children. However, it obscured an important point, which was brought to the fore by an influential article by sociologists Judith Stacey and Tim

Biblarz in 2001.[49] In their meta-analysis of these studies, they found that in actuality there *were* some differences between the children of heterosexuals and the children of homosexuals. It seems intuitive, even, that children will be affected by who their parents are—just as the children of atheists will often be different from children of fundamentalist Christians. The important point was that these differences did *not* amount to harm; they took the form of personality traits like openness to difference and greater feelings of gender equity, things that should arguably be *valued* rather than diminished. Granted, the goal of helping parents and children by showing the sexual orientation of the former has no harmful effect on the latter is an admirable one. But those researchers who glossed over any differences set up a fundamental problem, which was also contributed to by attorneys' arguing that gay/lesbian parents were not any different in their parenting from heterosexuals in theirs and therefore not harmful to their children. That is, researchers started from a position that these differences would necessarily constitute *harm*. Likewise the logic in assuming that children are harmed by not being raised by two heterosexual (married) parents, as well as the denials of this assertion: by adhering to a set of assumptions about the marital configuration that benefits children most, we take as a starting point the assertion that a non-normative configuration—for example, one that does not involve marriage or that involves more (or less) than two parents—will be harmful to children. We therefore cede to a certain framework for the normative family, which still takes the heterosexual family as its starting place.

The second potential argument to be made against the normative claim embedded in the work of Kurtz and others takes on the question of whether marriage as traditionally conceived and practiced is necessary for the well-being of individuals and society. As Badgett points out, even in those societies where children are often born to non-married couples, the families often remain intact—at greater rates than in the United States. In the Netherlands, for example, 91 percent of children born to non-marital couples are still raised by both parents, whether they are married or not. Also, many of these couples go on to marry after the birth of their children—so the ingredients of the traditional family are there: they simply occur in a different order. Beyond that, Nancy Polikoff points out that there are many nations where "marriage matters less"—in other words, where a couple's or individual's rights, such as rights of survivorship, medical decision making, social security, and inheritance, are not based on their marital status, whether gay or straight. Polikoff and others have found no harm resulting from these non-marital arrangements, and in fact the evidence seems to suggest that many of these countries, particularly those European nations with a strong welfare state, serve their population better by providing greater access to health care and having fewer children living below the poverty line than in the United States.[50]

Moreover, this trend is not limited to the Netherlands and other countries with same-sex marriage laws. For example, in her book *Unhitched*, Judith Stacey discusses the Mosuo of southwestern China, where the tradition is for a child to be raised by his or her mother and the maternal family, with little if any involvement from the biological father.[51] Marriage is likewise not the norm here—rather, men and women practice *tisese*, sometimes called "walking marriages," where men and women partner sexually with no expectation of marriage, cohabitation, or monogamy. In Japan, Singapore, and Hong Kong, for example, greater access to education and high status employment has increased women's autonomy and, coupled with the traditionally onerous expectations of married women in East Asian families, has made marriage a less attractive option. Yet none of these cultures have yet experienced the dire consequences predicted for either the children of these relationships or the fabric of society.[52] Does this then mean that same-sex couples who are barred from getting married are not missing anything? The answer is no. The data show us that marriage brings many, often unanticipated, benefits to couples who seek it as well as to their children. What it does mean is that marriage and family do not have to happen in a certain prescribed way in order to benefit children and society.

This assertion is buttressed both by the developmental studies discussed prior and the more recent empirical studies of legal same-sex unions in Europe. One of the first was Eskridge and Spedale's 2006 book, *Gay Marriage: For Better or Worse?* In it, the authors present data from the Scandinavian experience with legal same-sex registered partnerships (akin to civil unions in the United States), particularly those in Denmark, which has the longest history of any country in the world of offering these partnerships. Much like the current study, they surveyed and interviewed Danish couples about the benefits they hoped to accrue by registering their partnerships. These ranged from the tangible legal and financial benefits that one commonly thinks of, such as employee and health benefits and inheritance rights, to the more personal benefits, such as an expectation of monogamy and longer lasting unions as a result of having made a public commitment. The latter finding is also supported by Kathleen Hull's 2006 study of same-sex commitment ceremonies in Illinois, prior to the legalization of same-sex marriage.[53] Moreover, the children of same-sex couples benefit from the formalization of their relationship under the law.[54] Eskridge and Spedale additionally cite improvements to the couples' relationships with their families as well as broader social effects, such as easing the burden on the welfare state and attracting skilled workers whose home jurisdictions do not offer these benefits. Although these findings are based on registered partnerships rather than marriages, they are certainly suggestive of the types of benefits that married couples in the United States also might experience, perhaps to an even greater degree.[55]

Where Eskridge and Spedale's study leaves off, with legalized registered partnerships in Denmark and elsewhere, Badgett's study picks up with the legalization of same-sex marriage in the Netherlands. She examines not only the effect (or rather lack of effect) of same-sex marriage on the rest of the Dutch population but also the effect on the couples themselves, as assessed based on her own experience as well as that of the nineteen Dutch couples she interviewed. For example, she found that her subjects experienced a change in terms of their feeling free (and likely) to express their commitment in front of other people, which results in a greater feeling of commitment, as suggested also by Eskridge and Spedale and Kathleen Hull. Marriage also reduced the harm of social exclusion and potentially the "minority stress" experienced by these couples. In some ways, the respondents felt that marriage had "normalized" them in Dutch culture, in a way making them less "queer" and more run-of-the-mill. This was buttressed by modern Dutch culture's willingness to now apply the same model and norms of marriage to same-sex couples—as Badgett terms it, the population's recognition of gay and lesbian people as "marriageable."[56] But it did not change the division of household labor or the arrangements of labor outside of the home. Most couples remarked that not much had changed in their day-to-day lives. And same-sex married couples were no more or less likely than heterosexual couples to divorce in the first two years of eligibility in the Netherlands.

In the America context, analogous research documenting the effects of same-sex marriage and its equivalents was in relatively short supply even a decade after the first legal same-sex unions occurred. Hull's 2006 study of the functions and effects of same-sex marital commitment ceremonies, even though the research preceded the legalization of same-sex marriage, remains an important contribution in telling us about the ceremonial, affective, and cultural aspects of these rituals. In participating in such a rite—even when it is not legally recognized—couples achieve, as Hull argues, a quasi-legal status by enacting the cultural markers of law in its absence. They not only engender public support for their union and a sense of permanence in the relationship but also allow for a culmination of the "coming out" process. These findings suggest that the cultural reach of marriage, and law, are great: they operate even where legal same-sex marriage does not exist. In addition, a series of articles by psychologist Esther Rothblum and colleagues have also added to the empirical knowledge base with both longitudinal studies of couples entering civil unions in Vermont, and comparisons of couples who had entered marriages (in Massachusetts), civil unions, or domestic partnerships in 2004.[57] They found, among other things, that those in civil unions had reported fewer breakups but otherwise very few differences from their un-unioned counterparts. This suggests the power of a legally binding connection, but also the relatively limited sociocultural effects of a status that stops short of marriage.[58]

We know that marriage has a long, varied history and that it most likely means very different things to different people, at different times and geographical locations. Despite the persistence of certain distilled versions in legal and public discourse, we also know from histories of marriage that it has had—and continues to have—many functions. Moreover, although the trends and transformations that would eventually make it possible have been in the works for many decades, we know that the path to legal same-sex marriage has not been linear. Rather, it has been necessarily marked by abrupt (and sometimes more subtle) shifts, both legal and cultural, in attitudes, tactics, and responses. The subsequent chapters of this book pick up the story at one of the more dramatic moments of change—during the years immediately following the "Summer of Love" in San Francisco and the first fully legal same-sex marriages in Massachusetts. This book seeks to address these specific questions: Why do same-sex couples seek to marry? How do their reasons differ depending on the couple (or even the individual)—and how do their reasons differ once they actually arrive at the altar? What do these reasons tell us about how they view the law, its role in their life, and their own place in society and the civic order? What does legal marriage bring to these couples, and how is it similar to or different from commitment ceremonies, civil unions in those states that offer them, or Scandinavian civil partnerships? With a better understanding of where we have been and how we got here, we now turn our attention to the voices of some of the first married same-sex couples in the United States, and the story they tell us about today and the future.

3

The Rite as Right

Marriage as Material Right, Marriage as Strategy

It's rights, it's love, it's security.
—Scott and Mike, Walpole, Massachusetts

Despite its varied past (and present), the right to marriage is one that has been treated in modern western history as so vital that is deemed "fundamental" in United States law. The Supreme Court has upheld the right to marriage for interracial couples, deadbeat dads, and those convicted of a felony. Like becoming a parent—also a venerated and protected status, and one carrying many rights and responsibilities—the state does not traditionally place many barriers or restrictions on marriage, aside from age and blood relation; this is one reason why the Defense of Marriage Act and other explicit limitations on marriage stand out so markedly in the American legal lexicon. As the Court waxed eloquent in the landmark marital privacy case, *Griswold v. Connecticut* (1965), "We deal with a right . . . older than the Bill of Rights—older than our political parties, older than our school system. Marriage is a coming together for better or worse, hopefully enduring, and intimate to the degree of being sacred." This belief was further entrenched two years later in the landmark anti-miscegenation case, *Loving v. Virginia* (1967): "The freedom to marry has long been recognized as one of the vital personal rights essential to the orderly pursuit of happiness by free men. Marriage is one of the 'basic civil rights of man,' fundamental to our very existence and survival."

Given this romanticized and venerated status, it may seem odd, even profane, to orient to marriage as a way to access a right or rights, to save money, to acquire necessities such as health insurance, or to enforce legal protections. Instrumentality should have very little to do with love, intimacy, and the "sacred." But this is the bizarre paradox of legal marriage in the twenty-first-century United States and what Martha Fineman has called the "sexual family."[1] By making marriage the apex of intimate relationships and the primary site for interpersonal rights and responsibilities (well over a thousand of them according to sources cited in chapter 2), we virtually ensure that marriage is not "just" an intimate relationship or sacred institution but a nexus of the personal and the instrumental, the emotional and the legal. It can be whimsy and romance, but it can also be strategy and financial respite. Until your life partner lies dying in the hospital and you are barred from the room, or you lose your job for taking time off to care for (and possibly grieve for) her, it may not be so immediately and painfully apparent how instrumental marriage rights are. It is striking, in fact, how quickly "rights" come to the forefront of the discourse for everyone, when the matter for discussion is not simply (presumably heterosexual) "marriage" but is instead qualified as "*same-sex* marriage." Put these phrases into every day conversation and ones sees the point of departure: in a conversation among heterosexuals, the word "marriage" is most likely brought up when someone is talking about a "happy marriage" or a "bad marriage"—an upcoming wedding or, perhaps, a marriage falling apart. It is notably personal and relational. Add "same-sex" to the word "marriage" instead, and a political debate is invoked. It is no longer simply a personal relationship but a civil right, a "wedge issue," or a subject of litigation.

The articulation of marriage as a right—and specifically one denied to gays and lesbians as a class—is not itself without controversy. This became most apparent in the second wave of marriage litigation, with the *Baehr v. Lewin* case in 1993 and the Hawaiian campaigns for and against a constitutional amendment banning same-sex marriage, but continued in similar campaigns in California and elsewhere. Opponents of same-sex marriage have quite successfully been able to frame the pursuit of marriage equality as a pursuit of "special rights" for gays and lesbians. In the Hawaii case, this strategy was quite successful: opponents of gays and lesbians seeking marriage were framed as minorities trying to impose their new definition of marriage and thereby violate the rights of the majority. At the same time, they were seen as undeserving of the "minority" mantle, which had to be preserved for "traditional 'suspect classes'" (read: racial minorities) in a politics of scarcity that held that the state's limited resources (including marriage rights) should be reserved for those who need them most.[2] In a state whose majority is non-white, and lives with the legacy of colonialism and domination by a white minority, this rhetoric was compelling.

In what again became a popular refrain in California with the challenge of Prop 8, and in Iowa with the recall of the state supreme court justices who had joined the *Varnum* opinion legalizing same-sex marriage, the equal rights–based claims of same-sex marriage supporters were pitted against claims of sovereignty and democracy. As political scientist Jonathan Goldberg-Hiller notes, "Gays and courts were forcing an idea of marriage that the majority opposed—a clear case of 'judicial tyranny.'"[3] The repeated suggestion that these two emblems of American legal tradition—protection and inclusion of minority citizens on the one hand and government by the majority on the other—are fundamentally contradictory has led to what Shannon Minter has called, "The Great Divorce."[4] Juxtaposing two successive California Supreme Court decisions—the 2008 *In re Marriage Cases* case, which found that same-sex couples had a fundamental right to marry, and the 2009 *Strauss v. Horton* case, which upheld the validity of Prop 8 amending the constitution to ban same-sex marriage—Minter examines how it has come to be presumed that democracy and equality are fundamentally unrelated, and might even be contrary to one another. To take action to protect a minority group's rights against the will of the majority or to refuse to enact a policy favored by the majority, which would violate the rights of a minority, is anti-democratic. This action can be seen as even more anti-democratic when those doing the protecting are unelected judges who cannot be said to adequately represent the will of the people. Thus, from this point of view, it would have been improper to sustain same-sex marriage in either Hawaii or California, when the voting public was clearly against it, as expressed in a democratic process. Minter argues that in fact one need not divorce these two ideals from one another; he sees the two as co-constitutive: "social oppression can be as much a failure of democracy as an explicit denial of formal political equality would be." Put another way, "democracy is compromised by social inequality." Equal access to rights, including marriage rights, is as much an essential component of democracy as majority rule.[5] Therefore, by protecting the rights of minorities, one also protects the foundations of democracy. Admittedly, those gay and lesbian individuals or couples seeking the rights of marriage are most likely not doing so to save democracy; but in a culture which has steadily loosened the requisites of marriage, while still attaching a great number of privileges and responsibilities to it, it seems neither outlandish nor dictatorial to extend these rights to an additional minority group.

Small wonder—given the history of exclusion, the increasing availability, its status as a home of privileges, and the variety of historical contingencies—that some same-sex couples might orient to the "sacred" institution of marriage as a locus of legal and financial rights and protections. By the early part of the twenty-first century, and particularly in the midst and wake of the "gayby boom," marriage had become a sort of one-stop shopping goal for those pursuing expanded LGBT rights. Take just one example: In both California and Massachusetts, where the couples in this study resided, the right to second parent adoption—the ability for the non-biological parent in a same-sex parenting union to legally adopt the child without the birth parent having to give up his (or more frequently, her) rights—was already in place prior to same-sex marriage. This, however, is not the case in many states, and it remains a burdensome requirement compared to a marriage where both spouses are presumed to be the parents of any children one or both of them create. Likewise, older same-sex couples preparing for illness and end of life planning have spent untold thousands with financial planners and tax attorneys to figure out how they can protect themselves from the many financial pitfalls the surviving partner may encounter, which would all be subsumed (or would disappear) under the laws of marriage. While it is doubtful whether most couples would be able to name all of the rights they are excluded from as a result of not being able to marry, it remains such a palpable, material manifestation of the stakes of marriage that instrumentalism could be a powerful motivator, even in the abstract, for seeking marriage. In fact, one does not have to have been excluded from her dying partner's hospital room, or to have lost thousands of dollars in inheritance taxes, to understand and be motivated by the legal and financial benefits of marriage; one need only imagine these benefits (or their lack). Between the secondhand stories of others in the LGBT community and the electronic media saturation of LGBT advocacy groups staking these claims, it is a hard message to ignore that one is "missing out" on a great number of advantages if one is barred from marrying.

In interviews and surveys, couples seeking marriage licenses in San Francisco were surely not immune from these messages. These applicants were aware of the benefits of marriage, at least in the abstract if not more specifically, and some saw this as a primary motivation for standing sometimes for hours in line to get a license to marry. For many others, it was nevertheless an important consideration and one of a handful of motivating factors. In some cases this motivation was based on experience—having been denied one of these rights before they were married—but for many it was entirely anticipatory. At the same time, many—especially in San Francisco—were well aware that many benefits would not necessarily accrue to them as a result of their marriage that day. Couples in Massachusetts were often mindful that their marriage in their home state would not guarantee them access to the *federal* rights of marriage, or be recognized in any but a small handful of other states outside of Massachusetts. In San Francisco, rights awareness ran the full gamut from

two-thirds did not.[6] Indeed, particularly on the item dealing with security for one's family, women's ratings of its importance were significantly higher than men's, which makes sense demographically as more lesbian couples have children than do gay male couples.[7] Additionally, those couples of both genders with children also rated the item significantly higher. Interestingly, older couples, who might be more concerned with such exigencies as end-of life decision making and rights of survivorship, did not rate these items significantly higher than did their younger counterparts. In fact, on the item asking about family security, age was inversely related to ratings: *younger* couples were more likely to rate the issue as important. On the related item about taking advantage of the legal and financial benefits of marriage, there was a slight correlation between older age and higher ratings, but when answers to these two related questions about security and benefit were grouped, ratings of the pragmatic reasons as a whole were not significantly correlated with age at all.

Couples were also asked in two open-ended questions to explain in their own words their reasons for marrying. These reasons often mirrored those reflected in the close-ended questions, with more specificity and context. For example, couples with children expressed concerns in the event of tragedy or other adversity: "We need desperately to protect each other and our children here and if something ever happened to one of us," and "We have a child to raise and need our future to be secure for her," were typical responses among these couples. Those who did not yet have children but were planning to have them felt these concerns as well. One couple said, "Even though we don't have children now, we shouldn't have to worry if [we] do. Most people don't have to plan to fend off the state from taking their children away." The sense of urgency was compounded when a family member had medical concerns as well: "This is suddenly more important to our family as my daughter was born severely disabled."

Others did not necessarily have children but were concerned with protecting their connection to one another in other ways. For example, some couples' overriding concern for medical and insurance rights arose from one spouse's serious medical condition. One woman explained, "We've had some health problems and experienced what it was like to not legally be 'family.' My partner was having open heart surgery the following week and we really wanted this." Some couples faced threats not from disability or disease but from hostile family members: "My family opposes my being gay. I want to protect my wife in the event of my death and for her to be recognized as my wife whether others accept the reality or not." For still others, it was their nationality or immigration status that put them potentially in harm's way. A couple from Los Angeles feared deportation of the husband who was from Brazil. Ironically, they had avoided registering as domestic partners because they were fearful of the effect on his homeland security status, since the type of visa he had specified that he could not have an "intent to stay." When asked what their most important reason was for marrying at City Hall, they stated that they were "Desperate for our legal status to stay together in the country." In another sad bit of irony, they chose to marry and avoid domestic partnership because they thought that their marriage would carry more weight with the federal government, but domestic partnerships remain in effect in California, whereas their marriage was soon invalidated.

Despite the weak correlation between age and pragmatic rights-based concerns, a number of couples who ranked these as important reasons for marrying were in fact concerned with end-of-life and survivorship issues. One forty-six-year-old man from Berkeley said, "My husband's family will try to take away our house if my husband passes first." A San Francisco police officer whose spouse was a stay-at-home mom explained, "My partner and our two children are the most important people to me. I put my life on the line every day when I put on my uniform and I hope that if I die in the [line of] duty my fellow officers and my family members will support and protect my partner and my children for me." Echoing a common set of a concerns, one middle-aged female couple commented, "We are getting into our middle age and want to provide for each other. One partner's parents wouldn't hesitate to challenge an estate." These end-of-life concerns were pressing, again, for couples with children, regardless of age.

Many couples expressed dismay and resentment that their access to these rights was so contingent; the couples themselves communicated this dismay in the context of their pragmatic concerns, but to a certain degree they seemed to be tinged with a hint of protest. A male couple in their forties, from the Los Angeles area, stated that they "never wanted 'special rights' just the same as everybody else (which they take for granted)." Their concerns were clearly both practical and ideological; as one stated in the survey, "Absolutely—I want equal rights for equal taxation." In a sentiment echoed later in the interviews, couples were especially resentful of the never-ending number of forms and measures they had to take to approximate the status of marriage in even a piece-meal way. Two psychotherapists from Palo Alto who had been together for eighteen years and raised four children explained that it, "Took us nine legal documents (durable powers of attorney etc.) and two wills to even approximate a part of heterosexual marriage." A female couple from Alameda stated, "We luckily have supportive families but despite our almost twenty years together and stacks of legal documents we are still considered legally strangers by the law."

In interviews, couples expanded on many of these same themes with more in-depth examples. Kristie and Maureen, a couple from Southern California, ranked the legal protections of marriage as their foremost reason for getting married. They had been together eighteen years and are mothers of a school-age daughter whom they adopted in South America. However, because they were not able to complete a second-parent adoption (or dual-parent adoption), they were particularly concerned with the joint parental rights that they would be able to secure through marriage. They had taken a number of steps to secure their status as a family, including taking the same last name, becoming domestic partners, and, in their words, "collecting marriage licenses" everywhere they went. They had their own ceremony in a church in 1992, took part in the collective marriage by Rev. Troy Perry in the 1993 March on Washington, married in Vancouver, Canada, in 2003, received a marriage license at San Francisco City Hall in 2004, and finally were legally married in California in July 2008. They were so eager to marry, in fact, that when they heard about the marriages in City Hall, in Kristie's words, they "packed up in the middle of the school week, pulled [their daughter] out of school, called in to work, put the tents in the back of the car and just drove up there as fast we could." Still, they had great legal concerns: "[W]e feel that since we have a child and own joint property and come from VERY conservative religious backgrounds that we need the legal status to protect our family and our relationship." When I followed up with them in 2008 after their legal marriage, they expressed a tone of relief:

> Now because of this legal marriage we are both legal parents to our beautiful (now twelve-year-old) daughter. We now have legal rights for illness, death, or incapacitation. We both work in elementary schools and feel that this is also added legal protection for job security if there ever was an issue concerning sexual orientation then we can have a legal way to prove our long term committed relationship.

Andy and Bill, an upper-middle-class Caucasian couple in their mid-forties, moved to San Francisco together in 1999. They had no children, lived at the edge of the Castro district, and identified as "bears," both in conversation and in various signs and emblems around their home.[8] They had not registered as domestic partners at before 2004 because they had been advised it would not make sense financially for them at the time. But when California's more comprehensive domestic partnership bill passed in 2005, they decided to register to protect their mutual property interests in the house they had recently purchased together. They seemed very aware of the financial ramifications of their relationship status and resentful that they were not entitled to the same financial benefits and protections as heterosexual married couples. Andy and Bill lamented that they were tired of paying extra taxes on health care, for example: "Well, our medical insurance, we're self-employed, so our medical insurance affects—we can't get a family plan, so . . . we're probably paying a couple hundred dollars extra a month because we have to be looked at as individuals. [W]hy should I pay $300 more in taxes a year that he [Andy's heterosexual boss] doesn't, and he has more people insured? You know?"

Will and Andrew, an interracial white and Latino couple, were similarly motivated by property interests. A middle-class couple in their thirties, both in management positions, they had already been together for fourteen years at the time of their marriage. The practical implications of their lack of legal marital status struck them first when they had bought a house with another couple (a married heterosexual couple) the previous year, in a Tenancy-in-Common (TIC) arrangement. Will remembered, "We obviously had to get lawyers to help us create a TIC contract between the four of us. That's really for the first time where it hit us how different we are . . . because we're not married." This experience stayed with them the following year when the opportunity arose to get married at City Hall, in what they thought would be a legal marriage. Will recalled, "So, by the time February [2004] came around, we were like, 'no brainer.' Like we now know all of the things that we don't have benefits around because we're not legally married because we had gone through the process of buying a home." But they also remarked on smaller-scale changes in benefits afforded to them because of their newly married status. For example, Will was employed by a large retail clothing company: "I remember the next day, I went into work and I said, 'OK, well, I'm legally married, so Andrew can now get a discount card.' And, our admin assistant was like, 'You're right. Here you go.' And, he had an employee discount card."

One of the rights commonly associated with marriage, but rarely invoked as a specific concern for same-sex couples in their decisions to marry, is the spousal privilege of not having to testify against one another. This issue did come up in a handful of cases, though. Dale and Lisa were the last couple to receive a marriage license from San Francisco City Hall in 2004. They were from a diverse neighborhood in San Francisco and had been a couple for fifteen years. They had met while living on opposite coasts but both were working on the campaign of a mutual friend; they had eventually moved in together and started a family (they have one daughter). Both Lisa and Dale had professional backgrounds in law—Lisa was an attorney, and Dale had legal training and worked as a private investigator. As Lisa explained:

> [I]n practicing law I became increasingly aware of the fact that although married couples did have a privilege that my communications with Dale would not be privileged and I thought that was incredibly unfair. And it never came—push never came to shove on that issue for us, but when I was reading about that being one of the reasons I thought, "Well, that's kind of a significant thing."

More common were the day-to-day financial and logistical concerns of those sharing lives and property. When couples owned homes together, property interests were compounded by concerns about what would happen to the property and the surviving spouse, if one were to outlive the other. Nicola and Renee were also a younger interracial couple, Caucasian and African American from Sacramento. As Renee reflected on their reasons for marrying, "Well, it was important to me for property reasons, it was important to me emotionally, and socially, but it's also property reasons, medical reasons, benefits, and I'm thinking more of my 401k and things like that." Nicola added:

> We have one house together and Renee owns her own house as well and so if she were to die, I wouldn't get her house . . . and if we were to put my name on the house, on . . . the legal documents then we have to be two single women on there and our taxes and stuff as far as that is concerned is huge and so it's a difficult issue, whereas if we were simply married it would be a non-issue.

Concerns about end-of-life and incapacitation were common sources of disquiet, even for couples who were healthy and nowhere near the end-of-life. Bill and Andy of San Francisco had the following exchange:

> BILL: I mean it's amazing to think that when you travel you have to have that little medical power of attorney document stashed somewhere

so if you're not in a location that recognizes [same-sex unions] . . . I
don't think his parents would ever do anything, but if he became ill,
I don't—his parents could try to swoop in here and try to do things,
and we've done the best we can protect that from happening, but—
But it could happen today—

ANDY: So that kind of scared me into saying, you know, we have to keep
abreast of all the new changes and make sure we're doing what we
can.

Will and Andrew agreed, "if you don't protect yourself legally that way,
you can lose your house, your half of the house to someone else's family
and all sorts of horrible things can happen."

Ironically, the few couples who had the most reason to be concerned
with end-of-life issues did not necessarily prioritize these benefits and
protections as motivations to marry. Laura was from the San Francisco
Bay Area, and her partner Janet had passed away between the time they
were married at City Hall in 2004 and the time of the interview, and
before same-sex marriage was legalized briefly in California. They were
together for twenty-seven years and had three children together, all
jointly adopted (the youngest, a daughter, was adopted by one mother
at first and later by the other in a second-parent adoption procedure).
She said that they did not prioritize the instrumental reasons for marrying, initially, perhaps in part because Janet was an attorney and was
therefore, Laura felt, better able to protect them regardless of their status. They married primarily, Laura reported, because of Janet's desire to
protest unfair laws and her own desire to do something that was symbolically and personally meaningful. Even so, Laura endured terrible
bureaucratic ordeals after Janet's death—primarily with the Social Security Administration, when trying to access the death benefits due to their
children—because of their lack of legally married status. In fact, the day
after the interview, Laura had a scheduled appointment to appeal the
increased tax assessment on their house, which would cost her an additional $8,000 a year beyond what it would have if they were married.
Sadly, the rights of marriage came too late for her and her children.

Pat and Terry had been together for twenty-three years but had no children. By the time of the interview in 2006, Terry's cancer had advanced to the point that both women knew her time was limited; Terry was completely engaged in the conversation but was visibly fatigued by the end of the interview. They had seen an attorney when Terry was diagnosed and drawn up wills and other arrangements, but their attorney advised them against getting a domestic partnership. Unlike Maureen and Kristie, they had never had any sort of wedding ceremony or state recognition. As Terry said, "I don't think marriage is important at all, even for straight people. And I really mean that. But as long as straight people can do it and gay people can't, we should change that." So even though they hoped that getting married would help them obtain intensive care unit access for Pat when Terry ended up in the hospital, they were under no illusion that this or other rights would necessarily accrue to them as a result of their City Hall marriage in 2004. Moreover, such rights and benefits were notably absent from their explanation of why they decided to get married. When I tried to follow up with Terry and Pat in 2008, I did not get a reply—but presumably the rights of marriage had come too late for them, as well.

For others, marriage seemed indispensable because of the sheer number of rights and benefits associated with it. Dale, a legal professional, reflected on the vast number of rights connected to marriage: "There are probably of the 1,500—I don't think we're even sure. Maybe there are a couple hundred that we personally would care about, but as a matter of principle we care about all of them." This was a theme that first emerged in the survey responses: even when one might be able to assemble a will, a power of attorney, and other documentations, the enormity of the bundle of rights automatically conferred upon marriage left some couples overwhelmed with trying to make up the difference. As Nicola from Sacramento commented:

> And the difficulty is that with us, we have to—from a legal standpoint, we have to do everything individually. We have to have wills to will each other our property, etc. We have to have durable power of attorneys for

health care, so if that's an issue, then that pops up. It's all these little bits of your life that you have to deal with on a separate basis, whereas for straight people, you get married and it's all taken care of, it's an automatic thing. So that was a big thing for us.

A more general set of concerns revolved around the unarticulated legal benefits of marriage as evidence of a couple's ambition to be a family and a legal unit. Leilani and Nancy were a young couple from Oakland who had met and gotten together five years earlier when both were students. They had moved to the Bay Area from Massachusetts just months before the *Goodridge* decision legalized same-sex marriage there. At the time of the interview they did not have children or property together, but were planning both (by the time I followed up with them in 2008, they had had both a wedding ceremony and a baby). As Leilani, who has a legal background, explained:

So many times in family law cases you see things . . . even if they weren't legal they count somewhat in a case because it helps the court see all of these people really are trying to act like a family and sometimes they will honor that in a small way. And so, my thought was almost, if we don't do this . . . what might we lose a year from now? What might, you know, will a court later say if we are fighting or something or whatever that "oh they weren't trying to be like family because they didn't go for this marriage at City Hall thing." You know? . . . I didn't expect any direct benefits in the legal sense, but I thought there might be some indirect [benefit].

Nonetheless, Leilani was also convinced of the importance of marriage benefits and protections because, like Nicola and Anne Marie, she recognized the all-encompassing bundle of rights that coalesce in marriage. When asked about the importance of these rights as compared to other reasons to get legally married, she explained:

They're really important. I mean I could live with other things. . . . But the legal stuff, I mean, we can throw tons of money at it and make up contracts and wills and all sorts of things, or [*laughter*] or we can simply sign a marriage certificate. So, yeah that's really important. That's number one for me.

Many of the same thoughts of practicality were echoed four years later when marriage again became an option in California in the wake of *In re Marriage Cases*. In a follow-up with Jamie and Dean of San Francisco in October 2008, they were certainly concerned with "obtaining legal rights, such as hospital visitation, and forming a Trust together [which] is extremely expensive, time consuming, and inconvenient. That's one of the reasons we'd prefer to have legal recognition through marriage."[9] Yet despite these concerns, they initially planned to not get married immediately; they said they wanted to wait until after the election that November when the fate of Prop 8 and their marriage rights would be decided. However, their concerns ultimately got the better of them: three weeks later, on October 30 (days before the passage of Prop 8), Jamie emailed me to let me know that he and Dean had gotten married the day before. He explained:

> Our decision to go ahead now was based on the possibility of Proposition 8 passing. We didn't want to have to wait yet another five years, and wanted the security, rights, and benefits of a married couple. It's part emotional, part political, and part financial. But as before we both agree that it was the *right* thing for us to do.[10]

Mary and Kim, a couple for nine years, from the relatively conservative community of Chico, California, admitted that their reasons for wanting to marry had shifted between 2004 and 2008, when they legally married. They recounted, "When we married in 2004 in San Francisco, we did so for traditional reasons: family, commitment, celebration, love." This had changed by 2008, with Election Day and Prop 8 looming. Now their concern had shifted away from tradition and toward a practical concern with legal rights, admittedly combined with political motivations to make a statement (see chapter 4). Likewise, Linton and

Jeff, who lived in the East Bay Area, expressed increased concerns with such practical implications of marriage when we followed up in 2008. A young, professional, interracial (Caucasian and African American) couple, both transplants from the Midwest, they had been together for seven years at the time of the interview. Linton had only recently come to a set of political beliefs that valued marriage rather than resisting it as a heterosexist institution, and their ceremony at City Hall on February 12, 2004, was profoundly meaningful in a number of ways for both Jeff and Linton. They did have a long list of concerns about the protections they lacked due to their status after the invalidation of their licenses. Like Lisa and Dale, there was the issue of spousal privilege; Linton's employer was being sued, causing him great stress, and he could not discuss it at home, for fear that Jeff could be forced to testify about it. He exclaimed, "I mean, it's ridiculous that there's a lawsuit . . . that I can't talk about to my partner because he would be subject to be subpoenaed. However, if I were straight, I could say whatever I want and he couldn't be dragged into court. That's a simple fact." Still, they stated that they were not motivated by a desire for the legal protections and benefits at that time, and were skeptical that they would achieve in any case. Four years later, the story was much different, perhaps in part because of the prior experience and the seeming solidity of a California Supreme Court decision, their pragmatic focus was more pronounced:

> It was important for us to get married to protect ourselves in case either one of us dies. We were concerned about property transfer rights, and all the other legal rights that are afforded to married couples. Additionally, Jeff wanted to take my last name, and the only way to do so was to marry. Finally, it just feels good to be married![11]

Massachusetts

One might guess that the importance placed on legal and financial concerns would be more significant in Massachusetts where, unlike in

California, most couples did not have the option to enter into a domestic partnership or civil union to secure these rights and responsibilities. In the early 1990s some local jurisdictions, including Cambridge and Boston, had begun to offer domestic partnership registries with a limited number of rights and protections by city ordinance. These generally included the ability of city or county employees to extend benefits to their partners, the right to visit a partner in the hospital or county jail, and access to the school grounds and school records for children they raise together. Additionally, certain gay-friendly employers, such as the University of Massachusetts, opted to extend same-sex domestic partner benefits. However, under Massachusetts state law, there was no comprehensive—or even uniform but limited—domestic partnership or civil union option.

Neri and her spouse (unavailable for the interview) were a Latina couple in their thirties from Uxbridge, Massachusetts. Neri's spouse was a special-needs teacher and massage therapist, and Neri herself was disabled and not working at the time of the interview. They had met six years earlier through an online dating service, while living on opposite coasts. Six months later, Neri's future spouse gave up her residence in Los Angeles and joined Neri in Rhode Island, where she was living at the time. A few years into the relationship, having closely monitored legal developments on same-sex marriage, they decided to move to Massachusetts. As Neri explained, "as we were keeping an eye on things we decided, 'We both work in Massachusetts. Let's move there so we can get married.'" They experienced a full-scale life challenge as a couple when, early in the relationship, Neri was diagnosed with cancer and underwent rigorous chemotherapy and radiation treatments. Neri spoke of the difficulties they had to deal with when she underwent treatment for cancer, and they had no legal connection to one another: "[She] and I saw the other side of what you can run into when you're not married." She discussed all of the additional paperwork she was required to fill out so that her soon-to-be spouse would be able to visit her, receive her medical information, and make decisions for her in the event of Neri's incapacity, as well as all of the conversations she had to have with medical professionals, including some that revealed both spoken and unspoken biases. For example, when considering treatment options and how they would affect her, some doctors continued to view Neri as a single woman and assumed that, because of this and her lesbianism, she was not interested in having children—and therefore not interested in saving her reproductive system from the effects of radiation.

Bijan and his spouse were educated professionals in their thirties, living in a largely gay section of Boston, and fathers to a one-year-old adopted daughter. Bijan is half French and half Iranian, mostly raised abroad, while his spouse was from Minnesota. Both had come out in early adulthood and, according to Bijan, despite both being children of divorce they knew within months of meeting that they were meant to spend their lives together. They had been together for twelve years at the time of the interview, having already gone to Vermont to get a civil union in 2001 and Canada to get married in 2003. Unlike some of the other "marriage license collectors" I interviewed, Bijan and his spouse had never had a public ceremony because it felt "kind of silly" to them. Although the couple had considered moving to Vermont so they could take advantage of their civil union status there, they were acutely aware of the geographical and legal confines of their marital status. Bijan recounted an episode while going through customs when returning to the United States from their wedding in Canada. Having filled out a single customs form and presented it along with their brand-new marriage license to the Homeland Security official, they were told, "Sorry, this is American customs and your piece of paper is worth nothing." Like Neri, Bijan came to the realization of what the rights of marriage meant in a moment of crisis: in 2001, he had been struck by a car, and had, as he put it, "the usual story of being rushed to the emergency room and they wouldn't let [his partner] see me." He recalled:

> We were so infuriated. I think that is what kind of started the whole thing. We never actually thought about marriage until, you know, but then we realized wait a second marriage is basically this like 1,100 federal rights

and 860 state rights in Massachusetts. We were like how come we don't get that? Any straight person can go to Las Vegas, meet someone, get drunk and get married and have that. We have NO laws protecting us.

The experience so profoundly affected them that they began to become politically involved in the marriage equality movement in Massachusetts. They began volunteering for the Freedom to Marry Coalition, and, in Bijan's words, "started understanding what it was all about and then we started telling our friends that they all needed to wake up. You know, we are all asleep at the wheel here." Despite being politicized, however, they weren't looking for legitimation: "We didn't need society to bless us in any kind of way or whatever, but for us it is more about the protection. I mean it really is 100 percent why we got married. Otherwise, we really didn't need to do that." Still, however, there are places that Bijan and his family will not travel, including Iran where his father was, because of fears that their marriage will not be recognized.

Scott and Mike, another "Bear" couple who had been together for twelve years, did not have a traumatic experience but had also become deeply sensitized to their lack of rights as a gay couple when it came to marriage, prior to the *Goodridge* decision. Both in their early forties and natives of Massachusetts, they stated that they did not want to offend anyone with their marriage or "push anyone's buttons"; they purposefully chose to have a small civil ceremony at Cambridge City Hall for that reason and were adamant that they did not seek any kind of blessing, religious or otherwise. They explained that, as a gay couple, they did not have the same grand lifelong expectations of marriage that a straight couple might:

If your whole mind-set is that it's not an option you kind of change your whole life around that it doesn't mean what it might mean to straight people. As a gay person you just don't think there's ever that option so you don't look to that for your security. You make your own security.

And so they did. But in the wake of the *Goodridge* decision, between its release and its implementation, Scott was prompted to do some research and began to be aware of all the financial and legal benefits they were presently excluded from. As Scott exclaimed, "It has nothing to do with religion. I don't want to force churches to marry people; I don't want to do that. But I just want the taxes that we pay to be equal to [those of] straight people." He summed up, "To me it really is about the rights. It's not about the commitment because we had that. It's about being treated equally. That's what I want."

Like many of the couples in San Francisco, those in Massachusetts with children felt added attachment to the multiple protections included in legal marriage. Katherine and Daphne, both thirty-seven, were a middle-class, white, well-educated couple with two children. They had been raised in Catholic families in the south shore area of Massachusetts, met ten years prior through friends, and soon moved in together. They jumped at the chance to get married when it was legalized in Massachusetts, taking out a license on the first day they were available at Cambridge City Hall and applying for a judicial waiver to the standard three-day waiting period so that they could get married that very day, May 17, 2004. At the time of their marriage, their son was two and a half, and they were working on getting pregnant with their second child. Their children had been conceived with a known donor, who had surrendered his paternity rights to clear the way for the non-biological mother to complete a second-parent adoption and have a legal link to their son. Still, when they traveled out of state, they felt safe in their parental rights only if they brought a lengthy set of legal documents establishing their relationship to one another. Katherine described the experience of relying on all of this paperwork in dramatic fashion:

> I keep saying it's like—and this might be extreme—I feel like a Jew in Nazi Germany making sure I have all my papers in order. You know, make sure you have all your papers in order before you try to travel. Like

that's what it makes me feel like having to, you know, have all of that there just in case, god forbid, something were to happen.

They did not spend much time talking about particular rights or obligations related to taxes, property, and the like; aside from their concerns about traveling with their children, their only specific reference was to their newfound ability to share employment benefits, but they repeatedly stressed how important these benefits were to them, and how lucky they felt to live in Massachusetts and have the opportunity marry.

Beth and Isabel also had many reasons for marrying but focused on those related to parenthood. Both natives of New England in their mid-forties, their relationship already had a long history by the time they were legally married in 2004. They had met as young teenagers at a summer camp in Maine and became friends, but lost touch after their junior year of high school. They reconnected after college, by which time both women were living in Boston; they drifted in and out of each other's lives as friends for a number of years before beginning a romantic relationship in the mid-nineties. They had a commitment ceremony with family and friends in 1997, which they consider their anniversary to this day; two years later, they had a son. They explained that by the time they were able to marry legally their lives were already intertwined financially, legally, and socially to the point where they were very much a unit; they also had quite a bit of legal paperwork related to the birth and co-parent adoption of their son. Still, legal marriage brought them an added security that they could not resist. As Isabel explained, "We obviously wanted to get whatever protections we can for [our son], you know. To make our family as legal as it possibly can be." They also took advantage of the moment to change their names to a mutual last name; legal marriage made this process much easier and less expensive than it would otherwise have been. When Beth and Isabel were asked to rate each of the various reasons for marrying, the financial and legal benefits and security it brought to their family were the only items they ranked at the top of the scale.

Kristen and Ivy, too, were parents, which figured largely in their decision to marry. However, their life experiences growing up resulted in vastly divergent paths to this realization. Kristen was a Massachusetts native, raised in an intact Catholic family outside of Boston; she had a career as a software executive but was in law school at the time of the interview. Ivy was also an executive working in health and technology but had been raised in a non-observant Jewish home in the Midwest. Her early life was characterized by frequent moves and parental divorce, and she had spent time in the foster care system. Now thirty-five, she had been married in her early twenties to a man. Kristen, by contrast, had always been a lesbian and had had a commitment ceremony with a prior partner. She was, by her own definition, "the marrying type." The couple had been together for nine years but had never had a marriage ceremony with one another, aside from exchanging paper cigar rings on a trip to Vermont. They joked that Kristen had proposed repeatedly to Ivy, only to be shot down because, as Ivy was quick to point out, it wasn't legal. When the *Goodridge* decision came down shortly after the birth of their first child, however, Ivy suddenly came face-to-face with a dramatically altered set of circumstances. She explained:

> [E]verything changed with me when we had kids, right before [their older son] was born. . . . When I was trying to figure out, so "Let's say I died in child birth? What happens? . . . I haven't talked to my mother in twenty years. You're saying she can show up and grab my kid? Our kid?" . . . That was the biggest wakeup call to me.

Ivy had given birth to their son, and Kristen had not yet completed a second-parent adoption. She had never before felt an urgency or a reason to marry, but now she did: "Suddenly it put a lot of things into perspective like, of course, that should be something you can be able to do. And it actually does matter."

For Kristen, however, marriage had always been a priority. Her prior experience with a non-legal ceremony had left her unsatisfied; she reflected, "although it was recognized in the Episcopal Church as a union, it wasn't a union. I mean, it wasn't legally a union and they called it a union, but it still never felt—I don't know—complete." While she had always hoped to marry for the sense of fulfillment and commitment it brought, she conceded that having kids gave her "a completely different perspective on the matter." She also had a pragmatic concern of her own. Not long before they were married, Kristen's Massachusetts employer was sold to a midwestern corporation, who then eliminated the company's policy of domestic partner benefits. The only way to retain those benefits after a one-year grace period would be to get married. So while Kristen had broader relationship reasons for wanting to marry, she had immediate concerns as well. Ivy, however, saw things a bit differently from the start, as far as the purpose of getting married:

> I was committed before, getting married, and I felt like I knew where I was with my relationship before even having the option to get married. And it was really having our son that threw the wrench into that picture, where it said, "You have your little idealized view of what your relationship is and great that you have a nice, clear cheery picture of all is well in the world, but actually it isn't. Lots of people don't want you to be together. Lots of people think that's a really bad thing and, given the opportunity, that can affect your family in a variety of ways. So, it was really how important it was to protect our family.

Troy and Chuck were equally eager to get married. Troy was a marketing professional in his late thirties and had been raised Mormon before coming out in his mid-twenties. Chuck, fifty-one, was a Renaissance man of sorts; he had been in the military, worked in multiple professions, and held three graduate degrees in business, psychology, and theology, respectively. He had been a businessman, educator, consultant, and now a journalist. He was also spiritually eclectic, having been raised Methodist, converted to Roman Catholicism, and finally to Reform Judaism in later adulthood. The couple had met in 1999 at the Boston Marathon and moved in together six months later. They did not have children nor had had any sort of traumatic life event leading them to want to marry. Rather, they felt that they had simply come to a time in their lives when these things seemed to matter more. As Troy explained:

> I mean, we really were at the point in our relationship where, you know, we kept going back and forth on what we needed to do to, you know, kind of have all of your affairs in order. When you start owning property together and living together and sharing finances, you just need to get all your ducks in a row. And so, you know, getting married just kind of instantaneously takes care of most of it.

Although marriage was certainly important to them for other reasons as well—Chuck, in particular, discussed the emotional aspects that had affected him even as he read the *Goodridge* decision the day it was released—they were also very practical about its benefits:

> I think once you've decided to have the relationship and the commitment and the life together, you need all of the protections that go with it, whether it's a civil union or a marriage or just the legal protections that you create on your own. You need something, just out of, you know—just being practical about being together, you need all of those protections.

Chip and Keith, from Cambridge, were situated very similarly to Troy and Chuck. Both born and raised in the area, Chip was a self-made successful independent businessman, fifty-five years old, with roots in Ireland; Keith was African American, fifty-six, and a retired police detective. After originally meeting in 1979 and dating briefly, they met again and began dating seriously in 1981, and had been together ever since. Both had retired at forty-three; it was only at this point, once Keith was no longer a police officer, that he felt comfortable enough to fully come out to those around him (by then the couple had been committed and living together for some time). They never had a commitment ceremony or domestic partnership, did not have children, and never thought about marriage because they did not believe it would ever be legal in their time. Of the *Goodridge* decision, when they heard about it, they remarked "We thought we were about fifty years too early." But when it became clear that they would soon be able to legally marry, they jumped on the opportunity. Chip explained:

> [I]t kind of happened at the same time we got to an age where we needed to think of our own mortality and what happened next, and we have an imbalance in our income so that my . . . federal estate tax will really wipe everything out as Keith knows it, as opposed to if we were legally married in a federal sense. . . . So that's where the whole marriage really became important because we began to see how disadvantaged we were as [far as] a safety net, as a legal safety net.

They explained that although it was a special moment to be among the first married at Cambridge City Hall, particularly for Keith who had been born and raised in Cambridge, they did not need the legal license to feel married. Chip stated:

> It was the legal protections we were really after, 'cause we were already married. And I think we've all been to some marriages where the minister or priest or officiator will always say, "I'm just a witness, and this marriage is really between these two people at the altar, and they're committing to each other." And that's what we had done years before, so we were really already married, so it was more about legal protection.

Younger couples, in general, were more likely than couples such as Chip and Keith to have had or considered a commitment ceremony prior to having gotten legally married, and which ostensibly gave them the same sense of emotional commitment separate from their legal marriage. But it was nevertheless not uncommon for them to make the same distinction that Chip and Keith made between "feeling" married and what they later sought with a legal marriage license. Michael and John, for example, were both white and in their mid-thirties and lived in a predominantly gay neighborhood in the Boston area. Michael had grown up in Vermont and spent ten years in the education field before pursuing a doctorate in psychology. John was from Oklahoma, raised in a middle-class family and had spent most of his recent career working in education as well—he was at the time working on his second master's degree. They had in common roots in the Roman Catholic Church— John had actually spent three years in seminary before leaving after coming out as gay—but both had long since drifted away from the church. They had met in Denver and moved to Boston together after a brief time in California. Although they did not have children or specialized health concerns and were far from retirement, John and Michael were very clear about the purpose of their marriage: "We wanted . . . the health care protection and the legal protection that we thought was really, really important, and didn't want to lose that."

Michael continued, "I still see the marriage piece as a legal, contractual agreement. . . . I see what we did with the legal documents as a— not as a business agreement, but as a law thing." He admitted that this was largely a recent concern, as the result of his decision to give up his job and become a full-time doctoral student: "Going from a full-time employed person to now I'm not, and thinking about what's that going to mean for me in terms of access to health care for all these other things— that's been really—I've been reminded about that and I've thought nothing more than about what's going to happen with health care."

It was not uncommon, though, for couples to state an overriding concern for the protections and benefits of marriage, but lack either a specific compelling realization or fear propelling them to this decision, or a strongly voiced feeling about the importance of practical concerns. Glen and David are a good example. An upper-middle-class white couple of twelve years, both natives of Massachusetts and highly educated, they consistently stated, when comparing different reasons for getting married in the abstract, that the legal and financial benefits were foremost for them. They had had a marriage ceremony on their own three years prior, which they considered to be the more emotionally important date. They described getting married at Cambridge City Hall in the first days of legalized marriage as "a very exciting time," and David initially expressed equal concern with the individual rights and the broader political implications: "For me, it was the legal benefits and also I was getting very upset with the politics around it. And how they were trying to make it not happen right until the end. I became very upset about that, the tactics being used. So for me it was political as well as legal protection." But they admitted that they, as well as their family and friends, were mostly excited that they would now have access to rights of marriage. David stated that he didn't even care whether the institution was called "marriage" or had an alternative label, such as civil union, so long as the same rights and benefits were included. When asked to rate the importance of various reasons for marrying, they were very clear and had no disagreement: it was about the legal protections. But they did not express the kinds of fears or epiphanies experienced by other couples, such as Kristen and Ivy or Bijan and Matt.

Similarly, Jesse and David, both transplants to Massachusetts from North Carolina and Maryland, respectively, were also a professional upper-middle-class couple in their mid-thirties, together for twelve years. While Jesse was admittedly more ideological about the importance of exercising the right to same-sex marriage, and also was the more political of the two, David was a self-described pragmatic, concerned with health insurance and other spousal benefits. He explained:

> There was also the pragmatic . . . I was working for the city at the time, and Jesse was self-employed. . . . And we were paying out of pocket for Jesse's health insurance, as a small business of one. And as soon as we were married we were going to be allowed to get health insurance, and all those benefits.

While he also felt it was important as a matter of principal to be treated as an equal, David conceded, "But I think at that point, it was still the pragmatic 'we want the same benefits as everyone else has.' And domestic partner benefits could always be taken away and what not." Like Glen and David, there was no precipitating event or overriding fear; but when asked to rate various motivations for marrying on a scale of one to five, the only one that both men rated as a five was obtaining the financial and legal benefits of marriage.

Practical Consequences after Marriage

The lack of these responsibilities and benefits, and the efforts and motivation to attain them, are important in what they communicate to the bearers, the legal consciousness they represent, and their intangible consequences, such as feelings of insecurity and stress. But inevitably the question of most interest becomes: What does marriage actually bring to these couples, once they have it? For some couples, the effects were almost immediately evident and far reaching. Anne and Nancy were one such couple. A middle-class Boston couple in their fifties, Nancy and Anne shared a love of baseball and close connections to spirituality—Nancy described herself as an "unaffiliated Buddhist," and Anne, who grew up working class, was an ordained United Church of Christ minister. They had been a couple since 1996 and in 2000 had committed themselves to each other in both a lavish commitment ceremony at home and a civil union in Vermont. A series of encounters with serious illness, before and after marriage, rendered the difference palpable for them. Nancy had originally been treated for breast cancer before their marriage, at a time when she and Anne had no legally recognizable relationship in Massachusetts (their civil union in Vermont had no bearing in their home state). Anne had a difficult time communicating the nature of their relationship to the hospital staff, who, while not hostile, didn't understand Nancy's "partner" as her next of kin who should be getting all information about her condition. When the cancer recurred the year after their marriage, the ability to use the term "spouse" and produce a legal marriage license put Annie in a distinctly different position: "I didn't have to worry about any of that this time, you know, so you know, sitting around the hospital for eight hours through, you know, two surgeries, I didn't have to worry that nobody could ever *not* tell me what was going on, no matter what."

Kristen and Ivy also experienced dramatic changes of their own. Right after their marriage, Kristen was able to add Ivy to her health plan under her employer's benefits program for spouses. After the sale of her company and the elimination of domestic partnership benefits, she and Ivy were in a tough position and facing an additional $3,800 a month in health care expenses. Kristen explained that "there was a financial burden that was immediately going to fall on us because we weren't married. . . . And gay, straight, or otherwise, that's not fair. Because I have a piece of paper I should now have health care benefits?" Fortunately, *Goodridge* came down from the courts, and the couple was spared the additional expense. Kristen recounts, "And then, when I did get married I said, 'Here you go. I am married. That was your requirement.' They were like, 'Oh! We didn't see that one coming.'" Even more important were the implications after the birth of their second son. Their first son, born about six months before the *Goodridge* decision, was a "legal stranger" to Kristen until completion of a second-parent adoption. Their second son, born after their marriage, automatically had both parents' names on his birth certificate. This took even Kristen and Ivy by surprise: "We were shocked. We had no idea that that was gonna happen," remembered Ivy. This has had tremendous consequences in terms of their sense of security while traveling with the children. Likewise, Maureen and Kristie experienced the tangible benefits of marriage when they officially became legal co-parents to their daughter once same-sex marriage was legalized in California. Jesse and David, too, were able to identify an immediate financial impact: "We were directly affected by that paying thousands of dollars every year for Jesse's health insurance [before marriage]. And that's just one of the benefits, a big one." There were also less dramatic tangible benefits realized, such as Andrew's ability to receive an employee discount at Will's company, and Jeff's comparatively easy and inexpensive process taking Linton's last name upon their wedding.

Notwithstanding, however, most couples encountered very little in the way of particular identifiable material changes post-marriage. This may be attributable in large part to the fact that their marriages were not recognized by the federal government as a consequence of DOMA. Additionally, California couples in particular resided in a sort of marital limbo state until the California Supreme Court clarified their status in 2009. Indeed, those in California would *not* gain new rights in any event, if they were already registered as domestic partners with the state—a notable difference between these couples and their counterparts in Massachusetts. Yet, when asked whether they had experienced any tangible, practical changes post-marriage, surprisingly few answered in the affirmative in either state: only 8 percent of couples in Massachusetts and 9 percent of those interviewed in California were able to identify any such differences in their everyday lives. Because many of the new rights they sought to gain were anticipatory, these couples would not experience the difference until one of them died or became incapacitated, and it was a small minority of couples who had already had the kind of life-threatening experience that most feared facing without spousal protections in place. Typical were the concerns that David and Jesse of Massachusetts shared, as well as those of Andrew and Will of California: Andrew explained, "If you don't protect yourself legally that way, you can lose your house, your half of the house to someone else's family and all sorts of horrible things can happen." David specified in a similar vein, "There's the whole retirement thing, because I make more money than Jesse, there's all sorts of issues with that. I think still, if I were to die first, and he inherited my 401K plan, he would have to pay taxes on it." Jesse followed up with concerns of his own: "Back to my panics, God forbid someone try to bar me from David if he's sick. I mean there is going to be a scene. The notion that I can say 'I'm married to him,' and that has a . . . quality to it, it's pretty important to me."

What eventually became quite clear was that even for those whose prior motivations were instrumental in nature, once marriage became a reality they left the practical behind to a certain degree and began to experience these rights in ideological or emotional terms. The anticipatory nature of their concerns, dealing with life's worst fears, may have had much to do with this. Ivy, who did not see the necessity of marriage at all until the birth of her son, experienced a great relief that was in many respects typical:

> I was able to relax a little bit. It was just the ability to take a deep breath and exhale, which I thought was great. I didn't know that that would be coming until after we got married. And it just—by adding that security—it just exhaled a little bit. It was a little bit less stress in terms of what if, what happens when? Those types of scenarios. So, that was a big thing for me that I didn't know would be coming.

Anne and Nancy, having already experienced a brush with death as a result of Nancy's cancer, harbored similar fears: "God forbid, one of us goes in a nursing home, if we weren't legally married, we'd have to sell the condo. I mean, that's like incredible . . . you know, you'd lose your home, just because you couldn't be legally married. That one just really drives me crazy." On another hand, it certainly didn't take a near-death experience to elicit these feelings of fear; for Renee and Nicola of Sacramento, proximity to the health care field was enough: "Although it's not an issue for us, it was just the fear that something that can happen and working in the medical field, I know how it works." Although they did not have children, Nicola was also quite upset with the exclusion of unmarried couples from certain parental rights. She described her disappointment concerning the experience of a lesbian friend, who had a child with her partner of ten years but had, in Nicola's words, fewer rights than the sperm donor because she was not the biological mother. Nicola's response was vehement: "That just is obscene to me that, that's—I think in our society with so many gay people having children that the children have to have rights as well and the way that they get their rights is through their parents being married."

Beyond remedying these fears and "what ifs," marriage had unanticipated effects that went beyond the material. In some cases, the material benefits of marriage morphed into more meaningful devices of recognition. Both Linton and Will reflected on how angry it had made them that their partners were not able to take advantage of the discounts their workplaces offered to fellow employees' spouses. Both worked for otherwise relatively gay-friendly employers and knew, upon reflection, that it was not the monetary value of these discounts that most concerned them. Rather, it was what these benefits—or more accurately, the exclusion from these benefits—represented. The ability to later pursue these benefits as married couples had begun as a practical matter but had become a signpost of inclusion.

That marriage should bring emotional value and a sense of security in and of itself is not surprising; but couples themselves, who had long ago committed emotionally to one another in most cases, and had admittedly been motivated by financial and other practical concerns to make it legal, were surprised by the effect it had on them. One example was Greg, from the greater Boston area. He and his spouse, Robert, had been together ten years by the time of the interview and had gotten married on their eighth anniversary. While Greg was white with Scottish roots, Robert was of Armenian and Lebanese descent. They had similar backgrounds in many ways: both were in their late thirties, college educated, raised in the suburbs of Boston in Catholic families, which were still religious and harbored a mix of acceptance and apprehension about their sexualities and their marriage. Both admitted they had not seen the point of marrying unless it carried financial and legal benefits, but they finally had their opportunity when *Goodridge* was implemented. Although they talked about the community recognition that marriage brought, they decided to elope and had never actually had a public ceremony. Greg, who was trained as a librarian but unemployed at the moment, commented:

> When we got married, I was really thinking about the benefits of—I don't know. Employers are starting to—you have to be married to get health care through your—so those are the things—some of those benefits were important to me. But then when we actually got married sort of the emotionalness [*sic*] of it really hit me. It sort of surprised me, actually.

Will's experience was similar. As he recalled, "In the beginning, yes, it was more about the benefits and all the legal things that we just needed to worry [about] because we're not married. After the fact, the symbolic actually became bigger . . . the symbolic validation became really apparent, huge after the fact." His spouse, Andrew, again connected this to the fears of the future's legal and medical unknowns: "It's 'what ifs' and having to plan for it. Having the burden to have to plan for it." But it wasn't just about quelling fears, in the end, for either of them. It was a deeply felt validation of their relationship. Andrew remarked of their relationship after getting their marriage license in San Francisco: "It felt strangely stronger. . . . Well, I think it's just the perception from outsiders that, 'Hey, we're married and we're no different than anyone else.'" He told of an anecdote that underscored this sentiment. Shortly after receiving their marriage license, he showed the document to his sister, who is heterosexual and married. She remarked that it looked just like hers. Though obvious, this observation underscored Andrew and Will's sense of equality and inclusion. Will agreed, "I think to a certain extent, there was this high of what had just occurred and the validity and just that we were legally really married. So, yeah, there was this, like, high after the fact, where it just felt stronger."

Experiencing legal marriage firsthand, in effect, broadened couples' sense of its reach. Scott and Mike of Massachusetts, by no means lifelong marriage activists before, came to a deeper appreciation of what it brings. Scott remembers:

> Before, I thought a little bit about it. I just kind of thought it wouldn't be an option so it didn't affect me. After I realized and became more political and understood it I'm like "Wow, I found out what I was missing out on." Like health care . . . I thought "Why have I been missing out on this?" So it's very important now. Before I wouldn't say it wasn't important but I would say I wasn't aware of how important it could be.

Describing what their legal entitlement to marry meant to them now, Mike and Scott aptly summed up in an exchange that was lighthearted but also profound:

MIKE: Marriage is not based on sex okay, it's not about sex! [*laughter*]

SCOTT: It's so much more than that. It's rights, it's love, it's security.

Marriage as Strategy

Ewick and Silbey, in their much quoted treatise on legal consciousness, describe those citizens who position themselves "with the law" by gaming the system, playing it to achieve particular ends. While they resist a description of this as "instrumental," it is certainly strategic and material. And it should not be surprising that these same pragmatic considerations might be present when the right to enter a legal marriage suddenly becomes available. One can fully appreciate the security of those rights of marriage only when one is deprived of it, an experience shared by a majority of same-sex couples (and others who cannot or will not marry for whatever reason) but commonly overlooked by married heterosexuals. The experiences of Neri and her partner during her cancer treatment, Matt and Bijan after Bijan's accident, or Laura after the death of her life partner and mother of her children all serve as visceral reminders of just how important these relationship rights are. No wonder, then, that strategists and litigators have often focused on the material consequences of the deprivation of legal marriage rights when making their case: these rules and benefits are tangible, frequently quantifiable, and often quite consequential.

But one might also ask if it is surprising that we might see the idealized and romanticized institution of marriage as a vehicle for financial and legal benefits. One lawyer who helped litigate the California case legalizing same-sex marriage noted: "We initially relied heavily on rights-based arguments but realized fairly early on that very few people, gay or straight, view marriage primarily as a way to get rights and benefits."[12] Indeed, while few would choose to dispense with these benefits, they were not, at the end of the day, the predominant focus of discussion with the majority of married same-sex couples. Interviews and surveys reveal that while certainly important, this seemingly "most obvious" reason for same-sex couples to pursue legal marriage was in fact *not* the primary reason why most couples stood in line for hours to marry at San Francisco's City Hall in 2004. This is especially noteworthy given the primacy attributed to the rights attendant to marriage in public and political discourse on legal same-sex marriage. One might guess that responses in Massachusetts might differ because Massachusetts did not already have domestic partnerships in place (as in California) and because the marriage licenses issued there were on much less precarious legal ground. However, access to benefits was not the highest rated set of reasons for most couples marrying in Massachusetts, either— only fourteen of the fifty couples interviewed in Massachusetts cited such instrumental concerns as among their reasons for marrying at all. Even among couples in California, responses on the survey suggested the de-emphasis of marrying as primarily a way to secure rights. Comparing those couples that had already registered as domestic partners (and therefore did not need an additional status to secure state-level rights) and those who did not register, couples without domestic partnerships were in fact significantly *less* likely to marry for instrumental reasons. Moreover, despite the number of rights attached to marriage, it also does not account for much of the difference in how most people fared *after* marriage—notwithstanding the notable and invaluable difference legal marriage made to couples like Kristie and Maureen, Kristen and Ivy, or David and Jesse.

"It's rights, it's love, it's security"—a simple summary of a complex institution but no less accurate for its simplicity. Instrumental concerns can indeed motivate a decision to marry, but they are almost never isolated from other motivations or results. Curiously, same-sex marriage is one of the few contexts in which it makes sense to focus on legal spouses as bearers of rights, because many have been living as spouses and functional families for years or decades before it was a legal option. They may have been forced by necessity—through parenthood, illness, or adversity—to acquaint themselves with the legal protections that would otherwise be automatic and approximate them as best as possible outside of marriage. Ironically, in other legal contexts—in immigration, for example—the law requires that practicality *not* be the motivation for marriage. Inevitably, though, human relationships and motivations are never so simple. The material benefits of marriage often crosscut with other facets of the institution. In some couples' experience, they were motivated by financial or legal concerns but ultimately underwent transformations that were wholly expressive. For others, it was easy to underscore the importance of the many rights they would gain but harder to speak of the entitlements in isolation from other features they valued in their newfound right to legal marriage. The unmistakable conclusion is not just that marriage in and of itself is complex, but that law serves a multitude of purposes even within the confines of a single act. The men and women in this chapter are unabashedly (and perhaps necessarily) pragmatic, but they are not simply gaming the system. Their past experiences and present social positioning influence their orientation to the functions of legal marriage but do not confine them to a singular consciousness regarding its purpose or resonance. American history has seen other moments in which access to a particular legal institution—integrated public schools, the jury box, the military—carried more than one meaning for those traditionally excluded. Rarely are the consequences purely practical, and marriage is no different. Yet this moment in history helps us understand that the stakes in legal marriage are a unique mix of the material, the ideological, the political, and the romantic.

4

Marriage as Protest

The Political Dimensions of Marital Motivation

All of a sudden, we see riots, we see protests, we see people clashing. The next thing we know, there is injured or there is dead people.
—Governor Arnold Schwarzenegger's predictions for the Winter of Love in San Francisco

Given Schwarzenegger's prediction of the scene at San Francisco City Hall in 2004 when the first same-sex marriages occurred there, it would hardly be a stretch for the casual news reader to assume that these marriages were little more than an elaborate gay rights protest. Although those who were present saw far more celebration and singing than riots and protest, there were plenty of people, signs, and media. The scene at the Cambridge city clerk's office in Massachusetts a few months later, when that office began issuing the first fully legal same-sex marriage licenses in the United States, looked very similar.

Indeed, even well respected sociologists have asserted that these marriages shared both the motivation and the effects of a protest. In what was most likely the first published study of couples married at San Francisco City Hall in a major scholarly journal, the *American Sociological Review*, eminent sociologist Verta Taylor and colleagues reported that "[t]he overwhelming majority of participants considered their marriages acts of protest in which they were confronting the identity categories, values, and practices of heteronormative society [citation omitted] by enacting marriage outside the boundaries of state sanction."[1] The researchers found that 81 percent of those they surveyed cited political motives for marrying—an overwhelming number and far more than the percentage who cited these reasons in the current study (only 25 percent of the 1,469 couples I surveyed considered this set of motivations their primary reason for marrying).[2] While also reporting that a "significant number" of couples additionally had concerns for the practical rights of marriage as well as romantic or personal reasons for marrying, the clear and unambiguous upshot of the study is that the Winter of Love was a political protest event, in its causes and effects, both for those who engineered it and those who participated.

Similarly, in her 2011 book on sexual orientation and legal consciousness, legal scholar Rosie Harding explicitly references the San Francisco marriages as an example of what she terms "fracturing resistance." Harding dissects the concepts of power and resistance in response to perceived shortcomings in Ewick and Silbey's formulation of an "against the law" orientation of citizens to law—one that, they say, is typified by acts of resistance and avoidance. Harding, finding this model too simplistic and not particularly applicable in the lives of gay men and lesbians, further divides the "against the law" or resistant orientation into "stabilizing resistance," "moderating resistance," and "fracturing resistance." The first is the most benign as it is essentially a form of resisting through being: simply by residing outside the heteronormative confines of sexuality, gay men and lesbians parenting or in relationships, or just by being out, resist the dominant power structure. Moderating resistance is different in that it attempts to lessen the degree of effects of the power structure through affirmative acts, even if they do not result in a change in this structure: a march or a protest—most explicitly public acts that register disagreement with the government but don't necessarily change the source of disagreement in the immediate—qualify here. Finally, "fracturing resistance" actually disrupts or breaks the path of power—even if temporarily—often in the form of a riot or rebellion. Unlike the former two, this form of resistance necessitates a response of some sort from the power structure. Interestingly, the 2004 marriages in San Francisco and Mayor Newsom's exercise of power in authorizing them are the only nonviolent example of "fracturing resistance" offered by Harding. While Harding acknowledges that the marriages were "purely peaceful," she explicitly refers to them as a form of "civil disobedience." And she is not alone, nor is Verta Taylor, in thinking of them this way.

In probably the best known of the few studies of same-sex relationships and legal consciousness, Kathleen Hull takes a more measured approach to the question of marriage as protest. Hull's study was based not on a collective act, such as the San Francisco City Hall marriages, but rather on ceremonies carried out by individual couples prior to the legalization of same-sex marriage. Hull persuasively argues that the participants used these ceremonies to enact legality outside the boundaries of formal law—which at that point continued to exclude them from marriage—and in doing so presented a subtle but powerful form of resistance. But Hull is clear that she does not treat these ceremonies as *intentionally* political, as Taylor et al. and Harding do in regard to the San Francisco marriages, instead analyzing them as an "indirect challenge to the state's supremacy." As Hull notes, "this enactment of legality outside the law is not self-consciously political action but should be read as a form of political resistance nonetheless."[3] While Taylor et al. also looked at what they considered to be the enactment of legality (in the form of marriage licenses) outside the bounds of law, the setting was quite different, which most likely accounts for part of the difference in analytical outcome. Both, however, find oppositional political force and resistance in the act of marriage to varying degrees.

Clearly, some of the participants surveyed for this book agreed wholeheartedly; as one put it, "marriage itself isn't so important as the politics of it." But as is often the case, to accurately depict the motivation and legal consciousness of those same-sex couples marrying in San Francisco—as well as in Massachusetts—we must reconceptualize what is meant by "resistance," "disobedience," or what is considered "against the law," in Ewick and Silbey's terminology. Commonly, studies of legal consciousness denote as "oppositional" average citizens who either find their own ways to subvert or resist the law's reach, or "lump" it, avoiding law altogether. Hull's contribution to the literature shows us that this can also be done by not avoiding law but by explicitly *enacting* legality where it does not exist. Harding's tripartite model of resistance also helps to reach beyond traditional conceptions of "against the law" and thus demonstrate the spectrum of ways in which LGBT citizens might enact resistance.

Rather than fitting neatly into these preexisting models, couples interviewed for this book—especially in San Francisco where the city as a whole was resisting in a sense, but certainly also in Massachusetts—exhibited a way in which the act of marriage could be a political move of resistance to power, without necessarily being "resistant" to law. That these reasons were cited as reasons to *legally marry* at all may seem counterintuitive. One could hardly think of a greater intrusion than inviting the state into your romantic partnership. Admittedly, one might hear echoes of this if one were to interview those who made a conscious decision *not* to marry during the period when it was available. But for those who *did* choose to invite the state by pursuing a marriage license, the notion of positioning oneself *against* the law seems particularly unintuitive. And yet it happened, not only in San Francisco where the first set of marriages were widely considered a collective act of civil disobedience (or as one participant noted, more like civil *obedience*, since it was at the direction of the city and county government) but in Massachusetts as well; people who did not believe the law was their friend—and in some cases didn't even believe in marriage as a priority—got married. Further, rather than positioning themselves against the law necessarily, many individuals and couples highlighted political or protest-based reasons for marrying that nevertheless did not resist or avoid the law but instead fully engaged it as an *instrument* of protest. However, additional questioning revealed an interesting turn of events for even the most die-hard marriage critics: what began as a protest often became a deeply meaningful event.

Marriage as Political Statement

The couples that married in San Francisco, surveyed about their reasons for marrying, were asked to rate a small handful of items denoting an oppositional or resistance-based orientation. These included reasons such as "to protest the government's conservative agenda," "to make a political statement about gay rights," and "to change the institution of marriage." As a group, this set of reasons was rated slightly higher than the pragmatic reasons (see chapter 4), but not as highly as other sets of reasons (see chapters 5 and 6). It becomes clear that couples were most ambivalent about the statement regarding "changing the institution of marriage"—its average rating was 3.49 (compared to the other two items, which both had average ratings above 4.1 out of 5). In reading the open-ended comments appended to this section, it became apparent that the statement was interpreted in a wide variety of ways. While some reacted strongly in the negative, asserting that "changing" the institution most likely meant changing it adversely, others embraced the term "change" and interpreted it to mean that they would change it by making it more inclusive. Additionally, some commented that they wished to separate out the religious facets of marriage and make it a solely and explicitly civil institution. Thus, it's clear that the (intentionally) ambiguous wording of the statement provoked widely varying and often negative assessments, which obviously affected the ratings of these political or "oppositional" items on the whole. On another hand, it also revealed some interesting nuances in the way some couples positioned themselves, as either agents of change or agents of assimilation.

The remaining two items denoting political motivations—those having to do with "making a statement" and "protesting the conservative agenda"—also got widely varying responses but not because of any ambiguity in their interpretation. Comments in the open-ended section of the survey made clear that while everyone understood what it meant to make a political statement through marriage, there were differences primarily in participants' views of the desirability and efficacy of this route, as well as their own priorities in making this decision.

Nonetheless, ratings of these items were significantly higher than those asking about "changing the institution of marriage." The average rating for the statement about protesting the conservative agenda was 4.13 out of 5, while the item about making a statement about gay rights averaged a rating of 4.35, making it the single highest-rated item on the survey. Moreover, the ratings of each of these items were widely generalized: there were no significant differences in their respective ratings based on gender, domestic partnership status, income, or age (there was too little variation in participants' race to analyze its correlates in any meaningful way).

Some of these couples explicitly framed their marriages as acts of challenge, rebellion, and opposition. One of the very first couples to respond stated: "It was . . . based on [our] desire to commit civil disobedience and protest the U.S. government's conservative laws." A young male couple from San Francisco explained, "For me at least the City Hall marriages was [sic] a profound act of civil disobedience." While there were those couples who were shocked and saddened by the fact that their marriages did not last (in the legal sense at least), a number seemed fully expectant and aware that their marriages would not withstand legal challenge, a point of view which largely correlated with an orientation to their wedding as an act of civil disobedience. Almost twenty couples, in fact, specifically invoked the term "civil disobedience" in their optional open-ended comments on the survey. Some had more nuanced views of the "disobedient" nature of their marriage, in recognizing that it had been authorized by a government official. One male respondent from the east Bay Area exclaimed, "Absolutely—every chance I get. So exciting to have a politician (Newsom) mobilizing a pseudo-civil disobedience."

While some saw themselves as part of a broad-based societal struggle for equal recognition, other couples directed their ire and protest statement at President George W. Bush specifically; one said they married to "make a statement to our freaky president and his blind followers." This couple even went so far as to say: "Marriage itself is not so important as the politics of it." Several cited with glee the irony of their having married on President's Day; as one participant explained, "Standing in line on President's Day in the rain with all these other couples felt very political and very community oriented." A number of others described having been incited to political action by President Bush's State of the Union address in 2004, in which he announced his intention to pursue a constitutional amendment banning same-sex marriage.[4] As one female couple described, "Bush infuriated us when he announced his intention to pursue a constitutional amendment—he seems to like our tax dollars but not our lifestyle." One couple was motivated by similar antipathy aimed at Governor Arnold Schwarzenegger: "The turning point for us was when Schwarzenneger [sic] 'demanded' (his word) that the marriages stop and called us 'anarchists.'" In an admittedly unique case, a respondent was motivated by his partner's father, who happened to be a key conservative political figure and the author of California's Prop 22—the law that was explicitly challenged by the City Hall marriages and later by the In re Marriage Cases case. At least two couples sent wedding announcements to the First Lady and President Bush. Admittedly some cited this personal protest as one of many reasons for marrying, but other couples singled it out as their primary motivation.

Many couples, however, were motivated less by personal animus against a political figure than a more global sense of injustice and resistance, spurring them to political action. The directness of the approach appealed to many; as one couple, who had flown from Tacoma, Washington, to get married, stated, "Getting married was a concrete action we could take to voice our view on this issue and LGBT issues in general." For some, the goals were quite specific. A lesbian couple in their thirties, both educators, explained, "We hoped to push political boundaries—activism . . . we also hoped it would, indeed, go to the state Supreme Court" (their hopes were, of course, vindicated in 2008 when the state Supreme Court decided In re Marriage Cases). These and other participants were unequivocal in the political nature of their decision to marry. Invoking particularly potent historical imagery of rebellion, one respondent who had come from Las Vegas commented, "this is perhaps our generation's Stonewall."

The Personal and the Political

In interviews it became clear that while similar themes of protest and politicized motives were echoed in many cases, the statements and ratings on the surveys did not tell the full story. Indeed, several couples had gone to the City Hall in support of a political action—at least in part—and some felt that was their sole motivator initially. I spoke with a number of people, particularly women, for whom marriage had never before been much of a priority—or who had actively resisted it as feminists. But the more I talked to couples, the more I found that for very few were their marriages at City Hall *solely* an act of resistance and protest in the end. Rather, several nuances of both inspiration and experience permeated couples' descriptions of their reasons for marrying, their actual wedding, and its effects on them. Not all of the couples were fully expectant that their marriages would be annulled or believed that Mayor Newsom's action in authorizing them was illegal. Some couples did believe that this might happen and were not surprised when their marriages were later annulled by the Supreme Court. At the same time, even those who did believe they were legally married sometimes had political overtones in their discussion of motivations, and conversely, many who fully expected them to be overturned nevertheless experienced something beyond, or in addition to, what they characterized as civil disobedience.

For several couples the nuance of their experience started with their mixed feelings about marriage to begin with, even prior to its becoming (temporarily) available to them. For example, Dale and Lisa, who discussed the importance of rights that marriage brought them as legal professionals. Lisa saw herself as more deeply ambivalent about marriage from the start. She explained, "I had mixed feelings about the institution to begin with. I've never felt like I needed the state to sanction my relationship." Even when she first heard about the marriages at City Hall, she did not feel the need to rush to be a part of it. But her position evolved over time as people across the nation and the world reacted to Newsom's action. She said, "the fact that I felt the

Republican Party was really starting to turn gay marriage into a big platform issue and then the response to it, I think I began to feel like there was perhaps a political statement that needed to be made." Dale, who was also quite concerned with the practical rights associated with marriage, added:

> But we actually grew to feel stronger about the political statement. We were committed to that more and more. Not to the idea of marriage, but committed to the political statement both in terms of supporting what Newsom was doing and taking a position against what Bush was doing. And for me also it was a political statement . . . as opposed to a personal need or desire for it.

Dale and Lisa's experience, they explained, was also impacted by the fact that they were the *last* couple to marry at City Hall before the Supreme Court stepped in and put a halt to it. Because they were rushed through the process by officials who knew what was coming, they did not have time to make it an emotionally meaningful ceremony. Immediately after their rushed ceremony, they were surrounded by reporters who informed them what had happened, and this event only served to strengthen the political impact they felt, despite their earlier ambivalence. As Dale commented:

> [T]he political statement was strong enough I think to make us both not only feel comfortable but, at least for me, to feel really good about doing it. And as events progressed that became more and more true. I was thrilled to be part of the movement in that way and wanted to be modeling that for our daughter, and the importance and significance of it in history.

Twenty-seven-year-old Jeremy from San Francisco, interviewed apart from his partner of ten years, was more explicit in his rejection of marriage as an institution before 2004. Jeremy had obviously thought a lot about the politics of the LGBT rights movement and had well-formed thoughts on the sociopolitical dimensions of marriage. Very early on in the interview he stated unequivocally, "I just don't believe in marriage at all. . . . I think it's an outdated sort of, kind of like anti-feminist kind of a misogynist practice." At the same time, though, he set himself apart from gay anti-assimilationists who oppose marriage, because he reasoned that in order to have marriage "abolished as a state institution, it first has to be available to everyone." He was thus able to reconcile his disdain for marriage as an institution with the fact that he himself then got married, by taking the long view and orienting to it as a political action: "I felt like maybe it was something worth joining . . . it was a political stance to say like this is something we support. Well, the fact is that other people are getting rights that you don't have access to and . . . in order to dismantle that structure, it has to first become equal for everyone." Despite his ambivalence or disdain for marriage itself, he felt compelled to join in what he saw primarily, going in, as a protest—and sort of collective "civil disobedience as a city." He emphasized that the decision to head to City Hall was not a personal one either; instead, "this is not about us. It's about this political stance. You know, it's about having your voice heard and like representing sort of an underprivileged community." His experience once he arrived at City Hall did not dissuade him from this view; even the "flowers from the heartland," those marital bouquets from individual donors all over the United States, "added the sort of feeling of protest or like it was a very radical kind of action," he added. Jeremy admitted that he was personally touched by the "collective emotional experience" and—implicating the work of Kathryn Abrams—a "feeling of hope."

Patricia, also interviewed apart from her partner of fifteen years, had not been particularly interested in marriage before this event, but came to appreciate the political significance of this action. She identified her motivation for getting married as three-pronged: the emotional affirmation of their longtime relationship, helping to make marriage available for those who do feel strongly about it, and, as she termed it, the "civil disobedience act." Subsequent conversation clearly downplayed the first of these though. Patricia and her spouse felt that the longevity of their relationship spoke for itself in a way; they did not need a ceremony to affirm it. Patricia, at least, did not see any personal benefit that marrying would bring to them; rather, she commented, "this was much more of a political kind of statement enabling people for whom it meant a lot to, to enable them to do what they wanted to do." A longtime activist, she reflected on the political demonstrations of an earlier era and drew an interesting, if unexpected, analogy to the so-called White Night riots of the 1970s, following the trial of Dan White for the murder of San Francisco Supervisor and gay rights icon Harvey Milk, when the gay community and others raged against what they felt was an insufficient sentence for someone who had broken into City Hall and systematically murdered two officials (the other was the mayor, George Moscone). Patricia, who was present at City Hall in the aftermath of the Dan White verdict and ensuing riots, likened the two demonstrations as mechanisms for making much needed political statements. Referring to the riots and projecting into the future, she opined:

> Sometimes I do think that that kind of political statement needs to be made. But since it seems that people are not that willing to go to that kind of place now, that this [the marriages] is a better, or a different, way of appealing to the general population, let's say, in being recognized in a pretty innocuous way. . . . So I think that the impact on the national level had a big role in wanting to do this too.

Patricia stated that she did not think the weddings at City Hall were "disobedient" even though they were as "in your face" as some people felt they were. The Winter of Love was, in Patricia's words "pretty innocuous," but nevertheless constituted an important statement with a similar goal, which was to gain national attention, protest unfair conditions, and inspire change.

Though of a younger generation, twenty-eight-year-old Tudor of San Francisco's Castro district also drew analogies, as Patricia did, to politically tumultuous times of his past. An immigrant from Romania, Tudor had been born in the midst of a totalitarian Communist regime, which subsequently toppled during his teen years. The images of this period stuck with him, and he remained, in his words, "a starry-eyed immigrant" who assumed "you have to fight for every single right." When he heard about the marriages at City Hall, he felt a familiar sense of revolution: "It just felt so revolutionary; we were challenging such deep-seated beliefs in American society, I really personally wanted to be part of that . . . we were supporting a very important political idea of equality." He and his partner of five years headed to City Hall with no hesitation and married on Valentine's Day, just four days after the date they celebrated as their anniversary. There was no doubt that the act was personally and romantically significant for the two, but Tudor was very clear that he most relished the opportunity to challenge dominant images of couplehood in America and to take a public stand against an injustice. He concluded, "The public recognition and the public act of this—of disobeying current rules, I think, was a little bit of a bigger importance than having a piece of paper that said, 'You're now, you know, spouses.'"

Pat and Terry, discussed earlier, were initially unequivocal in their assertion that for them "it was a political statement." Like Patricia and Annie, because of their longtime relationship, they did not feel they needed validation or a symbol of their commitment. However, they balked at the term "protest," which they distinguished from the form of political and social activism they felt they were participating in. Pat explained, "If the world interprets our getting married as a protest, then it really doesn't have anything to do with us. I mean, you know, I did feel it was, like, contributing to some great movement in history." They explained that while "protest" connotes being *against* something, they were engaging in a social action *for* something. Nevertheless, they were clear as to the political underpinnings of their motivation.

Like Pat and Terry, Dawn and Sherri had been together for about twenty years, although they were younger (in their early forties) and had two children. The couple had a unique insight into the proceedings because of Sherri's position as a deputy city attorney in San Francisco. She had, in fact, worked on both the legal challenges to the City Hall marriages (her own included, which was eventually overturned) and also on the *In re Marriage Cases* litigation. Thus, like Dale and Lisa, they did not have much time to "savor the moment" of their wedding because, as a city employee, Sherri had to immediately return upstairs to do the legal work necessary to keep the weddings going. And like Pat and Terry, Dawn and Sherri described their wedding as distinctly political but not quite an act of "protest" or "civil disobedience." As Sherri explained, "You really felt like you were part of a political action. It wasn't that sort of quiet reverent ceremony that we had later that was really about us. It seemed like it was about something ever so very much bigger." Dawn added, in response to the suggestion that the City Hall weddings were a form of civil disobedience, "I didn't feel any disobedience about it." Sherri continued:

> Yeah. That was what was so amazing about it. That's why it was like this political action [where] there was no disobedience involved. You were there. You filled out your little bureaucratic form. You got your little bureaucratic license, and then in the middle of City Hall, some city functionary performed the marriage. That was what was so unbelievably revolutionary about it. I felt like I was doing something revolutionary, but not something that I would characterize as civil disobedience.

Although there were, again, clear political intents and implications, their wedding did not fit the description of what they would call civil disobedience or, in the classic sense "resistance." And, perhaps more importantly, as the interview progressed, it became clear that the wedding was not just a political event for them, either.

In this they were not alone. Even in the short length of the survey (and to an even greater degree in extended interviews), some ambivalence began to emerge about whether this was a solely political act, for even those who identified their motivations as protest-based or oppositional. Echoing what Hull and Harding have found about subtler and unintentional acts of resistance, one couple stated, "Homophobic policies should be protested, [but] marrying had a secondary benefit: simply declaring our love in this way became an act of protest as well." Another young couple similarly found themselves at the cross section of an event that was both political and deeply personal: "It was the Stonewall of the new millenia [*sic*] and we wanted to recognize our 6+ year long relationship in a crowd of lifetime activist and community members." This convergence of motivations took varying forms. For some, the marriages served dual purposes to begin with. One respondent, when asked how important protesting the conservative agenda was to her, responded enthusiastically, "Oh, HELL YES!!!!!! What an INCREDIBLE fringe benefit!" While exuberant, it is notable that the act of resistance was indeed a "fringe benefit" rather than a primary motivation. Other couples, in what became a common theme, described an evolution in their thinking about the significance of their marriage. A male couple in their forties from Los Angeles explained, "Our first reaction to the news that marriages were taking place was out of a sense of political statement. That, however, changed as we began the process." Even the male couple who felt like they were taking part in a "romantic's Stonewall" and likened their experience to the fall of the Berlin Wall, qualified their response with the following rejoinder: "But once you were there, you realized it wasn't political. It was all heart—an absolute blaze of love and commitment."

The same themes echoed, to an even greater degree, when couples were interviewed. Janja and Kim, from Chico, exemplified this phenomenon. When asked why they decided to marry, Kim explained, "Well I think we both wanted to make a statement to other couples to support gay rights and to be out and to you know take every opportunity that is given us to do something to help move equalization forward." They did not expect that the legal aspect of the marriages would last or that they would enjoy ongoing legal benefits as a result. Rather, as Janja explained:

> I think we definitely saw it as an act of civil disobedience. In fact at the time I was teaching a class on social movements and we were talking about, you know, my class was cheering me on and that I was going to get married so when I came back they wanted to hear every minute of

it. I think to us it was much more of a political protest than a romantic statement. I think the romantic thing kind of happened in the moment of the ceremony, but I think really we saw it as a political statement.

Janja, in particular, was caught off guard by how much it came to mean to her, a self-proclaimed "anti-marriage feminist." By her own admission she became quite emotional at something that she initially intended as an act of civil disobedience, surprising both herself and Kim; as she recalled, "I cried throughout the day." While before this experience she felt as if marriage was "this heterosexual thing and what did we care about that?" she explained that

> aside from all the legal rights that come with heterosexual marriage, I think at least for me once we went actually through with the ceremony and did the deed, so to speak, it became even more important to me. Then I really wanted it to succeed in the courts, and I really wanted people to understand why this was important and I really wanted to announce to everyone that we had done this and really made a point of doing it. And so it kind of changed my own view on it changed through the act of doing it.

She analyzed this in the context of the everyday experience and marginalization of gay and lesbian existence. The feeling of proclaiming their love publicly, and the significance of doing so "was heightened by the fact that as gays we aren't allowed to do that and there aren't many times in our daily life . . . because we are second-class citizens basically. So I think that even heightened it to be publicly doing this. It was incredibly moving."

Amy, a San Francisco resident interviewed apart from her partner of three years, recounted a similar experience. She commented, "I never even considered that I would ever get married. It just never entered my mind. But then when I heard that people were doing it, I just felt like, for me, it was more of a political statement or statement that I want to be counted." Amy explained that in the initial news coverage of the San Francisco marriages, she saw that most of the focus was on long-term couples like Del Martin and Phyllis Lyon. She felt it was politically important to represent younger and more recent couples in the LGBT community: "So that was kind of what I mean about a political statement, that I kind of wanted to support this and show this is the right thing to do, you know." She likened it to involvement in earlier civil rights movements, for racial equality or women's rights: "And then there's the whole civil rights angle as far as being part of a movement. . . . And this is a chance to be part of that or to be involved in that." After her wedding, however, she came to a different realization about the event's significance. She remembered, "It was something that I never thought it would be—could be real for me. . . . So it actually—if you had asked me the day before and the day after, like someday before, I was like, 'Oh, married, whatever, I don't care about that.' But then after, it was like, 'Wow, this really means something.'"

This multilayered experience of marriage—spanning the political and the personal—extended across demographic categories with a surprising breadth. Similar thoughts were expressed by middle-aged or elderly feminist lesbians, younger childless couples, and forty-somethings with children. In the latter category were Ed and Michael of San Francisco, by all measures a typical two-father family, with two children. They did not deny the validation or personal satisfaction and romance that came with the ability to marry. But, as Ed described it, the act of getting married in this particular setting and moment in history was also a profoundly radical political act: "You know, like the hell with the government, the hell with the federal government and their stupid laws and their absurd ideas and everyone's absurd ideas about gay people. Like this is my personal radical act to be married. It's my right to be married." He drew analogies to those who had worked for women's suffrage and to end slavery, who "had some kind of seed of radical act about them that made it personal and so that was their step into fully realizing that they were citizens whether it was engendered by laws or not." Ed recognized that the process would be a long one, and that his now-annulled marriage was by no means the end of the story of the struggle for marriage equality. But he expressed hope and satisfaction:

I do believe someday that gay people will have the right to marry in the United States . . . I don't know if I'll see it my lifetime. But, the fact that I did it, you know, the fact that I'll go down in history as having been one of those people who did it really means something to me too. That it's like a radical act of civil rights in some respects.

Living less than a mile away from Ed and Michael were Barbara and Betsy, a mature couple who had no children but similarly saw, and enjoyed, the radical potential of what they were doing. Retired and content, the two had been together for twenty-five years at the time of the interview, two years after their wedding. True to the traditional feminist creed, they had never thought or cared much about marriage. They admitted that the economic benefits interested them, but, as Barbara explained, "as an emotional or reflection of our commitment or some statement about our relationship, we've never felt that it's meant anything more than what we had." Marriage seemed more than simply superfluous, though: Barbara continued, "I think there's also some of the feminist perspective that emerges really sort of historically and you know, [that marriage is] detrimental to women. And I have some aversion to participating in, you know, that institution." As a couple of self-described "old political activists," they were eager to be part of what they considered an act of civil disobedience. Betsy conjured images of her childhood and teen years, in the 1950s, when one could get arrested—or beaten—just for appearing to be gay, let alone entering a same-sex marriage. She likened it to the civil rights movement that challenged racial inequalities. She saw her marriage as part of the very same civil rights paradigm and a "big statement": "one more little nail is a coffin of . . . homophobia." Barbara agreed, "Yeah, it was like going to a protest, you know, with adding your voice to a social justice issue and . . . one that could benefit us." Later both women confessed that they were surprised at the emotional reaction they also had to getting married after the fact, but the political dimension still loomed large in their narrative.

Not all couples, of course, agreed with one another on the primary motivation and significance of their wedding. Scott and Glen were one such couple. Both recovering alcoholics, they had met four years earlier at an AA meeting. Glen was a religious Catholic and was once in seminary, close to ordination at the moment when he met and fell in love with Scott, at which point he decided to leave the priesthood. Three months into the relationship, they moved in together and ritualized their commitment with a ceremony and exchange of rings. When asked about why they chose to go to City Hall and get married, even though they had already had their own ceremony and registered as domestic partners, Glen responded, "Because I thought it was important—I didn't think it would do anything to our relationship, really. I thought it was more of a political statement." Scott, on the other hand, disagreed; his reasons for wanting to marry were not in the least political. He said of his motivations, "None of 'em were political. Mine were more like—I just couldn't believe that we might actually, even for a small window of time, be considered legally equal citizens, equal partners, equal in a relationship." Still, even though he did not consider it an act of resistance or protest against the status quo, there is an element of civic and historical consciousness in his telling. However, for both Glen and Scott—as for many others—things changed once they went to City Hall and got their marriage license. Glen at first was nearly at a loss for words in describing what it felt like to get married in what he had initially deemed a protest: "It was so surreal. It was surreal, so surreal. It was like a dream. . . . And it makes me cry every time I think about it. It was the single most marvelous day of my life, single most marvelous day of my life. It was everything that I would want in a day ever."

The experience of marriage at City Hall in San Francisco was admittedly unique in its political significance, resonance, and controversy. For those reasons alone, and because of the less conventional legal route taken in San Francisco, one might reasonably expect that the "marriage as protest" theme would be far more present there than in Massachusetts. One couple who had married in both locales seemed to underscore this point. Ron and Jim had met in Washington, D.C. twenty-three years earlier and had been together ever since. They moved to San Francisco in 1997 and had been registered as domestic partners in both D.C. and California (as well as Hawaii where they had lived for a few years). With Jim's sister, who lived in Massachusetts, they had planned to marry there once it became available post-*Goodridge*. But then, as Ron phrased it, they "heard about the chaos down there" at City Hall and decided eventually to be a part of it. They were married on March 9, just two days before the California Supreme Court pulled the plug on the Winter of Love. In comparing the two weddings, Jim noted, "The Massachusetts thing was a family gathering and party as opposed to what happened in San Francisco, which was to me again a bit of a political statement . . . it was a really beautiful ceremony but again it was really more of a political statement as well as an affirmation whereas in Massachusetts it was just a wonderful party." Their assessment was attributable in part to their well-informed belief that the San Francisco marriages would not withstand legal challenge—Jim was a lawyer, and the couple had friends who worked for the California Supreme Court and who predicted as much. While both weddings were by their own admission symbolic—Jim and Ron knew that marrying in Massachusetts would not gain them marital rights in San Francisco, due to DOMA restrictions—their San Francisco wedding took on a distinctly more political tone because the route by which it was achieved seemed more rebellious, and because in Massachusetts there was more time to plan a family-oriented event.

This distinction was, however, far from universal. There were a number of couples in Massachusetts who did consider their marriages an act of resistance or politically motivated, at least in part—despite the fact that Massachusetts' weddings could not be considered an act of "civil disobedience" since the state Supreme Court had declared them legal. Images of the scene at Cambridge City Hall—the first in Massachusetts to open at midnight and offer marriages licenses to same-sex couples on May 17—do not look much different than those outside San Francisco City Hall. There were hundreds of people, singing and chanting; there were media and signs from supporters and detractors. Officials under both administrations, interviewed as members of married couples for this book, recounted similar experiences in the mix of chaos and uncertainty, unity, and jubilance. Both uniquely combined features of celebration and protest. This image, relayed vividly in filmed accounts of both events, is also clearly present in the firsthand accounts of couples married in Massachusetts.

For some, the political resonance was more well-defined than for others. Gilbert and Alex, who had met in 1991, were a highly educated and well-off couple with a two-year-old son. Although the two had different backgrounds—Gilbert was a non-religious Jew from southern California, and Alex was from a Catholic family and born in the Philippines—they instantly connected, and moved in together six months after they started dating. Alex had proposed to Gilbert back in 1993, and while living in California, they had become domestic partners at the earliest opportunity—but they had never had an actual wedding ceremony. For Alex, it was not for lack of trying; he was interested in the symbolism and community recognition of the wedding ceremony from the start and didn't feel the need to wait until it was legalized. Gilbert, on the other hand, did not see the point in a ceremony for its own sake and was more interested in acquiring the benefits of marriage to protect their family, particularly after the birth of their son. Neither was primarily motivated by activism, but Alex recognized a very real political undercurrent to what they were doing, by virtue of the very fact of their marginalization as a gay couple. He commented:

> There's a whole political dimension to all of these decisions that we're making. I think that a lot of people don't realize or don't acknowledge or don't recognize how political just being part of the mass culture is until you've been ostracized, unless you stand apart from the society in some way. Then you realize all of the things that other people can do that you cannot do.

The sudden ability to marry rendered this distinction quite clear, and provided a tangible reminder to Alex and Gilbert of their marginalization as a gay couple, despite their relative wealth. Alex stated:

> I think that just by being in this community it sort of makes you political or makes you aware of the political dimension that everyone else is participating in, and it gives you this insight into things like justice and

discrimination and all these things. So us getting married had a very palpable political dimension that we were already sensitized to just by virtue of being gay. So it was a life changing moment. I don't know that it
changed me politically but it was a very political act definitely.

For couples like Alex and Gilbert, then, while the political motivation was not paramount, it was nevertheless an inescapable part of the
experience. Others found themselves politicized unexpectedly by virtue
of the contrast between their life pre- and post-*Goodridge*. Nancy, who
with her spouse, Anne, discussed the practical benefits of being legal
spouses (see chapter 3), also felt a keen sense of political empowerment
but one tempered by a new sensitivity to what she had been missing
before. She commented, "[I felt a] sense of equality that I, that I had
unconsciously boxed myself out of and now I felt like a real, uh, it was
sort of startling to step back and say, 'Well, look how much you didn't
think you were, you were entitled to. You should be having them just
like these other people.'" In other words, although her motivations were
a combination of practical and ideological considerations, the legal
ability to now marry made explicit the structural inequality embedded
in gay existence with the denial of marriage rights.

For others, the political dimension of the experience was layered in
a different way, in that they distinguished between their legal wedding
and a prior commitment ceremony. Beth and Isabel, who discussed
their practical legal incentives for marrying, made such a distinction
(see chapter 3). They had held what they called a "festival of commitment" in their Unitarian Universalist church 1997, about a year and a
half into their committed romantic relationship. They were motivated
largely by their desire to publicly state their commitment as well as their
plans to start a family and, as Beth put it, have "a kind of traditional
order to things." Having made this public commitment and already having had a child together, by the time the option of legal marriage came
along, their purpose in marrying was different. They were indeed motivated in part by the practical and financial considerations, but there was
another more explicitly resistant connotation to the post-*Goodridge*

wedding as well. As Isabel commented, "I mean our second marriage felt like a political statement. Honestly. As opposed to . . . the wonderful spiritual ceremony that we had initially. And it was spiritual. But it was also political. It was sort of spiritual-political."

Gail and Betsy, a middle class Caucasian couple in their late forties, made a very similar distinction. They talked at some length about the ceremonial ways in which they had committed prior to legal marriage. First they had a private exchange of rings and moved in with one another, early on in their relationship—which they noted with reference to the stereotype of "U-Haul lesbians." Three-and-a-half years later, in 1994, they had a larger commitment ceremony with friends and family, integrating many of the wedding traditions from Gail's Jewish upbringing. It was at this time that the couple also legally took the same hyphenated last name, and many family members began to fully understand their relationship. Still, when the *Goodridge* case was finally decided, there was no doubt whether Gail and Betsy would get married. Upon hearing the decision, Gail hunted Betsy down in a local coffee shop and exclaimed, "Honey, we're getting married!" They sought a marriage license on the first night they were available in Cambridge and very quickly planned a large, public civil ceremony. But there was a clear distinction, again, between this and their prior wedding. As Betsy explained, "We didn't do religious stuff cause it was, it would have sort of felt like dissing our commitment ceremony. . . . We did it very [much] like a civil ceremony. . . . And we wanted to do it right away . . . because we really wanted to be part of the change right here where we lived." They explicitly framed their legal wedding as a political event:

BETSY: So it was very political—
GAIL: We just wanted it to be a rally.
BETSY: 'Cause obviously it wasn't sort of our personal marriage. That had already happened.

The event came replete with literature tables, speeches, local politicians, and representatives from several advocacy groups. They asked guests—250 in all—to make donations in lieu of gifts. When asked to rate the various reasons for marrying in 2004, Gail and Betsy rated the resistance-based motivations most highly: protesting the conservative agenda, making a statement for gay rights, and changing the institution of marriage. And yet, when reflecting on their wedding-turned-rally, Gail remarked, "It ended up being surprisingly romantic. . . . We didn't do it for that reason but it shocked us to heaven."

This distinction between ceremonies made by couples such as Gail and Betsy or Beth and Isabel was not the only thing that led couples in Massachusetts to view their marriage as an act of protest or political statement. A far different set of circumstances led one such couple, Johanna and Moira, to get married. Unlike Beth and Isabel, Johanna and Moira had never had, nor felt the need to have, a wedding or commitment ceremony. As Moira explained "marriage was never a big priority for us . . . I was kind of a hippy so marriage, to me, was sort of like establishment, you know, and do we really care about that?" They had been together since 1984 and had made a personal commitment to one another early on. In that time they had already adopted a child and purchased a home. A financial planner by profession, Johanna was well aware of the steps they needed to take to protect their finances. In a sense, marriage, to them, was superfluous; as Johanna stated, "we didn't need it" on a personal level. So while they awaited the *Goodridge* decision with great anticipation and celebrated it, it was as a political victory rather than a personal need (Johanna was on the board of GLAD, the organization who had litigated the *Goodridge* case; therefore she was highly involved in helping to spread word of the decision). They married very soon after it became possible, but as Moira explained, "it was more in solidarity. . . . It was like a political statement." Johanna agreed: "It wasn't some emotional thing like 'Oh finally, we can make legal what we've known in our hearts has been true for so long.'" Indeed, when rating reasons for getting married, the political statement was the most or one of the most important motivations for both women.

In the same vein, Larry and his spouse had never seen themselves as big "believers in the institution of marriage." In fact, in more than two decades together they had never had a commitment ceremony or any sort of event to mark their relationship—with the possible exception of a bureaucratic Norwegian equivalent of domestic partnership, which allowed them to access certain rights while living there. For them, getting married in Cambridge was "an expression of civil rights and an opportunity to be part of history." Larry maintained that the marriage did not necessarily represent a turning point of any sort in their relationship, but he admitted to being moved by the powerful and encouraging words of the *Goodridge* decision itself. He also took great pride in their being the fourth gay couple to marry in Cambridge—and presumably, in the state or country (excluding those marriages in California which were subsequently invalidated): "There's something really dramatic about that and it's a contribution, obviously . . . it was just like we were part of this great event. We did something that turned out to be perhaps a little braver than we were conscious of—and it was a very nice feeling." He admitted that in the end, "It was a little more emotional than we expected," but he maintained that he was well aware they were "involved in something that's much bigger than us as individuals. . . . The motivation is to be part of history, is to do something good for the gay rights movement." With the crowds and the television cameras, he said, it felt very little like a personal, private moment, even if he did acknowledge the emotional reaction they had: "History had taken over at this point. So I think that's, you know, so it's almost like you don't have a lot of control in a way."

Kim and Joanne also contemplated, initially, the political implications of marriage upon hearing about the *Goodridge* decision. In their late thirties/early forties, Kim and Joanne had met via an Internet dating service and had been together for almost five years. Kim was a doctoral student in public policy at the time of the interview, and Joanne was currently unemployed but had worked in human services; both were white, middle class, and considered themselves "recovering Catholics." Kim, in particular, was attuned to the politics of gay rights and marriage equality. As Joanne recalled, "Kim was very kind of like very political about it and I was starting to think like 'Oh, maybe we could get married' and anytime we had a conversation about it; it was more political than personal, right?" To which Kim responded, "Well, in the beginning, yeah." Kim and Joanne, unlike many of the couples I interviewed, did not immediately file their intentions to marry. In fact, they waited more than a year after the decision was implemented, marrying eventually in October 2005. Well before they got married themselves, though, they were taking part in marches in support of marriage equality. What began as a political interest eventually became a personal discussion, culminating in Joanne and Kim's decision to marry a year later. But whereas Joanne stated that the romantic impulse to marry was the most important motivation for her, Kim maintained that although she loved Joanne and also wanted the benefits of marriage, the political statement it made in support of gay rights was her overriding consideration.

Similarly, Anita and Emily had always considered themselves activists and viewed both same-sex marriage and civil unions through a political lens. Both in their mid-fifties, raised in self-described WASP households, educated, and trained as journalists, they had already been together for nearly twenty-five years by the time they legally wed. They were avowed liberals and although they had not focused their activist efforts on same-sex marriage specifically prior to *Goodridge*, they were certainly attuned to LGBT civil rights and gender equality issues. In 2001 they traveled to Vermont to obtain a civil union, with the very realistic assessment that they would not actually be able to take advantage of any of the rights it afforded in Vermont. As Emily explained, "We have no rights in Vermont, we live in Massachusetts and we're very political people; we really did it for political reasons." Three years later, when their home state became the first to legalize same-sex marriage, their reasoning was much the same. In rating their reasons for marrying on a scale of one to five, when it came to "making a political statement about gay rights," Emily rated the item an exuberant 15. While both admitted there were more personal (and for Anita, community-based) reasons for wanting to marry as well, the activist currents in their thinking were clear. Emily commented:

Well, as many of us have said over time, it was among the world's longest engagements. I love Nita, and certainly was happy to share that with everyone, but it was mostly political for me . . . I never wanted to get married, ever, even when I thought I was straight.

At their wedding, they made sure to have a friend speak specifically to same-sex marriage from the activist perspective; as Anita explained, "The political context was very important to us, and just sort of set the stage as to why we were doing this—in addition to the fact that we love each other and we wanted to share that with people. But there was a whole political element to it."

Unlike some couples, these urges toward political resistance remained constant throughout the process; though like other couples, Emily and Anita emerged even more politically energized about the issue of same-sex marriage. Anita noted, "It was a political thing and it became even more so afterwards." She and Emily soon became convinced that marriage equality was the paramount issue at the threshold of political equality for LGBT citizens: "Because once you legitimize a relationship between people of the same gender, then you cannot discriminate against them, you have no basis for discriminating against them on any other plane." At the same time, she—to a greater degree than Emily—was equally moved by communitarian sentiments and a desire for validation. When asked what the most important reason was for getting married, Anita responded, "It's the standing with the community—not so much that if affected our own relationship, but how others see us. I think that's very important to me," to which Emily quickly added, "Which is sort of political, too."

For most couples, indeed, their motivations were a combination of factors. Robyn and Peg, both forty-eight, lived in a predominantly gay and lesbian subsection of Boston. Transplants from other states, they had met while living in Cambridge and had been together for ten years. While they kept on top of recent marriage equality events, learning of the *Goodridge* case in process after the Vermont *Baker* decision, they had never thought about marriage as an option for themselves. They didn't have any sort of wedding or commitment ceremony on their own because, in Peg's words, it was "too much hassle." They had registered with their municipality as domestic partners only when Peg's self-pay medical insurance became prohibitively expensive. Robyn explained that her attitude toward marriage was framed significantly by her standpoint and political awareness as a bisexual woman. She explained, "And as someone who identifies as bi, I had made a decision back in 1990 or so that I would never get married. I would never take any privilege given to me in a relationship with a man that I would not have in a relationship with a woman, so that if my life partner ended up being male I wouldn't get married." In that context, she said—as to her reasons for wanting to marry Peg and its significance—"part of it was to acknowledge and get recognition for what already was. And part of it, getting married felt like a *radical transgressive act*" (emphasis added). Robyn went on to discuss how transformative she felt the act of marriage was for two people of the same-sex; she explained that "it was an odd combination of joining the club and transforming the club. Because I also think that once you remove the male/female requirement from a marriage, it really changes marriage." She quoted a favorite comic strip by Alison Bechdel, which featured a same-sex marriage proposal with the text "Will you simultaneously reinforce and deconstruct the dominant paradigm with me?" So while there were certainly personal, material, and symbolic reasons for marrying—and the pair had difficulty distinguishing one or even two most important reasons for marrying—they considered the political implications, as complicated as they were, to be at or near the top of the list.

Some other couples, similar in a sense to Robyn and Peg, suggested that their use of traditional marital language and symbolism was transgressive and an act of political protest in itself. Jen and Jennifer,[5] an upper-middle-class couple in their forties, lived in Cambridge and had done a very traditional wedding ceremony in a church in 1991, about five years into their relationship. They had a child together (in addition to Jen's child from a previous relationship). Interestingly, Jen's prior heterosexual marriage was undertaken for solely financial reasons—to get more financial aid for college—because, in her words, she "so politically

objected to heterosexual marriage." In talking about why it was important to her to marry Jennifer, then, and to do it in a very public way
with all of the traditional markers, Jen explained:

> I have always believed . . . that marriage is an extremely political sub-
> ject. . . . I would say "my wife." You know, and people would stop and
> be like, "how can that be?" . . . [T]hey just could not grasp it. So it was
> taking a term that was commonly used and applying it in a different way
> so people would think about, "oh, right, gay people might be able to have
> long-term . . . relationships." So . . . for me, it was a very political thing.

Jen, in fact, used the term "wife" to describe her relationship to Jennifer
from the time of their commitment ceremony in 1991 on. Jennifer, however—who was on the board of the Freedom to Marry Coalition and
was centrally involved with much of the organizing—did not feel comfortable using the term "wife" in the same way until they legally married in 2004. Ironically, when it came to the first night in Cambridge to
file their intentions to marry with the county clerk's office, Jen balked at
the act and the language of the marriage contract: "I was standing right
there reading that oath and I was like 'oh, excuse me, I don't believe in
this stuff. That's not why I'm here' [*Laughter*]. I'm here for a political reason." Much like Robyn, she felt the deep contradiction of marriage as a
conservative heterosexual institution (with, as Jen put it, "thousands of
years of baggage about women being oppressed and not having rights"),
but one she felt it important to enter with another woman, largely so
that it could lose some of that heterosexist baggage. In other words, Jen
oriented to this opportunity to marry as a transformative experience,
not necessarily because of any personal transformation but because of
its capacity for structural transformation of gender roles and heteronormativity. Still, when asked what was their most important reason for
marrying, Jen immediately stated "the politics," while Jennifer said, "the
rights," and neither woman disagreed with the other.

April and Penny, somewhat like Jen and like Robyn, also had some
conflicted feelings about marriage. The couple lived in the heart of

Boston and had been together for almost nine years. They had met at a bookstore where both worked, at which time Penny was in another committed relationship. But when that relationship dissolved, the two got together and moved in shortly after. At the time of the interview, April was working as a bookkeeper, and Penny was unemployed and looking for a career transition. They described themselves as cash poor but otherwise relatively advantaged: "We are very privileged and we haven't got any money right now." Both felt ambivalent about the institution of marriage initially; as Penny reported, "We are not really into it as a concept." Penny was first to warm to the idea and stated, "I mean . . . it exists in our society and it offers all of these privileges that are attached to it and you would be stupid not to take advantage of them if you could in some cases, so we did. But mostly I felt like I wanted to do it as a political statement and also because I am so romantic." Penny, in other words, attached multiple meanings to marriage, spanning the practical, the personal, and the political. But there was another element of protest that was most clearly articulated by April:

> I didn't want to get married, I didn't believe in marriage, it is just that the political situation changed so fast that, and Penny evidently wanted to do it and I told her it would take me a couple of weeks to get used to the idea and then I just woke up the next morning and I was like "We should do it." And then right after that President Bush said something about gay marriage being wrong and so we were like, "we have to do it now."

Like couples in San Francisco, and Mayor Newsom himself, President Bush's famous words in his state of the union address, in which he proposed a constitutional amendment banning same-sex marriage, galvanized the couple to a degree beyond what they already felt. As April put it, "I think the main thing about it for me was always, like, 'I didn't ask for this fight but people are so opposed to it that I don't have any choice but to just be up in their faces about it.'" Penny then added, "Yeah like, 'you know what, we don't even think your marriage institution is that great a thing but damn it, if you are going to give it to us you are not taking it away." April described her conversion to marriage supporter as a "really strong political motivation" driven primarily by a desire "to be against the conservatives in the government," while Penny's interest in marriage was also political but more multifaceted.

In many ways, then—with the exception of tending not to invoke the phrase "civil disobedience" and not benefitting from the same number of materials results—couples in Massachusetts were not markedly different from those who married in San Francisco. In both locales, it was not uncommon for the same act to be simultaneously an act of protest and an act of either protective self-interest or personal significance. At the same time, the dominance of the protest narrative was not as clear or as prevalent, even in San Francisco, as some other studies have suggested.[6] Couples often rated my question about them having gotten married "to protest the government's or president's conservative agenda" very highly in the abstract, but when questioned about it in more detail, or when they responded to a more open-ended question asking their most important reason for getting married, they often retreated from this stand. In some situations the couples were aware that they had more than one reason for marrying, as in the cases of Robyn and Peg and Jennifer and Jen. For others, they came to discover of the course of the interview that this "protest" quality was really more of a desirable side effect than an actual reason for having gotten married. This was clear in respondents' tones in the interviews as answers to this question were usually shouted very quickly in response, and when the respondents were asked to elaborate, they often retreated from their initial exuberance on further reflection.

This was clearly the case with Massachusetts couple Joan and Cecilia. Joan, a Massachusetts native and technical consultant, had met Cecilia, a Mexican American financial analyst from Texas, while both were working at M.I.T. Unlike many couples, marriage was in fact something they had given thought to prior to being able to do so legally—even though they had never had a ceremony on their own. Like Jen, Cecilia had been previously married to a man for six years. Joan, even before she came out, knew she would never marry a man, but still saw it as an important rite of passage.

Still they did not marry the second it became available because their relationship was relatively young, and they wanted to be sure they were marrying because it was the best personal decision for *them*, rather than simply because they *could*. When asked to rate the various reasons for getting married, the first to elicit an answer of "very important," or 5 out of 5—and an animated response at that—was from Joan when responding to the item about marrying to "protest the government's conservative agenda." She, in fact, nearly shouted her reply. However, when questioned further about it, she retreated from this and offered a slightly different explanation:

> Well, it's more about to make a statement. So yeah, I guess that is kind of a protest in my head. It's like, "I don't care if you say no. I'm gonna stand up and say yes." So I would call that a protest. But I didn't get married to protest. That was just a benefit.

In the end, after much discussion, they settled on both romance and validation as their most important reasons for marrying. Still, they imbued aspects of the act with political meaning and importance. For example, they explicitly chose to apply for a marriage license in their relatively conservative hometown of Medford rather than in a more progressive locale like Cambridge or Provincetown. They did this, they said, because they knew that it was important politically to not have all of the same-sex marriage statistics coming from only liberal bastions. Of their choice to get the license in Medford they said, "That was a statement. . . . Because we live here, dammit." They also likened marriage, in this context, to the ability to vote—you must have your own reasons for doing it, they explained, but assuming that you do, once you gain that right, "If you don't exercise your right to vote, then you won't be taken seriously."

To return briefly to the experiences of those in San Francisco, there were many couples whose narratives about their rationales for getting married paralleled very closely. For example, Nicola from Sacramento (see chapter 3), stated: "I wouldn't have done it simply for political reasons, but we really enjoyed being involved in a political act; an act

Cecilia and Joan, married in Massachusetts, October 2005

of civil disobedience was really appealing to us, but we could show to everybody that this is our belief. We believe in equal rights for all. So that was a big deal." Her spouse, Renee, in speaking about the moments at City Hall before their wedding, related, "It was really a unifying activist event with all the people in line and everybody's experiences coming together and the fact that everybody was there for equality and justice and we thought that it was wrong; the system was wrong." They eventually found, however, that the experience of the ceremony itself was disarmingly emotional for them. As Nicola recounted:

> [T]he political act, when we actually got up there and we had the lady do the ceremony parts of it in the middle of City Hall, it became hugely emotional right at that moment, so after that I think I was expecting it to be an act of civil disobedience, but afterwards it was very emotional. So the aftereffect was it really gave our relationship greater depth.

Nicola's post hoc reflection, in fact, turned out to be a common theme. Most of the interviewed couples that spoke about this and rated political or protest motivations highly, whether in California or Massachusetts, then commented that their reasons for marrying actually evolved from the political (e.g., marriage as a form of protest) to the personal (e.g., because they wanted to show their love for their partner and solidify their bond). Even couples who had expended a great deal of mental energy on marriage found this to be true. Andrew and Jim, a white couple in their forties from San Francisco, had been together for fourteen years by the time marriage came along. They had never had a wedding or commitment ceremony together but had discussed doing so, ironically, just the week prior to the start of the Winter of Love. By this point, Jim in particular was heavily involved in local LGBT activism: he was already on the board of a LGBT Democratic club and had joined Marriage Equality California. Because of this involvement, he had an inkling that it might be a significant event when they showed up at City Hall on February 12, 2004, for what they thought would be a peaceful political protest with a small group of fellow activists at the county clerk's desk. When asked what the greatest motivator was for them to go to City Hall that day to get married, Jim answered plainly, "It was to make a political statement. That was our reason." Andrew, by his own admission, was "really being dragged along to this political rally." They were taken by surprise, however, when the clerk actually issued them a license and then, in the assessor/recorder's office, were married by an officiant, in front of CNN cameras. As Andrew reflected, "We thought that it would be much more of a political statement, 'Yeah, we'll do this. We'll get married.' But once we were there holding hands and saying our vows, it was very personal." Jim, the activist, concurred:

> I still actually said when we were getting married that we needed to do this; it was a political statement, a very powerful political statement. . . . I didn't think the ceremony itself would have much significance because I already thought we were a very committed couple. . . . [But] while it was happening, it just became a very emotionally powerful ritual and experience that just took us both by surprise.

Jim and Andrew's experience—with the exception of the first-day excitement and news cameras—was not unique in this regard. Back in Massachusetts, Karen and Martha, from the western end of the state, were also taken aback by the significance their marriage took on. Karen and Martha were both from Episcopalian midwestern families and had met in graduate school fifteen years earlier. They had never had a commitment ceremony of their own other than a private, low-key exchange of rings and felt no use for anything else. They were both college professors who had spent considerable time thinking about the historical, social, and symbolic dimensions of gender and marriage, and generally found themselves skeptical or indifferent if not entirely opposed to the institution of marriage. Martha admits that she was "very sympathetic with the marriage critique that it wasn't the kind of paradigm that was automatically something I would embrace. I just thought it was a strange thing to want for myself. So we just didn't." Karen's opinion at the start was one of relative indifference: "There was no . . . proactive political consciousness that therefore I wanted in on this. . . . I'm mad [about] the privilege accorded the straights. But this is something that's sort of apart from us." At some point, however, when marriage became a reality in the state of Massachusetts, both women's outlook changed. Karen remembered, "I guess I started thinking . . . you can have a critique of marriage, but this is so profoundly political in the context to today's anti-gay politics." Martha added, in thinking about going to the county clerk's office to get her marriage license, "It was amazing. It felt important to kind of undergird that political sentiment with numbers that would then show the state nothing was gonna collapse or crumble." In other words, both women went from relative indifference, even hostility, to marriage to an understanding of same-sex marriage on a broader scale and of their own involvement as an important form of resistance and activism; Martha stated, "I would call that as purely political. . . . It was a political calculation. Absolutely." But this sentiment, too, was not the end of the story for Martha and Karen. Going through with the wedding itself—which by their own choice was a very small, private, family affair with just themselves and their children— elicited a further transformation in their experience of the significance of their marriage. Karen explained:

> I would say at the moment we decided [to get married], it was a kind of between a protest, like a protest act and kind of sense of bringing our family and household together. But then once it got going—'cause I cried through the entire ceremony. I mean that's really something I'll always remember.

Martha added, "And so, therefore, the kind of demonstration of the staying power of our relationship didn't feel particularly legal either. It didn't feel political." These words echoed closely the experience of marriage skeptics Johanna and Moira, discussed earlier. Despite having considered their marriage "really a political statement" and something that they did not otherwise particularly need, they were also struck, in retrospect, at how deeply it had affected them. Johanna explained, "But then . . . there's a deep emotional significance of that event, that it's not just politics because it did make me burst into tears every time I really actually am able to think about it. You know, the fact that—I think, for me, what may be at the root of that is the notion of being considered a *full human being*" (emphasis added).

The Politics of Marriage

Marriage: one could hardly find a more conservative institution to serve as a vehicle for political resistance. The likely comparison, when it comes to gay rights, might be the military's onetime policy of "Don't Ask Don't Tell" (DADT). However, even those servicemen and women who defiantly came out of the closet and were discharged from the armed services under DADT did not claim to have joined the military in order to enact resistance or as a political protest. On the contrary, both surveys and interviews suggest that in both San Francisco and Massachusetts, some couples—certainly, some coupled individuals—were motivated to marry by an idea of resistance and "making a statement." They came to this point of resistance-through-marriage by a variety of paths. Some felt energized by what they saw as a mass movement and a moment in history, as suggested by Taylor et al's analysis of the Winter of Love. Some came from a vantage point informed by feminist and queer critiques of marriage as heterosexist, anti-egalitarian, and overly assimilationist, which, ironically, led them to get married as a way to transform it. Others were compelled to react against what they saw as a reactionary backlash of conservative political and religious resistance to gay rights, personified in George W. Bush's 2004 State of the Union address. Some—though by no means all—came with a prior commitment to activism and political action around gay rights; many did not.

In its least complicated form, this call to action was personified by those who had otherwise no intention of getting married and did not think they would reap any financial or legal benefits; they did so at San

Francisco's City Hall out of a desire to enact what they considered to be civil disobedience. Patricia and her partner, Annie, were one such couple; Patricia, a seasoned activist, clearly oriented to the marriages in much the same way as Rosie Harding in her concept of "fracturing resistance," albeit in a relatively benign form. Several other anonymous survey respondents agreed, often with great fervor. Some, like Patricia, remained in the civil disobedience camp from start to finish and did not attach any other meaning to the event than collective political protest. As it turns out, however, she was in the minority in this regard.

Far more common were couples like Janja and Kim, who began with political motivations but were transformed by the experience; or like Pat and Terry, whose reasons for marrying clearly had political overtones but did not necessarily see it as a protest or as civil disobedience. Most couples, in fact, demonstrated a consciousness that was far more complex than "against" or "with" the law. Couples like Pat and Terry, as well as Sherri and Dawn did not deny the political significance or motivation of their weddings, but they also resisted any implication that it was "against" something, even the prevailing order. Sherri pointed out that the marriages could not be termed "civil disobedience" because they were sanctioned by the city government—a fact that, ironically, made the event "so revolutionary" in her eyes.

The transformations that many couples described in recounting their weddings and the aftermath underscored the complexity of their motivations and experience. A common refrain heard from couples on both coasts was that they had begun the process as a political statement but ended up with something that was meaningful to them in a far different way. Self-proclaimed anti-marriage feminists like Janja and Kim in California or Martha and Karen in Massachusetts had never felt personally or politically drawn to marriage, but when presented with the opportunity they felt the pull of the political and historical opportunity to take part in what they assumed would be a large-scale gay rights protest. Much to their surprise, in most accounts, they found themselves in the midst of not just a protest but a profoundly personal experience. This came as a shock to many, like Amy—or like Martha and Karen—who had written off marriage as a heterosexist institution that they would never be a part of, or as something they were doing only to participate in a social movement they felt was important. Even for those who were not as explicitly anti-marriage but nevertheless were politically motivated to begin with, such as Glen or Nicola and Renee, found a more intimate sense of meaning reverberating throughout the experience.

A smaller but still significant number of couples had the converse experience: they started off thinking they were getting married for the rights or the romance—or were uninterested in marrying altogether and emerged politicized by the experience or by the reactions of others. April and Penny, for example, admitted that they had very little interest in marrying until they heard the religious Right's reaction to the *Goodridge* decision. Dale and Lisa, whose interests to start were primarily pragmatic, were equally galvanized by the political discourse in the aftermath of the marriages and came to feel more strongly about the significance of their marriage in political terms. For several survey participants and interviewees, like Joan and Cecilia, the significance of their wedding as an act of resistance came to them primarily in retrospect, as what they came to understand, upon reflection, as a much desired "fringe benefit."

As might be expected in the context of a state-sanctioned institution as legally laden—and at the same time as personal and intimate—as marriage, many people's narratives of their experiences and motivations evinced a complexity and multiplicity that might not be easily summarized in either/or terms. For many couples in both states, the personal and the political blended together to such a degree that it was hard to tease apart which, if any, was primary. Beth and Isabel, finding this to be true for them, termed the experience of legally marrying in Massachusetts "spiritual-political." Jen and Jennifer, as well as Robyn and Peg, explicitly recognized and sought the transformative political potential of gaining public recognition of their private bond as two women. While Emily was explicitly political in her motivations, her spouse, Anita, felt most moved by the desire to "stand with [her] community"—which, Emily pointed out, was not only a matter of social validation but also political in its own way.

It should come as no surprise to feminists of any stripe that the old adage "The personal is political" turned out to be true in two of the first locales to offer same-sex marriage licenses en masse. One need not interview one hundred same-sex couples to find that this is true; it is evident in the legal and political skirmishes playing out on the public stage in states across the United States in every year since the *Goodridge* decision in 2003. It is by design, as well, in that the state has seen fit to regulate who may enter a legal marriage. That their personal commitment would turn out to also be occasion for a politically galvanizing event may have not been foreseen by some of the couples who married, in San Francisco and in Massachusetts, but it was not entirely surprising either. What might be seen as less predictable is the reverse—that more often than not the political turned out to be quite personal. Even the most politically astute of participants were often taken off guard by how deeply felt their reactions were upon marrying their spouse in what was in some cases initially conceived of as taking part in a mass protest. While one might reasonably assert that marriage, of any kind, cannot help but be an emotional event, their experiences are incomparable from a heterosexual perspective due to the explicit historical and present proscriptions of formalized gay and lesbian relationships, it is necessarily politicized, often not by their own choice. And yet the unexpectedly personal dimensions for even those who set out only to make a protest statement, those that had never previously desired to get married, underscore the degree to which legal rights can transcend both the practical and the political. Indeed, the act of marriage is often powerful because it is not *just* political and not *just* personal. How these elements intersect and also emerge in many couples as a sense of civic validation and re-enfranchisement, is addressed in chapters 5 and 6.

5

Marriage as Validation

Subjects before (and after) the Law

Today is quite powerfully about saying "yes." . . . More than
simply claiming the rights and responsibilities of marriage,
on a fundamental level, Jason and Richard are telling us
today that they believe in the power of this most timeless of
human institutions. Their desire to claim this institution is
predicated on their need and acceptance of its *power*.
—Eric, officiant at the wedding of Jason and Richard,
August 14, 2004

The modern institution of marriage lays claim to many meanings: commitment, love, responsibility, family. But is it also power? Certainly the use
of the marriage ritual to enact resistance or make a statement for gay rights
leads us to believe so—at least symbolically. From the privileged position
of heterosexuality, though, "power" is not something that comes to mind
with marriage: linking oneself to another, legally and financially (not to
mention emotionally) would seem, if anything, like a *dilution* of personal
power, perhaps even a diminution of autonomy. But committed same-
sex couples don't come from this same position of privilege. Unlike their
straight counterparts, they have instead struggled to make themselves
a unit, to establish formal links to one another and their children, and in
many cases to communicate their status and their inexorable link with one
another to their loved ones or community. To be able to do so through official legal powers, therefore, represents not so much a loss of power or freedom but a gain in resources and in validation, pride, and inclusion as well.
The Ninth Circuit Court of Appeals, in its 2012 *Perry v. Brown* decision

invalidating California's Prop 8, agreed that "it is the designation of 'marriage' itself that expresses validation, by the state and the community, and that serves as a symbol, like a wedding ceremony or a wedding ring, of something profoundly important."[1]

In many ways, the law's ability to serve as a source of validation lies at the crux of legal consciousness scholarship (see chapter 1). Early work in this tradition (and even before it) emphasized the legitimizing function of law. Low-status legal actors, as described in the works of sociolegal scholars Sally Merry, Ewick and Silbey, and others, sometimes look to the authority of law to authenticate their problems as ones deserving of public attention.[2] For example, some works have found that this function is particularly appealing for women looking to extricate themselves from domestic violence in the home and to get others to understand their problem as a legal rather than a private one. Their success once they do is far from consistent, as has been shown.[3] In fact, there is ample evidence to believe that low-status actors who engage the courts to solve their problems will often be disappointed, even if their actions in the aggregate ultimately transform the legal lexicon and positioning of claims-makers, as was found by Michael McCann in his landmark study.[4]

The couples interviewed and surveyed for this book differed from most of the participants in these earlier studies of legal consciousness, however, in at least one important capacity; with the exception of those very few who became named plaintiffs in the cases that led to the legalization of same-sex marriage in Massachusetts and California, they did not need to face the hurdles involved with litigation in order to invoke the law as a source of validation. Rather, the law, in effect, came to their doorstep (at least for those living in state). The most significant deterrents to legal action, therefore—the monetary and time costs associated with the often long, difficult process of adjudication, as well as the possible sense that they lacked the legal status or expertise to prevail—were essentially waived. Others, such as legal advocacy organizations and the *Goodridge* plaintiffs in Massachusetts, and Mayor Newsom and his administration in San Francisco, had taken on this burden, thus freeing interested couples to seek legitimation via marriage license without the impediments faced by working-class civil litigation complainants. That is not to say that the couples did not have to work hard to realize the tangible benefits of having a marriage license or even educate others on what it meant for their family status. But it almost assuredly did increase the attractiveness of pursuing formal legal validation for their couplehood.

Usually focused on the context of commitment ceremonies or civil unions, the existing literature on formalized same-sex unions buttresses the claim that couples do indeed seek validation, and often gain it, through legal or quasi-legal institutions. Badgett asserts, based on the experience in the Netherlands, that same-sex couples experience reduced "minority stress"—the alienation and other ill effects stemming from legal and social exclusion—when they are allowed to marry. Eskridge and Spedale found that the Scandinavian registered partnerships they studied helped to foster understanding between the couple and their social network, increase acceptance of same-sex unions in the broader community, and promote greater tolerance and equality for alternative sexualities and families by fostering dialogue and helping others to recognize the couples' commitment to one another. Hull found that even public commitment ceremonies not sanctioned by law had the goal and the effect of approximating legality for the purpose of gaining validation, cultural integration, and recognition as a couple. She concluded that although couples were able to enact a form of quasi-legality in the shadow of law through these ceremonies, ultimately her data pointed to "the unique cultural power of official law" in conferring not just rights and privileges but the "social and cultural legitimacy which some believe only official law deliver."[5]

Affirmation at City Hall: The Experience of Marriage

Both in surveys and in interviews, the symbolic and civic validation that marriage provided was a fairly consistent theme. Although there were some objections by survey respondents to the wording of questions dealing with this theme—a sizeable handful remarked in the comments that they "are already legitimate"—the underlying leitmotif of symbolic validation and civic authentication was pervasive. In the San Francisco survey, couples were asked to what degree they were motivated to marry by the following sentiments: (1) "we had always wanted to marry and could now do it officially," (2) "having only domestic partnership makes us feel like second-class citizens," or (3) "to legitimize our status as a couple or family to ourselves, our families of origin, and/or our community." As a group, this was consistently the highest rated group of reasons as a whole—in other words, there was less variance between the highest and lowest item means included in this grouping. Individual mean ratings ranged from 3.98 for (1) "we had always wanted to get married . . . " to 4.16 for (2) "having only domestic partnership . . . " When respondents were asked to state their single most important reason for marrying, moreover, these two motivations were the most frequently cited, in both San Francisco and Massachusetts. Again these findings generalized across genders—men and women rated these items similarly. Likewise, there was no significant variation according to socioeconomic status. There were, however, differences in ratings of some items along other dimensions, such as age and domestic partner status. Notably, younger couples were significantly more likely to agree strongly with those two motivations, and there was no appreciable difference in ratings of the item about gaining legitimacy as a couple according to age. Those without domestic partnerships were also generally less likely than their registered counterparts to rate highly the statement that they had always wanted to get married "officially," and, to a lesser degree, that they felt like second-class citizens. Interestingly, when asked to choose their single most important reason for marrying, there was no difference between those with and without domestic partnership in their propensity to indicate one of these reasons reflecting a desire for validation or "official" status. There was, however, a significant difference according to age: those under the age of forty were more likely to rate these motivations as primary in their decision to marry.

A look at the qualitative data helps to shed light and add context to some of these trends. Many couples commented that getting married at City Hall had helped them to better perceive the difference between marriage and domestic partnership, having now experienced both. One female couple from San Francisco commented, in a refrain echoed by many others, "We will never be acknowledged as a family and a married couple until we can legally marry. I'm sure there is not a married couple in America who would be satisfied to be called DP [domestic partnership]. No one understands what that means and it certainly doesn't reflect our marriage." Some couples directly commented on the notion of domestic partnership as a form of "second-class citizenship." A well-educated female couple in their sixties commented, "Until we exchanged our marriage vows, we didn't fully experience how second-class domestic partnership really is." These respondents also resisted any definition of marriage that did not involve legal recognition; as one put it, "[we] had already had a religious ceremony plus domestic partnership—[but] this didn't make us married."

An important piece of this validation was the fact that it came from a segment of government (even if only on the local level); there was a sense that legal marriage gave them validation as a couple in the public sphere. One couple explained:

> The City Hall symbolizes the government. The government is perceived as the body that protects the common good of all within its jurisdictions. Marrying us by a representative of the government/ inside a legitimate government building like a regular civil wedding is at least in symbolism an acceptance and equal rights.

Another couple emphasized, "To show our commitment to each other AND being recognized by the State was very important." The fact that they held "that official license piece of paper," as one couple put it, was an important factor in helping them to feel a sense of full citizenship. This was, in fact, a common theme; many considered it an "act of public recognition" and oriented to the ability to marry legally as a signal that

Joe and Mark, married at San Francisco City Hall, 2004

they were finally seen as equal citizens. As one respondent from San Francisco stated, "We had a very brief taste of 'full citizenship' while we were technically married." It meant a great deal to them that representatives of the government (especially Mayor Newsom) whom they considered "political leaders were finally standing with us and standing up for our rights as equals." Equally important was the sense that their marriage enabled them to escape the constraints of what they considered their otherwise second-class status. Several more spoke of a newfound sense of feeling "official" or "equal"—even, in some cases, after their license had been revoked.

The degree to which the public and the personal overlapped was palpable when people spoke about the importance of the validation of legal marriage in their lives as many placed great symbolic and emotional weight on the imprimatur of legitimacy given by legal marriage. A male couple from San Francisco stated, "The emotional 'high' from having a *legitimate, legal marriage* was the most meaningful experience!" One female couple from Southern California voiced this in a way that captured the multifaceted character of this feeling: "There was a window of time where we tasted the freedom that many other Americans assume. It felt magical and spiritual and real." Some couples located the source of this intersection of personal and public validation in the internalized homophobia they had endured during the length of their same-sex partnership and before. As one female couple from rural Northern California, together for more than a decade, explained, "We live with a lot of internal homophobia as a result of society at large and have had lots of therapy to deal with that. It's nice having the 'blessing' and acceptance of people around us and not always having to be hyper vigilant." Conversely, several couples commented on the sense of pride and empowerment they felt receiving a county-issued marriage license. As one middle-aged professional female couple put it, "I think this is where a lot of pride comes from legitimacy."

An important element of the validation their marriage license brought was the couples' sense of respect accorded to their relationships and the ability to adequately convey its depth and seriousness—to be "taken seriously, if only for a moment." Marriage became an indispensable vehicle for conveying to others their relationship status and the seriousness of their commitment, especially for those who were younger or had not been together for long, had children, and the like. As one young couple from Dallas observed, "Not being legally married can lead people to take you less seriously as a couple. We want it to be clear to our families and friends that ours is a permanent relationship." Another young couple from Phoenix explained, "Because gays and lesbians are not able to solidify their relationship by marriage, there are no clear boundaries. This means in the world's eyes, a gay person in a committed relationship may still be viewed as 'available.' Our families do not view our relationship as seriously as that of our heterosexual married siblings." Importantly, this recognition was distinct from the material rights of marriage. One couple noted, "It somehow made our relationship seem more legitimate even though we knew our rights wouldn't be upheld legally. I guess we're too used to not being taken seriously. Sad but true." In a theme echoed later by interviewees in both California and Massachusetts, it also turned on access to the commonly held linguistic markers of marriage. One man, from Los Angeles, reflected that, "More than I expected, it allows us access to a common language that had been missing."

The desire to access the common cultural and legal language of marriage was often linked to what scholars and many feminist or queer activists might call these couples' assimilationist aspirations: they wanted to be seen just like any other (straight) married couple. As one female couple with four children stated, "We feel it is important to be a part of the 'larger' community and for our children to integrate not as OTHER but as a family of the twenty-first century based on love and respect!"

In some ways, it didn't actually matter that the marriage licenses in San Francisco were invalidated because the couples involved had at least been afforded the opportunity to put their names on this legal piece of paper. A Presbyterian couple in their forties reflected, "We still treasure the now defunct 'real' license. To finally be able to get married just like my brother and sister were allowed to marry as heterosexuals."

Seeking Validation

These trends were remarkably consistent in interviews in both California and in Massachusetts. On both coasts, couples not only underscored the desire for validation but also were quick to make the distinction, both practical and symbolic, between domestic partnership and marriage. Furthermore, many of those who had not entered a domestic partnership remarked in interviews that this was precisely the reason they had not: it did not hold the same meaning for them in terms of civic inclusion and validation as marriage. As Neri, the cancer survivor from Massachusetts (see chapter 3) put it, "I prefer a legal marriage over civil unions or a ceremony because, one, I feel I'm worthy of that, and that's what I want and should have." Mindy and Julie of San Francisco had already been together for nearly twenty years and had adopted the same last name by the time they married at City Hall in February 2004. They registered out of perceived necessity with the county of San Francisco because Mindy worked for the school district (they had never registered as domestic partners with the state of California for these same reasons as well as some practical considerations). They were adamant about the difference between domestic partnership and marriage; when asked how they differ, Mindy became very animated: "How is it different? It's different because it's different. It's *not marriage* and *that's the point*. . . . How is frozen yogurt different from ice cream? [*yelling*] It's different!" Julie added, distinguishing the two, "I feel that domestic partners are my legal arrangement in my life and I feel that marriage is my emotional tie," whereupon Mindy followed up, "You know it's part of how human beings have put themselves together for how long. I don't want some newfangled label. I don't want to be put in a different category. I want the same category as everybody else."

Like Mindy and Julie, Jeffrey and Art, an interracial couple also from the San Francisco Bay Area, had originally registered as domestic partners a year into their six-year relationship in order to access health care benefits through Jeffrey's job. In retrospect, they perceived domestic partnership as perhaps a step toward marriage but by no means an equally significant one:

> [W]hen this is all sorted out and we have full and equal marriage rights,
> I think we'll look back on domestic partnership as the beginning of that.
> It was sort of like the foot in the door that allowed us to say this isn't
> good enough. This is separate and unequal.

Jeffrey and Art had considered going to Canada to get married the previous year, when it was legalized there, but were overjoyed when same-sex marriage came to their own backyard. Their reasons for marrying were clearly distinct from both their domestic partnership and their hypothetical consideration of a commitment ceremony (which they had never done); Art explained:

> I think the validity of getting married and getting a marriage license . . . I
> do know that when I had that in my hand, I felt that was the most incred-
> ible feeling and validation because it's everything but—my parents have
> one and I needed one. . . . And I just thought it was very real. It was actu-
> ally a legitimate license, which meant that I was really married. Because
> we could have a ceremony, we could do all that, but this was different.
> This was like having what everybody else has available to them.

Again, Jeffrey took the long view in discussing the significance of their
San Francisco City Hall marriage. Although he agreed with everything Art said about craving the same recognition that had come to his
straight married parents and siblings, he also did not expect that their
marriage license would go unchallenged. He saw this as "all part of the
process," a necessary stutter step toward full marriage equality, and still
quite validating at that.

Carolyn and Mona, of San Francisco, had been together more than
twenty years, had no children, and had not registered as domestic partners at the time of the City Hall marriages. They had had a very simple,
private commitment ceremony and exchange of rings many years earlier on their first anniversary, and had taken the same last name. Like
Art and Jeffrey, they agreed that neither domestic partnership nor commitment ceremonies conveyed the same validity as marriage. Carolyn
felt that a ceremony, without the force of law, would be unnecessary—
they already knew their commitment to each other. As for the idea of
domestic partnership, "It's like somehow this relationship is not quite
up to snuff. You know, being married is the real thing, and you guys are
just playing house or something." Carolyn clarified that it wasn't just
that domestic partnership carried far fewer rights than marriage when
it was first introduced in California (although that also had an impact
on their decision to not register); it was that, symbolically and socially,
it "seems lesser . . . certainly in the eyes of others it's lesser." Even when
Mona had experienced significant health problems a few years earlier,
they were not tempted to enter a domestic partnership. But by contrast,
they jumped at the chance to marry at City Hall.

Amy, who in chapter 4 spoke of her desire to make a political statement by marrying, particularly as a representative of younger gay and lesbian couples, remarked on the cultural importance of the difference between the language of marriage and that of domestic partnership:

> If I say, "This is my partner," then it conveys something. But what it really conveys is that we're not married, and we're not married because we're gay, so it conveys our inferiority. When I say, "This is my partner," it conveys the fact that I am a pervert, or I am a freak, or I am not normal. Well, when I say, "This is my wife," then it's the opposite. It's that she's my wife, just like my mom is my dad's wife. It's the same level of commitment, the same validity.

Importantly, Amy also noted the universality of marriage—and the language of marriage—as a marker of status: "When you say you're married, everybody knows what that means, whether you're in California or in . . . New Zealand or China, every language has a word for marriage. Every culture knows what marriage is."

Those interviewees who had access to relationship rights through domestic partner status or their workplace—and even those who did not—clarified that this access alone did not confer the same sense of full citizenship and legitimacy that did their marriage license. Neri from Massachusetts commented: "[M]arriage runs much more deeper [*sic*] than all the legal benefits, than of the financial benefits. It really is—for me, it's a sacrament." Likewise, those who had had their own ceremony in the past also drew a distinction. Amy, who had not only registered as domestic partner with her spouse but had also had a small ceremony with family and friends, articulated the difference: "At City Hall, it was like something new, something we didn't have before. It was like gaining something or something that was just bigger. Because this—I mean, if it would have held—this is a marriage recognized by the state or by our country."

Some of the respondents were even surprised at how symbolically important the access to legal marriage had become for them; one middle-aged survey respondent commented, in a way that probably applied to many lesbians of her generation who got married, "No matter how far or liberated or radical we'd become, that inculcated desire to be married was still there." In interviews, several people commented on how the validation they felt upon being legally wed took them by surprise. Particularly for those of the baby boomer generation and even for those over forty—they had been raised to believe that marriage was for heterosexuals, and did not foresee the possibility for them to be included in it in their lifetimes. Mindy and Julie were one such couple. Mindy discussed the mental shift she underwent as she realized she would be able to marry Julie at City Hall:

> And I never knew how much I wanted it. I never realized, "oh I can?" . . . suddenly, I could join my tribe and it was huge. It was just huge. Part of me, as I get older, it is about rights. That's part of it but there's a much more profound layer to this that I'm not articulating very well.

California natives Kimball and Margarita were in a state of shock when they learned that Mayor Newsom had made it possible for them to get married at City Hall—though for neither was marriage an altogether foreign thought. Kimball had been married to a man previously and had two children by that marriage, whom she raised with Margarita. Margarita had also, at an earlier time, come close to marrying a man, since, as she put it, that was "how I conceived of being an adult, how I conceived of raising a family" in the 1980s, before she met Kimball. In 1990 she met Kimball, who was by then divorced, and the two began a life together as an "instant family" in San Francisco. When they finally determined on February 12 that it was not some sort of media hoax, that they would indeed be allowed to marry one another, they rushed to City Hall the very next day and became the fifty-fifth couple to marry in San Francisco. Kimball explained the significance in an interesting way:

> I liked having, even though it's so prosaic, the bureaucratic imprimatur on it because effectively that's what it is, a blessing . . . even though it's so

kind of dry, meant a lot to me. . . . With us [as a same-sex family we have needed] all this stuff to kind of back up our validity. So, our relationship has always needed extra bureaucratic work . . . so I think for me, being able to be in City Hall and having all of that stamping and numbers, it meant so much more to me. Which is not very romantic. [*Laughter*] But, you know.

The nature of their family had necessitated a great deal of concern for the otherwise mundane bureaucratic protections and formalities available by law, and when it came time to marry, the bureaucracy of applying for an official marriage license at City Hall was at once mundane and exciting—an official imprimatur of government validation that they had come to find very important.

Other couples commented on this same sense of meaning, derived from the otherwise banal procedural formalities of legal marriage. More to the point, the quotidian nature of the license application process—applied in this extraordinary circumstance—gave couples a sense of having finally joined the mainstream, which in its own way felt revolutionary. Mindy phrased this as having "joined the tribe"—and talked about how validating it was to have straight people inviting and encouraging her and Julie to "come on in," as she put it. San Francisco resident Neil, who married Mark, his partner of eleven years, also remarked on this feature. Mark and Neil had met when they were both students in a conservative community in Southern California. Although they lived with each other fairly early on, their relationship was initially stilted by the fact that Mark had not yet come out to his parents. Based on their conservative upbringings, he feared their reaction, and instead let his parents believe that Neil was simply a roommate. Both men agreed that their relationship really began to blossom only after Mark finally came out to his parents; it was at that point that they began to plan for their future in earnest. Although they hadn't made specific plans to marry in a commitment ceremony—it was something that Neil had wanted but Mark was resistant to because of the lack of legal validation—the weddings at San Francisco City Hall galvanized them to make a firm plan to get married. They ended up flying up two consecutive weekends, the first to get their marriage license and have the legal ceremony, and the second to have a more traditional wedding and celebration with family and friends. Neil discussed what it was that was different about his City Hall wedding, as opposed to their later celebration with loved ones:

> There was very visceral and powerful feeling that came from that that most people wouldn't get from just signing up for their wedding certificate and everything, so I don't think it's necessarily that different than a straight couple who goes and gets their license beforehand and then has their ceremony . . . but just that kind of mundane experience for most straight people was such an amazing opportunity that that was the heightened significance for me.

His spouse, Mark, felt differently going into it—he initially oriented to City Hall, much like participants in chapter 4, as a form of civil disobedience. As was often the case, though, this attitude changed over time. He explained that "when we got married at City Hall that totally flipped; it was such a powerful experience for both of us." Much of this, Mark noted, had to do with the setting and the process; he commented, "I mean yeah, it didn't escape me that we were a gay couple in this government building having a ceremony; a wedding ceremony, it was —I mean yeah, it was validation." Both agreed that the actual paper license itself was a large part of that validation; as Neil commented, "That to me was so surreal. It was so official. I'd seen a document like this . . . and it had both of our names on it. I never thought I'd see something like that . . . that was a very powerful experience."

More than one couple made the observation that the power of the experience was the *sameness*, a point ironically made, as discussed earlier, by anti-assimilationist critics of same-sex marriage as well. Leilani and Nancy met on a blind date five years earlier while both students at different Ivy League schools on the East Coast and had been a couple ever since (chapter 3). Now living in the Bay Area, they always had intentions to marry; both reported that they had a visceral experience when filing their marriage license and paying the license registration fee. Out of curiosity, they flipped back through the records on file to the year Leilani's parents had married. There in the book, in the very same files where their own license would eventually appear, they found her parents' own marriage license. This was a profound experience for the two of them (so much so that they took a picture of the page). In a sentiment echoed by both women, Leilani said, "there was a weightiness to it that was absent before." Nancy added, "Yeah, there's definitely a part of it that was about, this was, you know, some small piece of the *establishment*, if you will, officiating." They were not surprised, but were deeply hurt, when the Supreme Court later invalidated their license— though they did not hesitate to get legally married once again in 2008 when it became legal.[6] Their experience in this sense was similar to that of Will and Andrew from San Francisco, who discussed the importance of the material consequences of their marriage (chapter 3). They also recognized an important element of what Andrew termed "societal validation," largely driven home by a seemingly innocuous comment made by his (heterosexual) sister. Upon viewing their marriage license, she remarked, "It looks just like mine." Andrew reflected in response, "It's the same. It was—it's a legal recorded document. It's separate from religion, a civil marriage . . . it's a recording of our relationship and the rights that are afforded to each other."

An irony of the San Francisco weddings, and one often overlooked in discussions of the initial Winter of Love marriage licenses, was the degree to which participants attached their subjective sense of its significance to their perception that this represented a legitimate—and legitimating—act of government. This stands in stark contrast to many observers' assumptions that most participants knew full well that what they were doing was not legal under state law and therefore constituted a massive act of civil disobedience, albeit one in which the city was complicit. It is abundantly clear that some people did in fact hold this view, but it does not necessarily follow that *most* people knew that these marriage licenses would not be legally valid. The comments made by many couples, when discussing both their motivation for participating and the significance of it, belie this assumption. Diana and Joan, a middle-aged couple from the Bay Area, did not diminish in any way the personal significance of the commitment ceremony they had had with one another several years before. But they made an unambiguous distinction between this and the validation they later felt at City Hall. Joan said, "When we did our ceremony it was for us. . . . Now what we were getting was something from a government body that was validating our commitment that we had already made to each other." They described the excitement they felt at the realization that "we're being married; we're getting a marriage certificate. This is no longer on a whim, this isn't just for fun; this is actually now going to be something that is a marriage certificate that they give everybody else that makes this commitment."

Even those who realized intellectually their marriages would probably be voided still felt, in a sense, the imprimatur of legality. Colleen and Louisa, a young couple in their twenties from the San Jose area, had already registered as domestic partners and gotten engaged to one another at the time they decided to marry at City Hall. A few months before their interview in 2005, they had a large traditional wedding ceremony, in which they both wore white dresses. This was in part motivated by the fact that their marriage at City Hall had been too last minute and rushed to be able to include family and friends. They admitted that the knowledge that the licenses would probably be voided made them feel "awkward" but, at the same time, felt that they were finally going to be "taken serious and be taken officially." Although Colleen was clear that "our relationship is about us and we don't really need any kind of recognition from the government to know that we love each other . . . it was still like an official little bit of acceptance that was really cool to feel." They were gratified to note that other couples in line with them at City Hall in 2004 also seemed to be taking the experience very seriously, rather than simply as a whim or an exercise in civil disobedience.

Consistent with the experiences of couples in chapters 3 and 4, many saw that the full impact of their marriage, and the sense of validation they derived from it, took them by surprise. Glen and Scott, who disagreed about whether their marriage was politically motivated (for Glen it was, for Scott it was not), nevertheless agreed in retrospect that something fundamental had changed as a result of this marriage, which made them "legally equal citizens." Glen, in fact, remarked that it was "the state saying, 'Yes'" and that it was "more than [he] ever expected." He went on to reflect, "I guess I didn't realize that for so long, as gay folks, we hardly ever get legitimized officially. We're usually tolerated at best. . . . For something to say that, from the State of California and the City of San Francisco, to say that 'you are equal and you're okay and we recognize the love that you share.'" This validation had a profound effect on both men: "But there was something intrinsic in it which I never gave it to. As I was reflecting . . . about it, we were different. That moment—" and here Scott interjected, "We were real." Scott later concluded, "It was a consummation of sort. It was the drying of the cement. I hate to keep using the same terms, but we were legitimized." They both confessed that, although it felt awkward to state, they had craved this approval:

GLEN: Part of me did need it even though I didn't know I needed it.
SCOTT: And part of me did, too, I guess.
GLEN: I didn't realize it until I—
SCOTT: Yeah.
GLEN: We were just equal.

Linton and his spouse, Jeff, who in had expressed concern over their lack of legal rights such as spousal privilege before they were able to legally marry, underwent a very similar experience (chapter 3). Linton, in particular—accustomed to a lifelong experience of exclusion as a gay African American man—went into his marriage at City Hall half hoping to gain the rights he and Jeff were missing but half, much like Glen, as an act of protest. He admits that by going to City Hall he thought he was making a "social statement" and by his own admission did not expect that it would have any effect on him other than to "defy the rules." With the benefit of hindsight, he reflected that the effect, not only in scope but in character, had been much more dramatic than he would have ever anticipated: "It's about our civil rights, but I guess it's also about acceptance and realizing that we are part of this whole experience [of marriage] . . . I finally got a taste of what it was like to be part of this right. And it was like somebody believed in you. . . . *Finally, someone believes in you.*" At this point in the interview Linton began to tear up, much to his own surprise. He explained that as much as he might have thought he did not need that acceptance, he realized only upon gaining the right to marriage just what he had been missing in terms of validation as a gay man.

Although they phrased it somewhat differently, Aleda and Anne Marie were similarly transformed by their marriage at City Hall. Already together for more than a decade and registered as domestic partners at the time that they married at City Hall, they had just moved from a small apartment in San Francisco to a larger home in the suburbs. They were still adjusting to the move when they heard that they might have the opportunity to get married in their old city. Aleda admitted that there was a civil disobedience quality to it that appealed to her, and a sense that it was something she wanted to be a part of even if the marriage did not hold up in court. Anne Marie, who did have some concern for the legal rights of marriage given that she was not an American citizen, was not as much of a "protester" as her spouse. Nevertheless she did not expect the sense of validation that she ultimately got: "I was thrilled with the marriage specifically and a sense of legitimacy that I hadn't missed because I hadn't known it and I wasn't expecting it because you know, the likes of us were told we're already too naughty to get stuff like that." She and Aleda agreed that this legitimacy was felt primarily after the fact:

> It was an aftereffect of a real sense of legitimacy and being part of a big picture that I hadn't really thought about before. It's like you just dismiss something . . . you may want to be part of it but you know that you can't be . . . there was just something incredibly legitimate about it that I finally got to experience. . . . It was a lovely feeling.

Aleda, too, realized only in retrospect what she had been missing: "Having that experience for the first time really made me realize, although I knew kind of intellectually . . . how on the outside I felt we were as a couple just by virtue of the fact that we were kind of operating by a different set of rules." She summed up her view on what they had gained by say-ing "it was to kind of be a part of a legitimate, kind of legal binding you know, [a] socially recognizable contract." She distinguished this from what the two might have been able to accomplish without the interven-tion of Mayor Newsom and San Francisco: "Every day is a commitment ceremony you know, we've made that commitment to each other. In my mind anyways, the whole marriage thing is really just a legal contract but clearly there are social implications to it."

Edie and Pam had been a couple since the mid-1980s and had expe-rienced their share of anti-gay discrimination and approbation before coming to San Francisco. Like most other couples of their generation and especially those before them, they had never considered marriage a real possibility and were shocked when the opportunity arose. Still, there was some hesitation as Edie, trained as a legal professional, shared a concern that getting married at City Hall would adversely affect their domestic partnership rights in California. But the moment proved too exciting for the couple to pass up. Edie explained, "I don't feel the need to have a religious person . . . say, 'You are a couple in the eyes of God.' I don't care, you know? But to have my city say, 'We recognize you, and we honor your relationship, and we recognize your relationship,' I was really—I was surprised at how quickly I wanted to jump at it." Pam agreed, and also articulated how being allowed to legally marry gave her a sense of civic validation that she realized she had lacked. Because she had grown up in Texas with Southern Baptists, Pam stated that

> my sexuality made me question my citizenship and my equality. . . . At the time that I was acknowledging my own sexuality, I did not under-stand that at the same time I would need to consider my citizenship, you know. But years later when I realized the ramifications, you know, I was forced to question, "Am I equal or not?"

She explained poignantly how getting married at City Hall had finally allowed her to answer this question in the affirmative: "[Now] we were full citizens and *fully human*" (emphasis added).

Across the country, in Massachusetts, longtime couple Anne and Gretchen also did not anticipate ever being able to legally marry. An upper-middle-class couple—Anne was a lawyer, Gretchen a marketing executive—they had realized fairly early on in their nineteen years together that this was more than just another relationship, despite their age difference. They both agreed that had it been legal, they would have married years before, within the first five years of their relationship. Even so, Anne explained:

> I think we both thought at the time that it was a formality. It would be great to have the opportunity but we never expected it in our lifetime. If you had asked us we would have said we were married before it was formally recognized. I guess I was surprised that even within the relationship taking that step really made a difference.

Gretchen added, "I think it adds a level of legitimacy in all aspects having to do with relationships. . . . To the outside world, I think it was really important to us to exercise that and take advantage of the full benefits that we deserve. . . . I think we both kind of woke up the next day and said I didn't think it would make this much of a difference but it did. It just underscored something."

Kathy and Andrea, by contrast—like Garrett and Dean (see preface)—were of a younger generation and fully expected, one way or another, to marry in their lifetime. They did, however, recognize the fortuitousness of the timing; as Kathy reflected, "We are still saying how lucky we are to be living in Massachusetts in the time that we are. We are so lucky to have met each other in the time that we did because I think it would have felt like second best or a fake marriage to have a domestic partnership . . . [or] commitment ceremony." Both middle-class, well-educated professionals in their early thirties, Kathy commented that even before it was legalized, marriage was "definitely something we had thought about and discussed." She traced these discussions to an experience they had a year into their relationship, when Andrea had accompanied Kathy on a business trip out of state and had ended up in the emergency room.

Kathy described the panic she felt at not having a recognizable status vis à vis Andrea, in order to be able to be with her in the hospital once Andrea was unconscious. It was after this that Andrea proposed, and the two decided they would find a way to marry. Kathy acknowledged that before they got married, she was primarily concerned with protecting their rights and that she would have settled for an analogous legal status; however, in a familiar refrain, this soon changed. She recounted:

> It was really an amazing thing to go to City Hall and pick up our license. I felt almost as moved by that than at any part of the ceremony, to see this official form that was stamped with our names on it and our parents' names on it, our address and that it said "legal." It said we were married as if solemnizing this document. That was an incredible thing.

It also became clear that a legal commitment by any another name (domestic partner, etc.) would not suffice in producing this feeling. Kathy commented, "I think even if they have the EXACT same laws and rules the fact that it is not the same name just really draws attention to the fact of you don't deserve marriage. You don't have the right to have this part of life. This part of humanity. . . . To me, it is almost like saying you aren't allowed to vote." This allusion to marriage as a marker of full citizenship was echoed in the after-the-fact reflections of Garrett and Dean, who had married in Cambridge. Dean reflected, "I think that the [*Goodridge*] decision and what we knew logistically it would mean for us is much less important to us than what the spiritual, if you will, impact of the validity and the social movement and the civil recognition as a component of society that it provided for us. It took weeks, I think, to really settle in intellectually." He went on to comment that "it became an issue that transcended our codification of our relationship in whatever enumerated rights and benefits and responsibilities might be appurtenant to it, to be much the way that we identify ourselves as active citizens participating in our society, really."

This newfound sense of full citizenship was a natural extension of a feeling of civic inclusion that very much mirrors the goals of assimilationist gay rights strategies, perhaps not surprisingly in this context. Courtney and Lelia, both in their early forties, were one couple who expressed this wish for inclusion very clearly. They had met in 1994 in a class that Lelia was teaching and experienced what they both considered "love at first sight." Four years later, they had a large traditional wedding ceremony with family and friends, complete with white dresses and traditional rings. This was important, the couple said, to publicly acknowledge and affirm their relationship, itself a form of validation through their personal community. After having children a few years later, the couple also adopted a common last name. Still, even with all of these markers of marital status in place, when legal marriage became an option they jumped at the chance and did so at the earliest opportunity. When asked why it was important to them, given that they were already married in the eyes of most of their family and friends, Lelia commented that it was to communicate that "I am a part of the community. I belong, along with everybody else. That I am not different! And that my relationship with the person that I love and my family is not different. We are part of this community, a part of this society, and that we are recognized." Courtney expanded on the difference between this and their earlier commitment ceremony: "The . . . ceremony validated our relationship to the closest people in our lives. The legal wedding validated our relationship to our society." Although they acknowledged that it was comforting to now have all of the same legal rights as other married couples, they maintained that the primary importance of their legal wedding was "more about becoming part of society as a whole and validating our relationship within our society as the same as our neighbors." Courtney maintained that it was important to, as she phrased it, peel back "yet another layer of that mystique that gay relationships are different somehow." Both women felt it was important to emphasize how similar their family is to other (heterosexual) families. For this reason, they agreed with others that a civil union or analogous status would not suffice. They insisted, in Lelia's words, that "it's about being the same and being included and part of the society and not separated or different or, you know, marginalized somehow."

Katherine and Daphne, who raised concerns about their lack of legal rights while traveling (chapter 3), were in many ways similar to Kathy and Andrea and Courtney and Lelia, both in their orientation to their marriage and in the role that it played, and in the events that brought them to want to solidify their bond to one another. Like Kathy and Andrea, a medical scare had prompted them to think about the long term together. Coming through this ordeal together cemented the couple's sense of permanence with one another and a desire to be married, even though at the time legal marriage was nowhere on the horizon. For a variety of personal reasons—including a general distaste for ceremonies—the couple did not have a commitment ceremony on their own, but they privately exchanged rings the following summer. Again, this couple underscored the importance of marriage in similar terms to Lelia and Courtney: they wanted to be just like everyone else. Katherine reflected, "I think it helps weave you into the broader fabric of society instead of keeping you outside of [it]—you know, I not only have the same rights but I now also have the same responsibilities as any other married couple." She pointed out that this was especially important given their status as an "invisible minority" and their resulting ability to "pass" for the majority; they could easily, after all, be mistaken for roommates, friends, or sisters. Getting married, with its outward displays—wedding rings, picture in the newspaper, spousal terminology—at once clarified their status as a lesbian couple and family while simultaneously integrating them into the social fabric of the mainstream "instead of being always outside and kind of the 'other,'" as Katherine put it; "I mean we're part of everyone else. It's neat."

Katherine underscored the public nature of marriage as an important piece of the affirmation she and Daphne felt in a way that resonated with many other couples as well. Longtime Boston residents Mike and Moe, despite being of a slightly older generation and having been together longer, expressed a similar sentiment. Both working in the health care profession, they had met at a conference on LGBT health issues in the 1980s. The two, like Lelia and Courtney, had a somewhat traditional wedding ceremony of their own exactly four years to the day

before getting married legally. Mike had initially resisted the commitment ceremony because he felt it was a poor simulacrum of a heterosexual paradigm—a "parody" in his words. He felt that if he was going
to get married, in other words, he wanted "the real thing." But that feeling gave way eventually to the reality that legal marriage was not forthcoming in the 1990s and the commitment ceremony ended up being
a very meaningful day by both men's accounts. Still, like many others,
the men did not hesitate to be among the first in line at Cambridge City
Hall in the early morning hours of May 17, 2004, to get their marriage
license. Mike spoke of his sense of what had changed since he and Moe
married the following month: "I mean, and I didn't know that there
was a feeling that went with being married, but there's something about
the commitment, both interpersonal commitment and then the publicness and the legality of that commitment that makes a difference to
my felt experience of being in the world." That the recognition was not
only public but positive in nature added to the affirmation and change
that they felt. Moe reflected, "Growing up in the '70s with all the sort
of messages that I received about what it meant to be gay: that I wasn't
legitimate. My relationships weren't legitimate, my lifestyle wasn't legitimate, but now it's definitely—there's been a complete paradigm shift
for . . . myself and people around me." He pointed to the legalization
of same-sex marriage in Massachusetts as acknowledgement that "we
aren't second-class citizens and we are equal." Mike added that this feeling could not have come from an analogous institution carrying all of
the same rights: "Marriage comes with a load of not only rights and
privileges, but with a certain psychological, an emotional legitimization
that a civil union does not have."

For some who thought they had dismissed the goal of assimilation
into a heterosexual institution, like Mike had earlier felt, the positive
feeling of validation from the mainstream came as a surprise. Robyn
and Peg, who discussed the odd feeling that they were at once joining
and subverting the dominant (heterosexual) paradigm by marrying
each other, admitted they were unprepared not only by the *Goodridge*
decision itself but by their own reactions in its aftermath (chapter 4).

Robyn described the experience of actually reading the decision after which she "suddenly realized that yes, in fact, we do deserve equality. And the decision was very compelling. . . . It changed my thinking." Six months later when the day came to get their marriage licenses, this sense was further cemented by their experience: "What happened on May 17 was that we were greeted by so much excitement and enthusiasm and recognition and positive affirmation. And I realized from the experience that that's something that we had been missing and that most same-sex couples don't experience." Peg added, "It's funny for me to say I wanted to become mainstream, but in a way to get that sort of mainstream acceptance. And I didn't realize how much that my underlying drive was that until the first year after we married." She described the experience of going to their first family Thanksgiving after having gotten married and bringing their wedding album for everyone to see. Peg realized then how much had changed and how much she valued the acceptance and affirmation—and excitement—their families now showered on them in the wake of their wedding.

Several couples felt that the legitimacy their relationship gained in the process of marrying—whether or not it was something they had actively sought—was powerful both because it was not something that historically marginalized gay and lesbian couples were used to experiencing, but also because it could be generalized to their broader existence. Troy and Chuck, who commented on the importance of the protections marriage brought as they got older, then made clear that it was not just these benefits but the legitimation in the eyes of the public that they valued: "Marriage is that package that does all of that for you," Troy concluded (chapter 3). Chuck commented on how empowering—and different—it was to be able to say they were married by power of the Commonwealth of Massachusetts: "It was civic empowerment for gay people to say that 'the Commonwealth' [pronounced them married]. . . . You know, usually people poo-poo the government, but . . . that was very powerful." Chuck also felt that it was equally powerful for gay couples like himself to be uttering the word "marriage" itself: "I mean, the word "marriage" is—there's a status with that that doesn't come with anything else . . . the euphoria of that language is so powerful. And I don't think people realized for gay ears to hear that is very, very empowering."

Emily and Teresa, like Chuck and Troy, connected the feeling of legal marriage as well to both a personal validation but also a more generalized sense of LGBT empowerment. Both were raised on the East Coast and had moved to the Boston area relatively recently before they met. A couple since almost the day they met in 2000, the two had, like Moe and Mike, what they considered to be a very meaningful and fairly traditional wedding ceremony in 2003, about seven months before *Goodridge* was decided. Because they considered this date in 2003 to be their "real" wedding, Teresa initially oriented to their legal wedding in 2004 as a renewing of their vows, combined with tying up loose ends legally—but was shocked to find how deeply the experience affected her. She said, "it affected me in a way that I never anticipated . . . it just became very permanent and very real." In a sentiment echoed many times over by couples in both San Francisco and Massachusetts, the two described how, in essence, nothing had changed—but at the same time, *everything* had changed. For Teresa, it was the sense of permanence and authenticity. For Emily, it was a more generalized feeling of safety and comfort, by virtue of the fact that their state had given their relationship a stamp of legal approval. She described how "I felt like I could walk a little more comfortable in being where we are now that our state has legitimized what we've just done . . . it just made me feel more comfortable talking about my own marriage than I might have otherwise." She went on to explain that being legally married, "gives us the license to be completely honest and, you know, people that still want to discriminate against you, screw them 'cause our state has now recognized it." This extended her sense of physical presence and safety in the community as well: "[since marrying] we can, you know, feel relatively comfortable holding hands or something when we're walking down the street because, you know, we're legally married and if . . . a straight couple would do it, we feel like we have the right to do it as well." The sense of equality and the security that engendered for Emily and Teresa could be generalized to the entire LGBT population. Emily commented, "looking at the suicide rate in teenagers and drug and alcohol abuse I think it's because we're not legitimized. And I think the more we become legitimized in the face of society, it removes some of that stigma and it might enable more kids to be comfortable with coming out." She felt that marriage equality alone would go a long way in accomplishing this goal and was in fact already palpable in its effects in the state of Massachusetts. Moe echoed the same sentiment: "All that internalized homophobia that a lot of us have obviously internalized—kids do the same thing, but this is just another way of saying, 'Wow! It's okay. We can be married.'"

Eric and Michael, although they phrased it in different terms, also discerned how their marriage had transcended the distinction between their personal transformation and a more macro-level transformation in terms of legitimacy for LGBT citizens. Michael, a biology professor from Germany, had met Eric, who worked for the Department of Public Health, in 2000 in an online chat room. Both were living in Boston, and what they did not anticipate would develop beyond an initial conversation ended up blossoming into a long-term relationship. They moved in together a year later and began to contemplate a more formal commitment within a couple of years—a step that, admittedly, appealed more to Eric than to Michael. What that step would look like, however, was unclear until after *Goodridge* was decided, and Eric, by his own admission, talked Michael into getting married. In order to plan the type of affair Eric had envisioned, they were legally married by a justice of the peace in July 2004 and had a large ceremony with family and friends a year later. In thinking about the significance of their wedding, Eric reflected, "I don't think either of us fully appreciated the subtle nuance of change that we would *personally* experience. But there was something about the sociopolitical legitimacy of the relationship. The buying into institutions . . . " Michael, in retrospect, agreed with him: "The fact that the marriage is really equivalent to what is accepted or standard in society, that you are accepted at the same level makes a huge difference." The two affirmed that this level of acceptance and validation was truly reliant on marriage itself—not some parallel form of recognition. As Eric a member of family, or not taking their relationship seriously, until they were legally married, even if only temporarily. One female couple from Marin County, north of San Francisco, noted in their survey, "Only after we were married did our family know and understand and were then able to celebrate our commitment. None of our family knew what to do with our Domestic Partner registration! Nor do communities, or friends. Marriage, people 'understand.'" Couples often noted the reaction of their families, which seemed to transcend other markers of relationship seriousness, including length of relationship, prior commitment ceremonies or domestic partnerships, and even in some cases children. One survey respondent commented, "Something shifted— even in the most loving, accepting members of our families/friends. Some—finally—began acknowledging us as married even though they had been to our wedding in 2001."

These types of stories of change emerged markedly in interviews as well. Garrett and Dean of Massachusetts told a story about visiting Garrett's grandfather shortly after their marriage. Garrett recalled:

My grandfather greeted us at the door and he handed two newspaper clippings. And the first was the newspaper clipping announcing his marriage to my grandmother, and the second was a newspaper clipping announcing my parents' marriage, and didn't say anything, just handed those to me as his acknowledgement of, "Your announcement of your wedding to me is the same as these two newspaper clippings. It holds the same validity in my eyes." . . . For me, that was a recognition that he respected us as a couple.

Garrett and Dean were certain this same recognition would not have been forthcoming without their legal marriage. A similar sentiment was echoed by Kathy and Andrea. Kathy remarked:

What I realized on the day [of their wedding] was the magnitude of the social component, that our families really accepted us on par with the other relationships in my family. It wasn't just Kathy and she brought along Andrea but "this is Kathy and Andrea, [they] are a couple and they are married.

Likewise, Jesse and David felt a visceral difference in their extended families. Jesse stated, "I definitely feel a real acceptance from David's mom and stepfather, that I didn't feel before the wedding. I feel very, very, very welcome in their lives, and I did not feel that, I think before. It [the wedding] meant a lot to them too." On Jesse's own side of the family, he told of an aunt and uncle whose position toward them also changed markedly. His aunt, whom he described as "wickedly severe about who is really family and who isn't, based on blood," came to accept them as married, and David as part of the family—in Jesse's opinion entirely based upon "the fact that with a legal contract, her husband being a lawyer, she has to accept it."

John and James, another upper-middle-class couple originally from Massachusetts, had, like Linton and others, gone into their wedding planning with an eye on the practical considerations. They had met nearly twenty years earlier at a gathering for LGBT students at M.I.T. and had been together ever since. A few years later they moved to Southern California, where James had taken a job as a faculty member at a large university. They had followed the legal developments leading to the *Goodridge* decision closely and began to have a sense with the 2003 *Lawrence v. Texas* decision that they might soon be able to legally marry. The couple had bought a second home in Provincetown, Massachusetts, and so they were able to marry there in spite of the residency restrictions Governor Mitt Romney had belatedly enforced. It was these practical considerations that had dominated their conversations, until the moment when they married. In retrospect, they were struck by two things: first, the sheer enormity of the emotional experience; and second, the effect on their extended families, particularly considering their long history as a couple. Although they did not have children and had not had a prior wedding ceremony, both families had had ample opportunity to get used to the two as a couple. It came as a surprise to John when, after their wedding, "My extended family basically stated they now saw James as a member of the family. . . . Given the reactions of some of the people in my family you would think that this relationship popped up a year or two ago—not that he had been around for eighteen years." They concurred that this would not have happened had it not been a legal marriage.

It was not only the contractual nature of their marriages, however, but the preexisting cultural construct of marriage—itself apparently inseparable from the legal status—that produced the differences in treatment that these couples experienced. Robyn and Peg, despite their equivocal concern with mainstream acceptance prior to their marriage, articulated this as a matter of framing and the availability of a commonly understood cultural category of couplehood. Peg stated:

> I felt like we gained an acceptance among the family community. We were always accepted, but they had a framework for us. They could understand us as a couple better when we became a married couple, that they didn't have a framework to understand what our relationship was before that. I don't think it was taken as seriously [before].

Robyn agreed, "I think it solidified what they already kind of knew, but it made it more real and more concrete and more official." Peg described the first trip home for Thanksgiving after they married and the experience of extended family gathering to view their wedding album as a pivotal point, even for those who had not been at the wedding. She continued, "Even [my] mom, who's an absolute liberal and open-minded and has loved the whole thing, I think it even gave her a slot to put us in. But definitely much more than the others. That's the framework they know."

Eric and Michael described a similar sense of the change they experienced in their relationship to others, as a result of the newfound availability of a cultural "slot" for their couplehood. Eric explained, "It makes it easier for people to assimilate the depth of our relationship. I think it is harder for people to truly appreciate a marriage equivalent as opposed to marriage. . . . So it has been easier for people to just start from the presumption of family, knowing that we are married." Michael and Eric identified a critical piece of this puzzle of validation: the importance of language. They and many other couples found that being able to use the legal language of marriage allowed them to access a shared social space of legitimacy in reference to their relationship. Michael reflected on what a difference it made to be able to refer to Eric as his husband: "Being able to talk about Eric as my husband feels immediately clear about what his significance in my life is. I can project it with a single word . . . I mean it's shorthand for the significance of the relationship." Eric agreed and offered that the language of marriage was one important reason why they would not have been satisfied, or fully validated, with a civil union status: "I am very, very aware of the perception and reality—perhaps reality created by perception—of language is very important to me and the idea of second-class citizenship or some alternative participation . . . is just not acceptable to me; it just doesn't sit well."

Other couples agreed and also commented on the importance of the shared language of legal marriage. Abby and Sophie, in their mid-twenties and both born and raised outside of Boston, had met in college, and almost immediately started discussing a future together. After eight months they moved in together, and shortly after began sharing a joint checking account, put both names on their utilities and lease, and essentially—for all intents and purposes—living like a married couple. However, for Abby and Sophie, the visceral difference of legal marriage came with the ability to use the word "wife" in reference to one another. Abby remarked, "when I say, 'wife,' it hits me. You know . . . Wow . . . even just that word. You know, that language used." She later continued, "language can make such a huge deal. I mean, clearly, but—that one, little word." Sophie agreed: "I think . . . our straight friends understand it more. Like she's not my girlfriend; she's my wife. . . . 'Okay, you're married. I understand that'. . . . They understand . . . the level of commitment, you know? . . . They respect it more and let us know." She also observed, "My boss is a Republican libertarian . . . I think he respects me more because I'm married, you know? . . . Because he—I mean, he understands that."

Just as the expression of community support and civic validation implicit in their ability to marry legally visited upon couples feelings of belonging and citizenship, the converse was also true. Couples in Massachusetts sometimes discussed the hurt and nervousness they felt at continued efforts to reverse *Goodridge* via constitutional amendment banning same-sex marriage. (This was still a possibility at the time of the interviews, although such efforts ultimately failed). The reactions of San Francisco couples whose marriage licenses had been invalidated by the California Supreme Court were far more visceral and immediate. An overwhelming majority of the more than fourteen hundred couples responding to the survey stated that they were not surprised but were nevertheless deeply disappointed and hurt by the nullification—even though not much changed materially. Many described a profoundly emotional reaction—many used the term "devastated" and some described it as the feeling of being punched in the gut. But there was also a palpable sense of disenfranchisement. One couple described feeling "Disappointed and tossed aside—back to the margins of society." Others said they felt "disenfranchised and dehumanized," "invalidated as a person," or "degraded and dismissed as a U.S. citizen." Several experienced it as having been failed by their government. One person said, "As a third-generation Californian, I felt betrayed by the state I'm so loyal to." Others stated that they felt, "an overall deep fear of being unwanted in my own country." Even those who anticipated the invalidation, in many cases, "felt kicked in the stomach like second-class citizens—worse than we thought we would feel since we really expected this result."

By and large, those couples who were interviewed also expected this result and understood it as one step in the political and legal process, but they still felt a keen sense of disenfranchisement, which was worse for having been given the right of marriage, only to have it taken away once more. Colleen, who had married her partner Louisa primarily to make a statement, reported that, "It definitely felt like a symbolic thing. Like the big government was saying 'uh, no, just kidding. You can't be official.'" Margarita, from San Francisco, having remarked on the meaning and sense of legitimacy she had derived from being subject to the same bureaucratic procedures of marriage as everyone else, was as shocked and disappointed by the reversal as she had been shocked and encouraged by Mayor Newsom's actions to begin with. She remarked that she had, as a result, lost a great deal of confidence in the legal system: "I've never been so disappointed in it. It just was so unjust. I just really feel like, how in the world could you have done that? I mean how legally could something be given and then taken away?" Leilani and Nancy, likewise, brought up the annulment and expressed a profound sense of disenfranchisement:

> It is very hurtful and . . . it's given me a feeling of having an "other" status that I did not have before, it's made me feel minority, which I never felt before. And it also gives me a distrust for the government that I didn't have before . . . now . . . I need to fight tooth and nail with the government because they don't, they're prejudiced against me.

A unique perspective was offered by Sherri, who had been one of the attorneys to litigate the case (chapter 4). She was certainly under no illusion that the mayor's actions were immune to judicial review, nor was she necessarily surprised when the courts found that he did not have the power to authorize same-sex marriage licenses. She was, however, deeply shocked and disappointed that the court chose to invalidate those existing licenses rather than retaining them until the underlying constitutional issues could be decided. She described in detail the transformation she underwent, having first acquired, then lost the right to marry:

> I was amazed, amazed at the power it had on me to have my government reach out and recognize me as a full citizen. I'm somebody who graduated from a top law school and did well and has a good job. . . . So you would think that I would feel very powerful and sort of central to society and stuff. But the act of getting married at City Hall made me realize quite concretely that I didn't feel central to society at all. I felt very marginalized still as someone who was denied very basic civil rights. I wasn't

even really cognizant of it. But I remember walking to work the next day after we got married and feeling like, "I own that sidewalk. My government stood up for me," and I could stand on that sidewalk with everybody else and be the same as everybody else and it felt just so different, I can't even describe it. It vanished when the Supreme Court nullified the marriages. *It completely vanished.*

Private Rite, Public Validation

One point can be gleaned quite clearly from all of this, and it is a point that was largely obscured for several decades before the modern same-sex marriage movement. Although marriage is clearly a personal commitment and contains a package of public benefits and responsibilities, it can also function as an imprimatur of public approval for one's relationship—and, by extension, one's personhood. Though this function is hardly needed, or even consciously recognized, in the context of most modern heterosexual marriages, it is of fundamental importance to couples who have been legally excluded from marriage. These surveys and interviews with couples in San Francisco and Massachusetts show that by far the most frequent change same-sex couples experience after they legally wed is the degree to which they feel that they are recognized and validated by those around them—whether family, social acquaintances, or public officials. Likewise, rather than becoming a tool of protest or mode of resistance, the legal institution of marriage is understood here as a bastion of legitimacy and validation. This point—particularly when put in the context of litigation—is not without controversy. For example, some public pundits, in reaction to Judge Vaughn Walker's decision in *Perry v. Schwarzenegger* invalidating Prop 8 in California, have protested that legal rights should not be conferred on the basis of anyone's "hurt feelings." The implication, more prescriptive than empirical, is that Sherri's loss of empowerment or Colleen's sense of disenfranchisement is not the concern of the state or of the law. Regardless of one's normative evaluation of the proper scope of litigation, the inescapable conclusion based on the evidence here is that the inclusion or exclusion of same-sex couples from the legal institution of marriage has profound effects on their sense of civic belonging, pride, and inclusion.

Whether the desire for inclusion was a motivation to marry from the outset, or was felt retrospectively after the fact, varied considerably from couple to couple, and even within couples. For some, particularly those over the age of forty, the initial shock that they would actually be allowed to legally marry in their lifetime eventually gave way to a realization that such a deep-seated desire for recognition and approval existed for them. Couples like Pam and Edie, or Gretchen and Anne, had grown so accustomed to making a life together without legal marriage that they had no conception of the degree of validation they were missing until they were able to marry. Others, like Glen, Aleda, and Linton entered the process with a demeanor of rebellion; they anticipated making a political statement but not seeking legitimation. It might have even seemed an anathema, as it did for some survey respondents, to consider that they would be seeking public approval for their relationship—they already considered themselves "legitimate" without that piece of paper. But again, the spirit of protest eventually gave way to a realization of how much the public validation of marriage did in fact mean to them, along with the sense of inclusion that they finally felt as a result. The unspoken and unexpected power of legal recognition, in other words, was not something they would have missed—or realized they missed—until they experienced it first hand. This aspiration for sameness and inclusion not only led participants to reject a substitute, such as domestic partnership or commitment ceremonies, but also highlighted the importance of access to the commonly understood cultural markers and language of marriage.

Indeed, when asked what the effects of their marriage were, or what had changed since, by far the most common response was the social reaction and recognition afforded to them by family, friends, and co-workers Countless couples, such as John and James or Peg and Robyn, recounted stories of extended family members, even parents, who finally "got it" and extended a welcoming hand to partners who may have, in practice, been part of the family already for decades. This was felt in both verbal expression and in more subtle gestures that had been observed in the time since the marriage: notes or gifts of congratulation after the fact, inclusion of a same-sex spouse in family events, acknowledgement of a spouse's birthday, and the like. Broader social circles, such as colleagues and friends, also demonstrated this newfound understanding, often by including the couple in "married people" activities or conversation. In some cases this, again, came as a surprise since these couples had already done so much together—including commitment ceremonies, buying homes, and having children—that should have made clear the nature of their union. Interviewees such as Aleda pointed out that, as welcome as these messages of inclusion and congratulation were, they served to demonstrate just what had been missing before. At the same time these were welcome changes for a population who, as Moe and Robyn point out, were not accustomed to receiving affirmation for their relationships.

The great weight of public affirmation for a quintessentially private act lies at the heart of this book. Although the feminist maxim that the personal is political is by now several decades old, it remains an important feature of most gay and lesbian rights issues, which necessarily depend on aspects of the participants' personal lives in order to define the affected class of citizens. To an even greater degree, the issue of same-sex marriage brings this nexus of the personal and the public into sharp relief. A common thread among the couples with whom I spoke was the degree to which their sense of full citizenship and humanity emerged as an embedded and intrinsic feature of their marriage—often to their own surprise. In some ways akin to the ability to vote, they found that their civic personhood was premised on their full inclusion in what many admittedly and ironically consider an institution whose contingency on state regulation is problematic at best. This conundrum, and the power invested in marriage such that its cultural and legal are nearly inseparable, are part and parcel of the most public and the most private of institutions, the most political and most personal of rights.

6

Making It Personal

Marriage, Emotion, and Love inside and outside the Law

We married aware that, as a married couple, we would still
be denied the rights, privileges, and benefits of marriage
according to others, so why did we do it? . . . We are hon-
ored that by marrying we were making a statement for civil
rights, but we married out of plain old-fashioned love.
—Carolyn and Mona, San Francisco

At first glance it might seem absurd that in a book about marriage, only
one chapter is dedicated to discussion of love and romance. After all, as
a number of couples poignantly point out, what other reason is there to
marry? The old saying that "love and marriage go together like a horse
and carriage," however trite, certainly holds true for a great number of
couples, whether gay or straight. At the same time, this is not—and cannot be—the end of the story. The simplicity of the formulation belies the
inherent complexity of the particular historical moment in which these
marriages occurred, and the convoluted intersection of law and love—the
political and the personal—that they represent. In the simplest terms, the
fact that same-sex couples have not had the *option* to marry—and still
do not in most states—necessitates a different approach. That the status
of their romantic lives is a topic of political and legal debate *at all* places
them in a unique position, one occupied most conspicuously in the past
by interracial couples and, to a lesser degree, the incarcerated. The law
and the culture—to the extent that those two things are distinct—have

dictated that the horse and carriage remain "unhitched" for same-sex couples.[1] Of course, some couples prefer it that way and have no desire to hitch their romantic lives to a state-regulated institution with a fraught past. For others, particularly those over the age of forty, their orientation to marriage has been predicated on the expectation that it would never be an option for them; it was simply irrelevant. When these expectations were suddenly defied, first in Massachusetts and then in San Francisco, the collision course between love and law accelerated.

The same-sex marriages that began in 2004, or even the debates over it prior to this, are certainly not the first instance of law and emotion intersecting. Scholars in the burgeoning field of law and emotion, such as Susan Bandes, Kathryn Abrams, and Terry Maroney, have analyzed multiple ways and instances in which the two bear on each other. Some focus on how particular emotions are, or should be, reflected in law or legal doctrine. A prominent example is Martha Nussbaum's and others' analysis of the role of *disgust* in criminal law as well as the regulation of sexuality and other realms of law.[2] Others have looked at what Maroney calls "affective forecasting": predicting how a particular legal outcome will make one feel (e.g., if a litigant predicts that a particular level of civil damages will make her happy in the future, she is likely to settle).[3] Still others adopt a legal actor-centered approach that focuses on how particular emotions affect the work of individuals involved in legal decision making—including jurors, judges, lawyers, and legislators. Shortly after the legalization of same-sex marriage in Washington and Maryland, legal scholar Ty Alper noted with interest the degree to which prominent (mostly conservative) political figures who had shifted their position to support same-sex marriage, almost universally personalized the decision, in often tearful accounts, as one driven by emotions such as empathy, shame, or love for their gay and lesbian family members or staffers.[4] His account proved prescient, when weeks later President Obama became the first U.S. president to endorse same-sex marriage, citing conversations with his daughters about their friends and schoolmates with same-sex parents as a precipitating factor in completing his "evolution" on the issue. As Abrams points out, law and emotion may intersect in a number of ways: law can "express or reflect [emotions], channel them, script them, cultivate them, and destroy them."[5] There have as of yet been no scholarly accounts of the way emotional and legal concerns come together for same-sex couples themselves. The closest to explore this intersection would be Cheshire Calhoun's "Making Up Emotional People," which, rather, focuses on (presumably false) cultural and legal constructions of same-sex couples' emotions—in particular romantic love—which are used to justify bans on same-sex marriage.[6]

The work of Kathryn Abrams and Hila Keren provides most likely the best model for thinking about how law and emotions are intertwined in the context of same-sex marriage. A primary departure in their work is its focus on positive emotions, such as love and hope, as distinguished from most prior research, which largely focused on negative emotions such as disgust or shame. Abrams points out that it is these emotions—often associated with the feminine—that encounter the most resistance in their intersection with the law (and more so when applied in the arena of family law), because there is a perception that the law (often gendered male) may be a corrupting or profane influence. In a separate work, she and Keren focus on the law's role in cultivating emotions—in particular, hope.[7] Although the particular empirical referents they use to study this (including the enactment of Project Head Start as part of the 1960s War on Poverty) do not involve family law, several of their observations provide foundations on which to think about the affective dimensions of law in the context of same-sex marriage. First, they point out that—far from isolating themselves from the personal—institutions (and legal institutions specifically) may be potent forces in cultivating emotions like hope, because of their rhetorical power and breadth, by encouraging particular ways of thinking to a broad constituency. This constitutes an implicit rejection of the common assertion that legal "rationality" and "the passions" are mutually exclusive. They also underscore the sustained social benefits that such cultivation can produce on a broader scale, in that its direct beneficiaries can then become forces for independently furthering the social change sought. Finally, their coda on the utility of contracts in facilitating positive emotions is particularly prescient in imagining how a similar analysis might apply to legal same-sex marriage: "Contracts not only facilitate the embrace of distant goals by permitting those within contractually ordered relationships to plan for the future, but they may also support the hopes of parties for the long-term social integration and acceptance of their nontraditional relationships."[8]

In this chapter we look at not only the emotions produced by the legal institution of marriage but also the role of emotions in channeling people's motivation to pursue such a legal contract. The degree to which romantic or emotional reasons for obtaining a legal marriage license (as distinguished from having a wedding ceremony not sanctioned by law) easily separate themselves from other motivations is debatable. Indeed, by this point it should be abundantly clear that the experience of marrying is a richly layered one for most couples, not only in terms of motivation but also in terms of the experience itself as well as its aftereffects. Thus, the type of civic and social validation couples felt (see chapter 5) might very well impinge on or produce heartfelt sentiments and emotional responses. Likewise, the sense of making history, produced by the political import of the event to some couples, often had an affective dimension. In still other cases, the decision to marry was uncomplicated: they simply loved each other and chose to express it in this way. That legal changes and procedures might be so emotionally laden and motivated might not be initially intuitive but becomes quite clear as one examines the narratives and experiences of the couples who married.

Marriage, Love and Law: Emotional Dimensions of Legality

Three items on the survey distributed to married couples in San Francisco rated motivations for marrying that were entirely external to law as it is most commonly conceived: "to be a part of history," "on a whim," and "for romantic reasons." These three types of reasons admittedly have little to do with one another; this is why they exhibit the greatest variance in ratings: average scores on a one to five scale ranged from a low of 2.01 for the reason that they "did it on a whim" to 4.42 for the answer that they married "for romantic and emotional reasons and/or to show my love for my partner." In fact, these two items were, respectively, the lowest and highest rated motivations overall on the entire survey. In other words, the most consistently cited "most important" reason for entering a legal marriage had nothing to do with the law: that of love and romance. This theme was consistent across demographic categories: young and old, rich and poor, male and female couples all ranked its importance similarly. The only significant differences were found between couples who had had commitment ceremonies on their own in comparison to their counterparts who had not, and to a lesser degree between couples who had registered as domestic partners and those who had not. Counterintuitively, those who had already done marriage ceremonies on their own—presumably for similar reasons, to show their love for one another—where actually *more* likely to rate romantic motivations highly when it came to later getting their legal marriage license. This tends to refute the assumption that a non-legal ceremony would serve the same personal and emotional purpose, or that the legal marriage—even one that is subsequently overturned, as in San Francisco—is superfluous. The emotional import of these legal marriages is especially striking given that more than half of the respondents had already had a marriage ceremony, presumably to fulfill these same purposes. Moreover, when taken together, motivations located "outside the law"—in other words, those having nothing to do with either benefits or validation derived from legal status, nor having any political purpose—accounted for the greatest percentage of answers when couples were asked what their single most important reason was for marrying.[9]

Notwithstanding the difference in their historical access to marriage and resulting differences in social position, surveyed couples often underscored their similarity to their heterosexual counterparts in emphasizing the essence of romantic marriage. As one longtime male couple from Iowa remarked bluntly: "Love—what other reason is there to get married?" Along with the complications arising from

their history of exclusion but highlighting a commonality with heterosexual couples, some surveyed couples stated that their marriage was
a long-deferred realization of a lifelong expectation that they had. A
middle-aged man from San Francisco explained that he had married
"to demonstrate my love for my partner and to be able to have that special moment of wedding ceremony that I'd dreamt of as a child." Some
intimated that, despite the rarity of opportunities for same-sex couples
to marry legally, it was a crucial step in the progression of the relationship. As one shared, "At a young age we are all told that love is cemented
in marriage. So, with that as our background, we just wanted to tie our
relationship in love and marriage."

That the ritual of marriage was a public act in this case contributed to its emotional salience for many people. Several couples commented that the chance to make publicly known their commitment to
their partner was a primary motivation for marrying. A working-class
woman in her forties stated, "My partner is the woman I plan to spend
the rest of my life with. Marriage is how we show everyone our commitment to each other." Notably, several people underscored the importance of this being a "legal wedding," even as they focused on emotional
rather than pragmatic or legal reasons for marrying. One young couple
from San Diego explained, "The most important [reason] was to show
our commitment to each other. It's one thing to say your commitment
out loud, it's another to sign your intent on a legal document."

Whether because of its cultural salience as a marker of commitment or its legal status specifically—and again despite the paucity of
its availability—marriage seemed the most appropriate way for many
couples to demonstrate their commitment to each other; in the words
of one man, an African American physician from the east Bay Area,
it was the "most natural statement of commitment to my spouse." For
some its significance as an expression of commitment came from the
knowledge that when given the opportunity, both partners were willing to take this step. As one man from a rural area of northern California explained, "Simply it's about love and knowing I could dedicate
my life to someone by my side. . . . [and] knowing he is willing to do

the same." The inexorable conflict between the couples' sense of marriage as an essential marker of their bond and its legal reality as something largely unavailable to them was difficult to navigate. How does one square with the notion that something is vital to your relationship when the relationship has, in fact, carried on quite successfully for years before it was an option? One professional male couple in their thirties addressed this contradiction, reasoning, "We didn't need it to validate our relationship, but going through the ceremony and process is inextricably linked to our concepts of how one demonstrates their [sic] emotional commitment. The expressions of love inherent in the trappings of marriage ceremonies are its power and why no one should be deprived the right to marry." Moreover, the prioritization of personal romantic impulses to marry was not always entirely separate from more macrolevel concerns discussed in prior chapters. Participants commented on the dual personal significance of joining with their life partner while also taking part in a historical event, or what they considered a defining moment in the LGBT community and rights movement.

There is no denying that purely personal motivations were at the heart of a significant number of couples' decisions to marry—perhaps surprising only in the particular historical context and setting. Indeed, in spite of the long lines, news cameras, continuing legal and political maneuverings, and unstable legal foundations, a large number of couples who married at City Hall in San Francisco found themselves motivated by purely romantic and spiritual sentiments. A longtime female couple from the east Bay Area, for instance, described their motivation: "It is really all about the love. 'I now pronounce you spouses for life' are the most romantic words [we] have ever heard." For others the event came at a particularly poignant personal moment. For example, one couple described how "after months of fighting aggressive breast cancer, we wanted to celebrate the joy in our life together. What could be more joyful than marrying the one you love?" This couple was so moved and motivated by the opportunity to marry that they flew from Ohio a mere ten days after the mastectomy surgery.

Celia and Paula, married at San Francisco City Hall, 2004

In addition to the sentiments and motivations expressed in the surveys, a handful of distinct common themes emerged from the interviews with San Francisco, which interestingly did not differ much from those who married in Massachusetts. One of these was a stark insistence that other considerations, external to the relationship, were not the couple's primary reason for marrying. Specifically, several people distinguished between instrumental or political reasons for marrying and their own more personal decisions. Julie and Mindy of San Francisco (chapter 5) typified this tendency. After some consideration, they had made a deliberate decision not to mark the occasion of their domestic partnership in any other way, out of a desire "not to go halfway." When they heard about the marriages during Valentine's Day weekend, there was no hesitation—they immediately made their way to City Hall, even though they were not yet convinced that people were actually being issued legal marriage licenses. Although they admit that they initially went to City Hall on a whim, they became determined once they saw what was going on. On learning that they would not be able to get married that day, Mindy "sat down on the curb and sobbed. I never—it was like I didn't even realize that I wanted to do that . . . so it was very profound." When they finally came back and said their vows, Mindy was struck by how starkly her experience differed from the legalistic or politicized expectations that many held: "How sweet and romantic and inclusive and wonderful and warm it all felt. . . . There wasn't anything angry about it. There wasn't any, 'damn it this is my rights I'm going to take it.' There wasn't any of that. It was so completely sweet and loving." Her spouse, Julie, agreed: "I have to tell you that standing in line and going through that for me wasn't about making a legal statement. It just wasn't. . . . The ceremony that we had had no overtones of, 'do I have or have not my rights,' you know, of being an okay person." Rather, they agreed, "It felt so natural."

Nan and Marie of Sacramento, whose relationship dated back to 1956, eventually came to a similar conclusion. They had started with a much different supposition—having already committed to one another and converted all of their property to joint ownership, Nan, at age sixty-seven, admitted that she initially was driven by the desire to make a statement: "It was really purely for political [reasons]," she stated, at first. She did not feel she needed this additional ceremony because she already felt married to Marie. Nonetheless, they agreed that the experience changed their views. As Marie recalled, "It was just a tremendous emotional moment, you know? I started crying and the man who was performing the ceremony started crying, but it was just—I mean, it was just more emotion than I could hold, you know? It was just wonderful." Marie was quick to add that there were no instrumental motivations; they did not stand to benefit materially. As she pointed out, "there is no benefit to us because everything we have is already joined, we don't have children, we don't work, we don't have the benefit of medical insurance. So, there's nothing in it except the two of us, you know?" The only thing they stood to gain, in Nan's words, were the "psychic rewards"—an opportunity to celebrate and honor their relationship and further commit to one another, in "a way that society provided to show a commitment."

Carolyn and Mona, despite their earlier concern for end-of-life rights (chapter 3), similarly made clear the distinction between what some might have assumed would be their motivation for marrying and what they actually hoped to achieve. Like Mindy and Julie, they had already been together for twenty years, had consolidated their finances, and had taken the same last name. In fact, as Carolyn explained, "getting married seemed, like, superfluous." Although they had never had a public ceremony, they already considered themselves married. By their own admission, they were under no illusion that their marriage license would go unchallenged. They were certainly sympathetic to the motivations of those who were making a statement for LGBT rights, but they were clear that that was not their purpose. Rather, with full knowledge that the license might be invalidated the next day, they married to deepen their commitment to one another; as Carolyn explained, "when you say, 'I'm married,' basically you're telling the world that you're there through the good and the bad." Still, Carolyn admitted, "I didn't realize that it would mean as much as it did."

Linton, too, who declared his desire to access the benefits of marriage to his spouse, Jeff, and his unexpectedly powerful sense of civic validation as a gay man was also shocked by the disarmingly personal emotional effect getting married had, and has continued to have, on him. In his interview, Linton—initially interviewed outside of Jeff's presence—discussed the process that began as him "making a social statement," and ended up being "an unbelievable experience. . . . And during the ceremony I stared into Jeff's eyes and I realized that regardless of whether this was legal or not legal, this was the person I wanted to marry. And I just broke down. It was really hard for me to get through my vows. And it was—I didn't think I was about to cry again, but it was unbelievable." He described his trying to make sense of the emotions that unexpectedly flooded in on the day of his wedding:

> And I still can't figure it out. I just—I don't know. I mean, because I knew I was going to marry, it was like an act of defiance. And I came out of there just—it was like disbelief that this could ever happen in my lifetime. . . . I mean, this was the right person. . . . This is the person I love. There's nobody else, and why should I not be partaking in this? And I was crying.

At this point, Linton again broke down in a flood of tears as he recalled the emotions of his wedding day. He was still surprised, nearly two years later, at the emotional reaction it evoked in him.

This, in fact, proved to be one of the most predominant themes to emerge from interviews: regardless of their initial motivations, couples were emotionally moved beyond their wildest expectations. Few couples epitomized this more than Don and Mark, who had driven from Los Angeles to marry in San Francisco in 2004. They had met in the late 1980s in Arizona, in what was meant to be only a one-night stand. But something about Don stayed with Mark as he drove home the next morning; he couldn't stop smiling and decided to call for another date. Twenty years later, they were still together. Although they wore rings and had registered as domestic partners, they had never had an actual wedding ceremony before their marriage at City Hall. Initially, Mark—who had been married and divorced from women three times before—acquiesced to the idea of driving up and getting married because he thought, "We might as well do it and get it out of the way. It will solve a lot of legal problems, that was my reason for doing it, and it will make Donny happy." He admitted, "I could have probably lived the rest of my life and never needed, on the emotional level that he did, to go through the ceremony. But uh, there are things that one does because it is important to somebody else."

Both men, however, were taken aback by how much the ceremony meant to them, and how emotionally poignant the experience was. Mark commented, "I think it blindsided both of us. I don't think either of us suspected how, on an emotional and romantic level, how important it really was to us." They explained:

> DON: It meant a great deal to me. It meant more to me than I had expected actually. To have the piece of paper in my hands afterwards.
>
> MARK: The funniest thing that I found is that—Mr. Sarcastic here who's been married so many times before, [and] really doesn't give a shit—I found it meant a lot to me too. That was what really surprised me . . . I found that it had far more meaning to me than I realized. I fell in love with him all over again.

And too, Don admitted that his initial motivations were more practical than emotional—he had already had the experience of facing challenges to his ability to make medical decisions for Mark, and had his own medical issues to contend with (both men being HIV positive). He explained, "Going in, I felt to some extent as Mark did, that it was about our legal rights and making the public statement about it. And I was initially surprised to find out how much it meant to me on a personal level." Much like many of those surveyed in San Francisco, he explained the emotional importance as a "confirmation of the personal commitment that we've made. . . . We have, in our circle, one of the longest relationships of anyone that we know that's remained intact. And yes it was really important. I don't know quite how to explain the feelings but it was overwhelming in some ways." Those feelings were so powerful for the couple, in fact, that they outlasted the legal life of the marriage certificate: as Don related, "It means a great deal to me still, even though legally it's been annulled. It was very powerful on a personal level."

Nancy and Leilani, who discussed both their tactical legal reasons for marrying as well as the validation they experienced from it, also emphasized the emotional impact getting married had on them. In describing their brief City Hall wedding, Leilani noted, "it really surprised me how emotional it was to like actually say the vows and stuff like that. That was, that was really touching." Nancy agreed, explaining how her emphasis had shifted from the legal to the personal:

> I think pushing the legal part has been so important for me for so long, but it's just like, you know, just like with getting married at City Hall, like it was an emotional experience and it wasn't my first time signing a legal document, but it was a big deal. It had a dimension that, that was surprising.

She continued, "It was a very cool affirmation of where we were at and where we were going. So for me, like, it has more of an emotional impact." In contrast to Don, Leilani added that the emotional element extended to the feelings of hurt they endured when the marriage license was invalidated by the courts: "It was very emotional . . . it was a little more disappointing than I expected when it was annulled."

Nicola and Renee, who discussed practical legal concerns and their interest in making a political statement, also found themselves taken off guard by the emotional resonance of their wedding (chapter 4). They elaborated on the evolution of their feelings about the experience, explaining that the great emotional impact they felt, while not entirely absent from their prior motivations, was primarily an aftereffect. The turning point was when they stated their vows, Nicola explained: "After the civil disobedience, the political act, when we actually got up there and we had the lady do the ceremony parts of it in the middle of City Hall, it became hugely emotional right at that moment. Renee elaborated, "the vows that they did became surprisingly emotional and very private in that moment, but prior to that it was really a unifying activist event with all the people in line and everybody's experiences coming together and the fact that everybody was there for equality and justice." When asked why they thought it had become such a deeply felt moment, transcending both politics and instrumental legal concerns, they ironically located the reasons squarely within the law. Renee offered, "I think for me, the reason that it was so emotional was that there was a . . . validation and a legal state stamp of authorization or legitimacy associated with that act . . . that I did not expect to see in my lifetime." She also noted the contractual nature of the commitment they were making, another distinctly legal feature: "You can state all those things [that you are committed to someone] and you mean that of course, but it's different when you actually are legally bound to someone. Just like if you make a promise, but you don't sign a contract." The emotional import of the moment was derived in part from the same sense of legitimacy that others described—a motivation that Renee and Nicola did not otherwise mention as a factor in their decision to marry.

Kim and Mary, of Chico, California, didn't know quite what to expect when they headed to San Francisco to get married. When Kim first heard about the marriages at City Hall, she expected the event to be a "flash in the pan." But as the days went on, and they saw that attempts to immediately shut the process down had been unsuccessful, they hurried to the city to fulfill what had been a hopeful but vague dream for them. They had already been discussing ways to officially mark their five-year relationship with an event of some sort, so it came at the perfect time. When asked what their primary reason was for going to San Francisco, Kim remarked immediately, "I think the biggest one was our love for one another. Just the fact that we were already thinking of doing this; this sort of gave us the platform. . . . I think it was more for family and for love and for us . . . more than political." They admitted that the politics of the moment excited them, particularly in contrast to the conservative community they lived in. But they both agreed that "this moment transcended the politics." Even so, they were disarmed by the level of their emotional reaction. Mary recounted, "We cried like babies. I could hardly choke the vows out, it was almost embarrassing, because I didn't realize I was going to be so moved like that. I'd never gotten married before, I don't know what it's like, and it was just this unbelievable, emotional, joyous, very happy experience." Kim agreed:

> I don't cry that easily but I was . . . it kind of choked me up when we said our vows and our family was all there and we exchanged rings and it was really a [big] deal. It felt very, very real. Very emotional in all those good ways that you would want . . . your wedding to feel.

The feelings continued to reverberate after the wedding. A year and a half later, Kim reflected, "Something does change when you get to say 'for better or for worse' . . . whatever those words are, forever we will be together and this is the one . . . it just deepens everything." Mary went further, describing the effect on the two of them, and for those around them:

> Just the idea that we had gotten married just so reinforced my love for her that it was just so fun to refer to her . . . as my wife. . . . It just was really reaffirming for me and I think for both of us and kind of publicly amongst our friends . . . they were just so happy for us because we were so freaking happy, we were like floating on clouds for months after this.

By the time I followed up with Mary and Kim in 2008 they had legally wed shortly after it once again became available in California, and their reasons for getting married had shifted since their first experience in 2004. This transformation was in part spurred by their outrage at the decision of their county clerk to discontinue all civil marriage ceremonies at the county courthouse rather than be forced to hold same-sex weddings. As they described it, "We still love each other as much as we did in 2004, but . . . what started as personal has become political."

Notably, one of the two couples I interviewed who had married both in San Francisco and in Massachusetts, Ron and Jim, echoed this surprise at how emotionally moved they were by their San Francisco wedding. The couple noted that this was particularly out of character for Ron: "I actually was much more emotional—and people would probably say I'm not particularly emotional—but even in saying the vows . . . I broke up during the vows, so I was much more emotional." He compared the experience to other weddings he had attended in addition to the two other weddings he had himself had by the time of the interview (one many years previous to a woman, the mother of his grown children, and the wedding he and Jim subsequently had in Massachusetts): "I just thought it was fantastic and I don't know of any ceremony I've ever attended that I've liked more. . . . Or become more emotional for." When asked why this ceremony was so much more moving, they cited two factors: first, Ron felt that the vows he spoke in San Francisco were not only lengthier but were more personally moving for him. Second, as Jim pointed out, it marked the first occasion on which they had celebrated their twenty-plus-year relationship with a public ceremony of any sort: "This was actually the first public affirmation of our relationship as well."

That the San Francisco Winter of Love gave couples the opportunity to publicly affirm their relationship and seal their commitment struck not just James and Ron but also many other couples as paramount to their choice to participate. This is not without irony since, as I have pointed out elsewhere, there would seem to have been nothing stopping couples who wished to from declaring their commitment in a public forum without legal status, through a ceremonial rite. Similarly, any couple in California and a handful of other states could make a legal and financial commitment via domestic partnership. Moreover, some couples (but not all) participated knowing full well that the marriage would likely be annulled. Still, many couples expressed surprise that one would even question why they wanted to get married, given all of these caveats. Joan and Diana of San Francisco, for example, when asked why they chose to come to San Francisco to get married, remarked somewhat incredulously, "Why did we do it? Because we could; and why? Because we love each other. Why do any two people get married?" Joan went on, "It really was because if you love somebody. . . . You want that commitment, you have that emotional tie, you have that commitment, you want to go forward with that commitment. You want to take it to the next level." Joan and Diana were not a couple who took for granted that their marriage would be annulled; they expected that this license would guarantee them a legal marriage. As Joan explained, distinguishing the event from their earlier "spiritual wedding," "This was a whole different type of thing 'cause now this was a firm document that I could hold in my hand that said I was legally married to this person and she was legally married to me. I had to take care of her, she would—you know—it wasn't just a partnership now, this was a marriage. You know, and this was the whole thing." And too, it wasn't simply a matter of being legally responsible for one another; in describing their relationship after their wedding at City Hall, Joan stated, "It really makes a difference . . . you finally get the opportunity to really be married, it's just really great. I can't explain it"; Diana's best attempt at description was, "Giddy . . . You couldn't wipe the smiles off our faces."

Leslie and Ari, of San Francisco, felt a similar degree of emotional resonance that was unique to this experience. The two had been together since the mid-1990s and had moved across the country together from Wisconsin to San Francisco two years later. They were in fact already planning a commitment ceremony at the time that they heard they would be able to marry at City Hall. In retrospect they admitted that they did have doubts buried deep in their minds about whether the marriages at City Hall would survive legal scrutiny, but at the time they were nevertheless immediately drawn to the opportunity to have what they considered a "legally binding" marriage. In telling about the unique emotional importance and effect of their City Hall wedding, Ari compared it to both their commitment ceremony and their later domestic partnership:

> The feeling is just different and I can't—it's almost hard to quantify that
> or talk about it, but it just emotionally resonates in a completely different
> [way]—getting married, even though I wasn't dressed up, even though
> we had very little time to plan for it . . . even though it didn't have all the
> sort of trappings that my commitment ceremony had . . . it felt different.

Leslie and Ari agreed that in a sense, it was practical legal protections
of marriage that actually contributed a depth of meaning to their experience. As Ari noted, "I think that there is something about the tangible, practical stuff that has, that contributes to an emotional resonance. . . . There was something about being in City Hall; it was just
unbelievable to me," even though, she freely admitted, the same tangible rights could be gained through domestic partnership or a series
of contracts. The two, in Ari's mind, were clearly intertwined: tangible
benefits that also carried symbolic emotional weight. In describing
the effect of both the marriage and its later annulment, she explained,
"Even though there's a part of it that's about the emotional peace, about
being legally married, that's emotional and not so much about the practical stuff, I think that lack of the practical stuff makes me angry which
is a piece of the emotional thing . . . it was just hard, you know, to have
that taken away." Here, Ari identifies what one would think would be a
primary departure between her experience and that of couples in Massachusetts. The differences, however, were not quite as pronounced as
one would think.

Love and Law in Massachusetts

In the months following the *Goodridge* decision in Massachusetts,
couples who had been together for years—in some cases decades—
were faced with a decision and opportunity that forced them to suddenly think about what legal marriage might mean to them. For those
motivated primarily by emotional and romantic commitments—as
distinguished from the practical, political, and symbolic concerns—
the thought processes and motivations were not that different from

commitment to Jerry in the form of marriage: "I came out in the '70s with all the disco and all the sex, and all of the wildness that I participated in, to finally say, 'This is what I'm choosing. Away from all of that madness, I'm choosing to have that commitment in life.'" He continued, "It made a difference . . . I feel like I'm a grown up here. I feel like I have taken on a responsibility that's gonna make me think twice about how I behave in this relationship, because . . . this made me think, 'You're married. You've got to act like a serious person and give what you said you would do in this formal ceremony.'" Bob admitted he cried throughout the whole ceremony, concluding that, "It makes it real . . . I was making an absolutely total, emotional [commitment]." Jerry agreed and appreciated that Bob wanted to make their relationship legally binding: "I think it was important to me to have Bob publicly acknowledge and legally acknowledge that I'm his partner. Even though obviously he does it in many ways, the fact that it's very public, that's just my lifestyle. We did it with grace, and love, and humor, and he was just incredible."

Donna and Dawn, both working-class Massachusetts natives in their forties, were equally excited to get married but for different reasons. The couple had known almost instantly, when they met in 2002, that they wanted to be together. The fact that Dawn had never been with a woman before—and was still technically married (though separated from) her husband of ten years—wasn't a deterrent to her; it was love at first sight and shortly after getting together with Donna, she came out to her family. Fittingly, when they were finally presented with the opportunity to marry, Dawn was the romantic: "I wanted to get married again because I loved her. I knew I loved her, and I liked being married." Like Don and Mark in San Francisco, the expression of commitment appealed to her: "I liked that stability of knowing that you're gonna be with somebody, somebody who loves you, and take care of somebody and . . . knowing that you have somebody there with you." Donna, by contrast—having never been married and never thinking she would be able to—was motivated initially by more instrumental and political concerns. She admitted, "I had very different reasons for wanting to get married. . . . I wanted to be part of the people that are starting to change—hopefully the world . . . [and] I wanted to get married—it was important for me for—god forbid, anything happened to her. . . . I didn't wanna lose my home, my things, you know, the bed that I'm sleeping in . . . I wanna protect myself . . . I didn't wanna be excluded." Donna had reason for concern: she had been barred from visiting her critically ill father in the hospital by his new wife who had told the doctors that he had no daughters. She lamented, "I've been a lesbian for my whole life, and legality counts in this country. It counts." But even the practically minded Donna was taken up in the romance of the thing. In the end, she married for these reasons but also for love; she felt a clear, if difficult to define, difference after marrying Dawn. She said, "It feels more real . . . now that I'm married. . . . I'm not quite sure how to explain it more than that. It's just more real." Donna had, in her words, wanted to "count as somebody in her life. I want to be as real as I can be, and you need legality with that." In the end, she got what she wanted.

Others, however, were actually quite specific that they had *not* married for only instrumental or tactical reasons. Cathleen and Carey, a professional couple in their forties from Boston, had been together since meeting on a blind date in 1992. They were surprised when legal marriage suddenly became an option for them, even though Cathleen was well-connected to the LGBT rights community—they had assumed that Massachusetts would legalize Vermont-style civil unions. They had never had a ceremony of their own and had not even discussed the possibility of marriage. As someone who had been agitating for LGBT rights and joined the crowds at Cambridge City Hall the first night, however, she was very specific that the decision to marry Carey was not movement-related for her. This, in fact, was the reason they did not marry among the first throngs of people at Cambridge City Hall: "If we were to get married it was more about *us* rather than a political statement. So there's a lot of layers in all that was happening because it was political in one sense, but then people still had their own personal choices about it." She underscored how long she'd wanted to marry Carey, before ever knowing it would be possible; Carey, for her part, said, "There was something that really, [in] your heart you just felt on this July [wedding] day. And it was a real mix love for Cathleen and . . . wow, this is really amazing we can do this."

Richard and Jason, an educated, upper-middle-class couple, made an even sharper distinction in their reason for wanting to marry. Because their primary residence was on the West Coast (they had a second home in Massachusetts which allowed them to marry there), their wedding would require a significant degree of planning; it was not only a matter of filing intentions during the initial rush at Cambridge City Hall, but the timing turned out to be significant. They had always said if they made it five years together, they would somehow mark the occasion; this came just as Massachusetts was legalizing same-sex marriage. Their ceremony melded the political with the personal (chapter 5): Richard was biracial (Caucasian and African American) and his parents had married during an era when, in some states, they could have been prosecuted for doing so. They were in the vanguard of change as were Jason and Richard. However, they made it clear that this was not their primary intent. Richard explained, "To get married, you have to be with somebody that you feel safe getting married with and that has to do with how strong your relationship is. Not being a hypocrite is very important so I couldn't just get married for political reasons to someone that it wasn't going to work out with or that I didn't want to try to make it work out with." Jason agreed, "It was much more personal and not very political, the decision making."

If there was any doubt in their initial motivations and planning, the wedding itself confirmed what the couple felt. Richard reflected on the moment he and Jason were announced legal spouses:

> I cried. It wasn't political. That part was not. The power part I did hear through all the tears, but it was the emotional, "I can't believe I'm doing this. I can't believe that I've come this far from being this closeted little gay boy thinking I was the only one in the world to a fabulous wedding . . . saying these things that I love another man in front of a hundred

people." . . . Beautiful, just a beautiful memory and there's nothing political about those memories.

Jason corroborated this and underscored that the same depth of emotion would not have been there had it not been legal marriage. Knowing that the *Goodridge* case had been decided the previous November,
Richard had proposed marriage publicly to Jason at a family Thanksgiving in 2003: "I really felt like the legal triggered the personal—it transformed the personal. Like, he wouldn't have been proposing at Thanksgiving that year a civil union or a commitment, 'Will you join me in a
commitment ceremony?'"

Jason and Richard, given their romantic engagement and their motivation, would be no more surprised at the personal resonance of their
wedding than any other couple, gay or straight. But for some couples
in Massachusetts, as with those surveyed in California, the emotions
took them by surprise. For Jake and Chico, marriage wasn't on their
radar screen at all (chapter 5). They were not politically involved or
optimistic but had settled into their relationship and the perceived reality that as a gay couple, marriage was never in their future. When it
did finally become an option, there was no formal proposal; by then
the two felt they were past the point of needing to ask whether they
would spend their lives together, and it was simply understood that
they would take advantage of this new possibility to marry. They went
through the conventional wedding planning process with little fan-
fare. But when it came time for the wedding itself, Jake admitted, "the
emotions of the ceremony blew me away. I wasn't expecting that . . . I
was doing everything I could to not be sobbing as I walked out there
because the powerful emotions hit me, and it was unexpected . . . the
emotions were extremely powerful." Chico, who had witnessed plenty
of antigay discrimination in his home country of Venezuela, also had
to hold back tears; he remembered, "The whole act of getting married
was much more important than I ever thought it was gonna be." He was
also pleasantly surprised, afterwards, at the understated but important
effects it had on them. He reported, "The biggest advantage of feeling

married is the sense of normalcy. . . . It's extremely important for us in that we struggled to just be like everybody else. Marriage gives us this tent, you know, of normalcy. And it feels great."

Eric and Michael of Boston also suggested as much when they spoke of the validation they experienced from getting legally married (chapter 5). Despite the fact that they intentionally underplayed their initial legal ceremony so that they could have a larger, more well-planned wedding a year later, the two were still taken aback by the enormity of their emotional reaction. Michael admitted that in the beginning, even after it became legally possible, marriage "didn't seem necessary" to him; Eric had to talk him into it. However, Michael's assessment eventually changed dramatically. He commented, "After the fact, it felt like the marriage made a big difference emotionally for us but I didn't see the importance going in." Eric felt that the fact that it was so low key contributed to their ability to fully realize the emotional importance of what they were doing. He recalled, "It was a pretty significant and emotional day when we got married and because we didn't have to worry about care taking and attending to guests or planning." But it went beyond that: "I think we both were shocked at the enormity of the experience and how much we felt different . . . we were extremely connected. It was also relatively profound how different I felt and how differently people immediately responded to our relationship."

Evolving Motivations

From these accounts and others, it soon became plain that many couples' reasons for wanting to marry evolved quite a bit, both during the time between when they found out that they would be allowed to legally marry and when they actually did so—and even during the short course of the ceremony itself. We have read in these chapters about couples who initially had political or instrumental motivations for getting married but only later came to realize the primary importance of more personal, romantic reasons. This theme emerged first in the surveys of San Francisco couples, who found they needed to qualify their ratings of personal versus other motivations for marrying based on the transformation they had undergone. One person, for example, rated romantic reasons for marrying highly after explaining, "We had previously ('98) had a commitment ceremony and got married mainly to protect our family and protest but found the event surprisingly emotional." Another stated, "Initially it was about making a statement but it became more about showing our love for each other." Two men who had decided to marry for the legal and financial benefits explained, "Although romance was not our initial reason, it became an unexpected, powerful result of the public declaration of our love and commitment." Likewise, a politically motivated woman from Berkeley, who had married her partner of twenty-three years at San Francisco City Hall explained, "This was not important to me at first. I decided to get married for political reasons. Once we were in the rotunda standing there looking at one another—all of a sudden political became very personal."

This reversal of the feminist mantra proved apt for several lesbian couples especially, such as Betsy and Barbara of San Francisco (chapter 4). They initially had very little regard for marriage but had gone to City Hall as an act of political protest. By their own admission, though, things changed at the moment of their wedding. Barbara recalled, "Particularly when we got to the ceremony part and you know, and said those vows. You know, it was like, well, yeah, this is—you know, it had weight, maybe a little more than I expected. We were pretty emotional through it." When Betsy pointed out that even their domestic partnership had an emotional component inasmuch as it was a statement of commitment, Barbara countered that their City Hall wedding was "more personal than that. . . . It was just, I don't know, announcing your love out loud and you know, if it did stand, I mean, we were married." Betsy agreed, "Oh, yeah. It is emotional. . . . It was a serious personal commitment."

One couple, Laura and Janet, turned out to desperately need the legal protections of marriage, and this became apparent only after Janet's death (chapter 3). Laura admitted that at first Janet had been the driving force: "Once we did get married and we started going through the process of doing it, I really shifted from doing it to please her to doing it because I truly wanted it and believed in it and it became political as well as personal." Indeed, the two—to varying degrees—were at first motivated by the desire to make a political statement. Laura recalled, "At first it was a protest but then it became very personal and I think what made it very personal . . . was when we did have the marriage ceremony it was so fast, we just made phone calls and emailed people and just geared up for it in literally four days and the response was so positive." Laura reported that Janet became increasingly politicized throughout the process, and that she "took it to her soul that we were married and because it's something that I think she always wanted." Likewise, she was "really emotionally devastated" when the courts invalidated their license.

Like Betsy and Barbara and Laura and Janet, Leslie and Dierdre had registered as domestic partners only the day before they married in 2004. They had met just before graduating from college back East and had been together since 2000. Just before moving to the West Coast, Leslie had given Dierdre a promise ring and told her, as a way of signaling the level of her commitment, that if they were able to marry, she would. This was a major step for Leslie, who had on prior occasions stated that she had no interest in marriage and never planned to wed. Just a year later they heard that Mayor Newsom was allowing same-sex couples to marry in their home city of San Francisco. Leslie admitted that her primary motivation was "fulfilling the sentimental need that Dierdre probably felt deeply. It was a way of fulfilling a promise I had made to her." Although she characterized Dierdre as a person who is not overly sentimental, this particular issue, Leslie said, "triggered such sentimental buttons for her." The political dimension also appealed to them—though Leslie admitted they went to City Hall largely on a whim, with very little forethought. It made sense, she believed, and would tie up a few loose ends. Of her actual ceremony, however—they were the last couple to marry on Valentine's Day—Leslie said, "I had no idea I was going to be so nervous, but I think that we were both shaking a little bit. . . . I think we were just incredibly moved in ways that we weren't anticipating." She conceded, "I don't think there were tears involved, but it was definitely very emotional." It was not surprising that Dierdre compared her marriage with the experience of becoming domestic partners. She came to the conclusion that "the saddest part about domestic partnership is that there is no emotional fulfillment that comes from signing domestic partnership papers. . . . They're very legal documents. There really is nothing emotional about it. It's just something you should be doing. . . . It's got no emotional component to it." The difference it made to be married, she said, was unmistakable: "I think that there's much more of that kind of absolute selflessness that I don't think we really demonstrated for each other prior to being married . . . sending our emotional commitment to the next level. . . . I think that we definitely experience marriage to each other on a daily basis."

The experience of having one's motivation for getting married evolve over the course of the experience was not unique to those couples in San Francisco; it extended to couples in Massachusetts as well. Gilbert and Alex had never had a prior commitment ceremony and had differences of opinion as to why they should get married: Alex desired community recognition and relished the implicit political statement they were making; Gilbert had more pragmatic concerns in mind, having to do with finances and protections for their family (chapter 4). Both were surprised at how much it came to mean to them personally to have a legal marriage. Alex commented, "Just having that moment was just a life-changing event really. I don't know if it's that way for straight people but it was very moving for me anyway . . . it really surprised me on the day of our wedding how much of an impact having it legally recognized actually had." Gilbert maintained his interest in the protections afforded by marriage but also now saw something beyond that: "On a very cold-blooded practical level that's important to me, but honestly if that was available through some other means that's equivalent. . . . Being married means more than that."

What a Difference a Day Makes

The transformations these couples underwent in the process of getting married, reevaluating their preconceived ideas about the purposes of marriage and what it would bring them on a personal level, presaged the emotional changes they experienced both individually and as couples. In general, couples in both states reported more closeness with their families of origin and greater inclusion of the spouse in the family. In this way, the social and community-level changes the couples experienced overlapped with the more internal, personal changes outlined here. Fifty-six percent of couples interviewed in Massachusetts and 30 percent of couples in California described notable differences as a result of marriage, either to their own emotional state or to their relationship with their spouse, which went beyond both the sense of social and civic validation and the tangible benefits. These differences emerged first in survey responses, even though the survey did not directly ask couples what had changed since they got married. In general, couples reported greater emotional intimacy after marrying. As one young San Francisco couple noted, "We are deeply in love and committed to one another. This made us feel even closer"; another noted, "We felt closer than ever after we were married—kind of a surprise to both of us." Another commonly echoed refrain was the sense that getting married had taken the relationship to "another level"—changing it beyond what they realized was possible. A middle-aged woman who had been with her partner for more than a decade maintained that "[the marriage] fundamentally changed our relationship" on an emotional level. She later stated that it saddened her when the marriage was annulled but did not otherwise have much practical impact; she said she "felt like our lives had been so changed by our wedding that the legal rights became almost secondary."[10] In articulating the content of the change, some discussed this in terms of liberation: one working-class female couple reported, "To make and exchange our vows in that type of forum was deeply emotional and freeing. Our relationship reached a different level by this experience." Others, conversely, characterized it as a greater sense of responsibility and commitment: one male couple from Berkeley commented, "It has made a difference in our relationship in that it has strengthened our sense of responsibility to one another and brings a clearly defined focus on why we are together."

In the interviews, couples were asked directly if anything had changed since they had married (in San Francisco this was asked again when following up with couples in 2008 after marriage was legalized). Commonly the initial reflexive answer was that not much had changed, because of the lack of federal recognition and their preexisting commitment (often marked by a commitment ceremony, exchange or rings, or domestic partnership). For many couples, though, as they discussed their wedding and their lives in greater depth, what often emerged in their description was a palpable yet not always immediately describable transformation in themselves or their relationship. Thirty percent of couples in San Francisco, and 56 percent of couples in Massachusetts reported changes after their marriage that they characterized as intimate, personal, or relationship-focused. While the particular changes ran the gamut from greater self-esteem to less fighting, the biggest internal shifts noted were an increased sense of permanence and stability in the relationship, along with a greater feeling of commitment and security.

These shifts were sometimes difficult to verbalize. Jeffrey, who had married his partner, Art, primarily because the sense of government validation appealed to them, tried to articulate this: "And what I was trying to convey that I can't really put into words was that, in terms of how we live our lives, absolutely nothing changed from February 27 to February 28, I mean absolutely nothing changed. But *everything* changed. Nothing changed and everything changed internally for me somehow." When pressed to explain further, Art offered, "There's a sense of—for me, there's a sense of contentment. I know I'm married, and . . . I'm very complete with that process. I think of my relationship with Jeffrey is very solidified." He added, and Jeffrey agreed, that this sense of contentment and stability survived the invalidation of their license: "I think what it did was, that peace that I thought I would never have available to me to say that I am married is there. I've done my part. That's how I see it. We've done our part to be married. And so I'm content with that. Everything else just has to kind of work itself out now." But even while admitting the difficulty in articulating what had changed, Art and Jeffrey tapped into what turned out to be a common theme: a greater sense of commitment, even when they had already considered themselves thus. Sherri, who like Jeffrey and Art spoke of the meaningful civic validation getting married had given her—and how devastated she was when the courts annulled her marriage—commented on the multilayered effects of the experience: "The ceremony in City Hall led not only to this kind of outward feeling more a part of society, but also this inward sense of committing and being an outspoken and articulate partner in a lifetime relationship, and that felt different." Her spouse, Dawn, agreed and admitted that this was surprising given how committed they already felt in the eighteen-year relationship.

Jim and Andrew, whose emotional reaction to what was initially meant to be an exercise in activism was noted, were also surprised to find how much difference it made to them to be married (chapter 4). Jim described the shock of feeling so sentimental as he said his vows: "I was choked up and it felt like 'Wow, I'm really committing myself in front of the whole world to Andrew and I'm happy to have that opportunity finally.' I was really happy to be able to do it. I did feel like it provided an extra glue to our relationship that wasn't there. It was a very profound experience." The implications of what they were saying did not go unnoticed by either one: by that point they had already been together for fourteen years and felt they had committed in every way possible. Why would they need any more "glue"? Andrew tried to describe where this sense of change came from even though they had never felt any change was needed. He reflected, "It seemed like suddenly we were, in a sense, thrust in to the position of . . . being a role model in a way, or just in the position where now we're actually married and we really need to take this relationship seriously." Jim added, "Not that we didn't before, but in the eyes of the world our relationship is sealed. It felt like we had an extra sense of responsibility to the world."

The weightiness of this newfound responsibility was a sharp contrast to its genesis: Jim and Andrew had shown up at City Hall to protest and did not know they would actually be getting married that day until minutes before filling out their marriage license application. As Jim summed up, "I didn't have much time to think about it but that's kind of how profound the experience was."

The increased sense of responsibility and commitment was frequently experienced by couples as a feeling of permanence that they didn't even realize wasn't there before they married. Mark and Neil, who described the sense of validation they got from marrying—complete with official paperwork, in a government building—admitted that most of what they felt during and after the ceremony came as a surprise (chapter 5). Even filling out the paperwork was an emotional experience, which they contrasted to the rather dry and emotionless experience of filing their domestic partnership. Both men reported that they felt significantly closer, more bonded, after their civil marriage. They reasoned that at least part of it was explained by the fact that they had never had a prior commitment ceremony or other occasion to publicly state their commitment. Mark explained, "All the promises that we've made, we've never had to voice out in the open in front of people and then so having that happen I think it hit me unexpectedly." It also helped, he said, that their families were finally witnessing their bond:

> Our families realized that this just wasn't a relationship that either one of us was just going to walk away from eventually . . . it made us feel closer knowing that our families kind of realized that we didn't consider each other boyfriends, we really were partners and so I think just having that happen, in the eyes of our family I think it just—we did feel really close.

Notably, it wasn't just a change in the perception of their family members—Mark and Neil *themselves* felt a greater sense of permanence in their relationship. Neil reported a lasting "absence of the sense of one of us can bail out." They had already mingled their finances as would a married couple and were registered as domestic partners, so it wasn't the practical implications of separation that led them to feel more inextricably linked. Neil explained how this newfound sense of permanence had played out in their lives. When it came to changes in career, applying to graduate school, and contemplating moves, rather than consulting with one another *after* the fact and hoping it would work out, they now approached these decisions as a team from the start. When identifying the source of this change, he pointed to the day they got their marriage license: "I think that cemented it. I think it was there before, but I think for me, it cemented it. That, okay well this is it; this is life. You know, this is for life."

Nicola and Renee from Sacramento were initially driven by a concern for legal and financial protections as well as political advocacy, but they were taken off guard by the depth of romance they felt at their wedding (chapter 4). When describing their relationship after that day, Nicola commented, "The relationship went to a different level; it was deeper and more serious." She discussed the fact that their relationship was in fact still quite young at the time when they got married. Although they had known each other and been friends since 1992, they had only begun dating the previous May—nine months before they married. This was atypical of the couples who married at City Hall (and in Massachusetts), many of whom had been together for decades, the average length of relationship being eleven years. Nicola explained:

> To . . . have a piece of paper and to be legitimized by San Francisco just gave it so much that I never felt in ten years with the other woman. . . . So after only months of being together really, nine months, I felt a depth that I'd never felt with anybody else before and I think the ceremony really, really helped that.

Renee agreed and highlighted the crucial difference their legal status made: "You can state all those things and you mean that of course, but it's different when you actually are legally bound to someone. Just like if you make a promise, but you don't sign a contract."

Don and Mark reported one of the more dramatic changes in their relationship after they wed. It was surprise enough, to Mark, that he was as romantically captivated by the act of marrying as he turned out to be—he thought he'd been doing it primarily to solve their legal problems and make Don happy. Beyond fulfilling a need to his longtime partner, though, he felt that getting married had reignited his romantic feelings, and Don reported the same. Beyond this, however, it caused them to make a rather dramatic change in their romantic life. Up to that point, Mark explained, they had had a tacitly open relationship; they had discussed monogamy but had not actually put it into practice. When they got married at City Hall and even after the license was invalidated they made a mutual decision that they would be monogamous; Mark described it as a "huge shift." This decision, while in a way surprising to both men, was indicative of a "change of heart by making this public statement that we were committed to each other, [it] really did change my feelings," as Don reported. He admitted that he had before had lingering doubts about the relationship that he allowed were not entirely logical; but "when we finally had that piece of paper and made that commitment, the doubt seemed to fall away. I just had this experience of . . . wonderful joy at the fact that I had been able to make this commitment to Mark. . . . [The] relationship to me meant so much that I was willing to sign my name to it." He summed up, "there is an emotional investment in marrying in San Francisco, and even though it's been annulled by the state, it still feels very real."

Aleda and Anne Marie, also originally motivated by both practical concerns and political commitments, reported far-ranging effects on both their relationship and themselves as individuals. Aleda commented, "I think there was a definite, kind of a stronger bond, more closeness there. You know, I mean kind of physically, emotionally, everything." Anne Marie agreed, "it gave us . . . so much more than we expected. I had no idea kind of how much fun it is to be married and it was just a wonderful sense of closeness and stability and safe[ty]." Aleda predicted that this would not have been the case had they gone through with a commitment ceremony, something that hadn't appealed to them in any case: "If we had just had a commitment ceremony . . . and there was no legal documentation behind it, I don't think it would have been as meaningful. You know, I mean it would have been like . . . kind of cool but you move on two seconds later." Anne Marie drew thought-provoking connections between the varied consequences of legalized access to same-sex marriage—micro and macro, personal and practical. She certainly cared about the legal benefits it gave her in terms of her shared property with Aleda and the end-of-life decision making along with the social approval and legitimation, but Anne Marie also recognized that these broader signals of acceptance and inclusion also impacted both her relationship and her own psyche. She commented, "I'm glad I have the legal benefits and the social benefits but it impacted me as well, not just on the outside world but . . . inside and it certainly drew us closer if that was even possible at the point." She and Aleda, like several other couples, were surprised that the experience of being legally wed could make them feel closer or more committed because they thought they were already as committed and as close as they could get. Anne Marie offered an explanation for how and why the ceiling lifted, so to speak: "I didn't realize I actually had some extra love. But I think it was love that . . . came out by sharing it [with] Aleda because, I didn't realize how it felt to be accepted. These are all just parts of the whole big picture." Her increased capacity for love and connection to Aleda was inextricably linked to the validation, both societal and personal, that the experience allowed her to access. She described her personal transformation—aside from the added depth of her relationship—as essentially an improvement in her self-esteem. She explained, "Because it was legitimized, [you] sort of feel better about yourself . . . we kind of liked ourselves a little bit more, not each other but ourselves; we were more accepted and there was at least a little bit more love that wasn't being held back, it just wasn't recognized."

Although participants did not always make the connection between their personal change and broader societal or relationship changes as explicitly as did Anne Marie, improved self-esteem was in fact a common theme, at least for those who felt that their marriage had led to any form of personal or emotional change. One couple who did make the connection between the broader sense of validation and the more personal transformation they underwent both as individuals and as a couple—and a family—were Ed and Michael of San Francisco. The pair had met in 1993 at the gym, bought a home, and moved in together two years later. In 2001 they adopted two children who were school age by the time of the marriage and interview. Neither domestic partnership nor a commitment ceremony had ever appealed to Ed and Michael in the past because it felt "less than"—it was not legal marriage. Although the proposal itself was spontaneous and somewhat flip—"do you want to go get married today?" over breakfast, with kids underfoot—it was actually an opportunity to fulfill a long-held desire. They felt that the other statuses available to them before did not confer the legitimacy of marriage—a position they held in common with many other couples. What they did not predict, however, was the degree to which they would be emotionally moved as a result, although they recognized that in their case marriage was both a "personal act of devotion and love" and a community action. Still visibly moved by the experience when talking about it two years later, Michael discussed the additional weight of responsibility he felt as a model of marriage and equal rights for his children. Although they stated early on that nothing changed after they got married—they had already functioned as a family unit before—they both backtracked on that statement later in the interview. They had difficulty articulating what exactly the change was, though Ed commented, "It did create a new light on it in the sense that I consider myself married and wear a ring. And, so, and I'm proud of that day and it changed my view at that point." This changed point of view had much to do with the fact that they had felt such widespread support from the community, and that provided "complete and absolute positive reinforcement" for their relationship, and in turn, themselves.

As distinctly as the themes of personal and relationship change emerged in San Francisco, the trend was even more common in Massachusetts. More than half of the interviewees reported personal or emotional changes to themselves or their relationships. This can usefully be compared to the 24 percent of couples in San Francisco and 6 percent of those in Massachusetts who reported no changes at all. Because the changes being reported were explicitly not legal or material, it is diffi-cult to say whether or to what degree this is an artifact of the legal valid-ity of the Massachusetts licenses as compared to those in San Francisco (only 8 percent in Massachusetts and 9 percent in California reported any tangible or material changes). Some of the same themes emerged, though: a greater feeling of responsibility and commitment, more close-ness, and more stability.

One of the individual effects that some couples in Massachu-setts reported in common with their San Francisco counterparts was improved self-esteem. Carey, who had married Cathleen purely as a statement of her love and because she finally could, found an unex-pected result: "I think it's increased my self-esteem too." She identified this as a consequence of the internalized homophobia she had always felt. This lowered self-image, which had been more or less a constant, appreciably diminished after she got married; as she described it, "That [internal homophobia] kind of keeps going through you and it's like, 'I'm married now and I'm not any less.'" Scott, after marrying his spouse, Mike, in May 2004, reported a similar transformation. He explained:

> I went through the whole, "Am I sick?" And "What's wrong with me?" So it was really, the validation from friends and family was really emotional for me. Then standing there and looking in to his eyes and everything was like "Wow." I was crying. It became very emotional for me . . . that we were accepted, and that's why I think it ties in to so many issues. It's important for your self-esteem.

The personal emotional effects of marrying were significantly inter-twined with the more social and structural issues raised by the real-ization of this newfound right alongside the history of marginalized existence for LGBT couples and individuals. Scott explicitly recognized this intersection: "The whole experience has changed me dramatically, politically, emotionally and self-esteem-wise."

Aside from gains in self-esteem and their sense of belonging and deserving, there were also several individuals who felt a palpable deepening of their commitment to one another, and a sense of relief and security at this dramatic demonstration of commitment. This was voiced sometimes in individual terms and other times as a mutual sense on the part of the couple. In the case of Jesse and David, who discussed the distinct effect that getting married had on their respective families and co-workers, it was Jesse who reported a profound shift in his internal sense of well-being in the relationship as well. As he put it, "It was a pretty significant change in my sense of relationship . . . with that ceremony, I experienced a real change in our relationship, that I did not continue to have the fear that David would just up and leave one day." Jesse professed to having a fear of abandonment, based on past life experience and observations, and that sense of disquiet stayed with him despite their decade-long relationship:

> I still had a panic that David would just look at me one day and say "I don't need this." Or something, and leave. And to think that David's commitment to me wasn't really ever in question, but by going through the process of planning a wedding and then actually going through with it . . . I thought "Alright, he really means it." It very much calmed an emotional storm in me.

The marriage proposal and ring that David had given him in 1999 had not accomplished this, at least in part because, as David confessed, he doubted he would ever be given the legal opportunity to follow through. The fact that he was willing to go through the relatively onerous process of planning a wedding—and legally committing—was what quelled Jesse's anxieties.

In a similar way, Eric and Michael didn't realize the effect getting married would have on their sense of commitment to one another until they experienced it. Eric reflected, "It really did alter our relationship. Although we always did have a really strong relationship, there was this omnipresent tension, different levels at different times, but it was omnipresent. Just, there was doubt of commitment." Although this was not entirely one-sided, they both freely admitted that Eric was the driving force behind getting married, and that Michael had more of a tendency to be commitment-phobic. Despite the differences in motivation or, more accurately, level of motivation going into the wedding, the effects were similar for both of them: not only the sense of validation and inclusion that they both distinctly felt from family and others but also a greater commitment to a shared sense of their future (chapter 5). When the couple faced the possibility of a job transition for one that would require a move out of state—as was the case at the time of the interview—their reaction to it was markedly different than it had been before they married. Rather than assuming a move out of state would end the relationship, they now treated it as a mutual decision. As Eric explained:

> It was much easier to say, of course, "this affects us. This is a family decision and we will figure it out as a family no matter what that means." So, everything that has transpired since has built upon that recognition. I think it was an important moment for us because it was very clearly stated even that day, "we are married and we are in this together!" Whatever that means, we are going to figure it out together. And I don't know how easily we would have arrived at that end result were we not married.

Thus, although it quieted Eric's fears in the same way it did Jesse's, it also transformed the character of the relationship as a whole in very personal and in a very real way. The same had been true of Kate and Theresa, who married in 2005, and like Eric and Michael faced a job relocation shortly after marrying. Kate, like Michael, was a professor and subject to the vagaries of the academic job market. Though neither Kate nor Theresa was initially enamored with the idea of marriage as an institution, their decision came down to romance and personal commitment. Like those before them, it ended up being a far more meaningful event than they had anticipated, particularly when it came to entering the job market as recent doctoral graduates. Kate remarked,

"It really is a difficult process and I think there would have been a lot of fear about how to navigate that if we had not been married . . . and I think in that sense we felt much more solid about our relationship because we had gotten married."

Some couples experienced quite tangible and noticeable differences in the dynamics of their relationships, likely as a direct result of their greater sense of permanence and commitment after marrying. Most commonly, this took the form of fewer and more quickly resolved arguments.

Jason and Richard had an somewhat comical exchange during the interview about how being legally married solidified their relationship. Their relationship had been on again/off again in the past and was generally characterized by frequent arguments. When they got married, however, this changed. By Jason's account, things got calmer; the reason had as much to do with the historic nature of their marriage as it did their internal sense of increased commitment:

RICHARD: There was a sense of, "Oh I'm really committed now." I do
   remember right afterwards—
JASON: It's the sound of the door closing behind you.
RICHARD: Thinking, "we can't be the first divorce." We have to make
   this last . . . and resolving arguments [became] so much quicker. I
   remember thinking after I was married, like, it's not going to be the
   end of a relationship. . . . And initially that really shortened the time
   for discussion.

Both Jason and Richard were surprised that "a piece of paper from the city" could make such a difference; Richard admitted that he doesn't think much about the law or their legal status. But as Jason put it, "we don't need that to have a commitment. And I don't need it, but it certainly made something feel more solid to me."

Two other male couples married in Massachusetts, Ron and Dan (who also married in San Francisco) and Troy and Chuck, reported similar experiences. Just like Jason and Richard, Chuck explained,

"You can't just say fuck you, I'm leaving, and then two days later come with a truck and disappear. You can't do that [*Laughter*]. There are consequences." Troy agreed, noting that when one is married, "you have to look for ways to make compromises and work things out." They cited the example of having been in marriage counseling to work through some difficulties they were having—both agreed this was not a step they would have taken had they not been married. Ron and Dan, both computer scientists, had begun their relationship via email in 1987 while living on opposite coasts. Education and professional obligations consigned them to different states until finally they both landed jobs at the same company in San Francisco in 1990; three years later, Ron proposed to Dan, and they vowed to marry when it became legal. Unlike Chuck and Troy, Ron and Dan had not been in therapy but did describe a similar transformation. While Dan was quite clear from the outset that his primary motivation for marrying was legal—he felt they needed the financial protections—Ron's had been romantic from the start. He drew a distinction between marriage and domestic partnership—which they also had—in this regard: "A domestic partnership is like the state granting you some legal rights but marriage to me was a spiritual experience." The emotional component, by his own admission, didn't dawn on Dan, however, until the day of the wedding. However, he was also the first to point out the personal changes in their relationship since their wedding. Like Jason and Richard, he admitted that he and Ron used to fight quite a bit, and Ron would often threaten to break up. This ended when they married. He also felt some of this had to do with the sense that they felt they could count on one another now that they were married; he commented, half to the interviewer and half to Ron, "It's gradually getting much better and it's much better because—I think it is partly the marriage because it is just knowing you'll be there."

Michael and Moe experienced a panoply of changes in their relationship, which were rather unexpected (chapter 5). As Moe recalled, "I thought it was gonna be more of a formality—but [once] I got [it]—it was very different. It was much more of a, 'oh, my gosh.'" The changes

Moe perceived were not only the sense of paradigm-shifting social and political validation they felt but also those of a more personal, romantic nature. Unlike Eric and Michael, or Kate and Theresa, Mike and Moe did not face a transition as dramatic as a coast-to-coast move or job change. But both men sensed a dramatic change nonetheless. At first the exact content of the change was difficult for Mike to put his finger on: "It's really interesting because I feel married. I mean, and I didn't know that there was a feeling that went with being married, but there's something about the commitment, both interpersonal commitment and then the publicness and the legality of that commitment that makes a difference to my felt experience of being in the world." Pressed to further describe the shift, he continued:

The most significant shift has been emotional for me in terms of deepening and deepening and deepening and deepening and that I didn't know—I mean, I would have said I loved him, I was committed to him, I wanted to spend the rest of my life with him and those would have all be true, but the felt experience of it is so much richer and deeper and that I think it's the kind of thing where I'm not sure how someone would know that without having the experience, you know . . . the felt experience of it is really different.

Moe agreed:

It was much more of an emotional deepening on many different levels where it really felt . . . the relationship just deepened in ways that weren't even tangible, but I think we became more honest with each other, we became much more available to each other, and it really cemented our relationship that I thought was pretty solid already.

Despite their far more traditional ceremony four years earlier and nearly two decades of commitment, Mike and Moe experienced as a result of their legal marriage something that they did not realize, except in retrospect, was necessary or even possible: more depth of connection.

Although prior research by Hull[11] has shown that couples who wed in (non-legal) commitment ceremonies reported similar feelings of increased commitment, greater accountability, and less relationship-related stress, couples in this study definitely felt distinctly bound by the legal aspect of their marriage and the historic nature of their marriages. Robyn and Peg, living in the greater Boston area, were keenly aware that their marriage placed them at the intersection of political history and personal milestone. As Robyn commented:

> I think the change has been so much bigger than any one relation-ship . . . in Massachusetts, the whole earth moved. . . . And the shift—when you look at the shift at the microlevel, at the one-on-one level, it doesn't seem that dramatic. But the entire world has changed here in Massachusetts. . . . It's hard to talk about on a daily basis because it's so fundamental and it's so huge. It's like the whole earth changed shape for us and we're just these little people. . . . So when I say how is my life different, it's not that different, but it's completely different. The world is different, here.

Love and Marriage

Amid these seismic shifts in the broader constitution of marriage, and by some accounts gay and lesbian identity as well, it might be easy to forget about the essential intimacy at its core. Although not all couples who love get married, most couples who eventually marry start from love. It is this indispensable fact that underscores their commonality with heterosexual couples who marry. Several couples commented that marriage, for them, was simply the next logical step in the progression of their relationship, or even an indispensable rite of passage that they had anticipated from an early age. Thus, the incredulous tone of some who answered the question of why they married—"Because we love each other!" For these individuals the tried-and-true aphorism of love, romance, and spiritual fulfillment was truly that simple. Yet by serendipity and sometimes by design, their nuptials—their deeply romantic moments—were also a moment in history, a social statement, a civil rights achievement, a validation, and yes, in some cases, a protest. That these weddings—many among the first to ever occur legally between same-sex couples in the United States—could provide an essential emotional milestone to these couples belies the extraordinary complexity of their place in the sociocultural and legal landscape. It also strikes an ironic chord in an era when there is increasingly skepticism and disinvestment in legal marriage not only among those adhering to the queer and feminist critiques of marriage, but among heterosexual couples in general—both in the United States and abroad.

For those who went into marriage drawn to and fully anticipating its emotional import, it became a tangible and culturally recognizable expression of commitment. Several couples experienced their once-in-a-lifetime San Francisco City Hall marriage, despite its short-lived existence, as a demonstrable way to communicate their depth of commitment to others or to their partner and even to themselves. Leslie and Ari, for example, were comforted to find that, when given the opportunity, they were both ready and pleased to make what they felt was the ultimate commitment to one another. The same was true in Massachusetts: couples like Bob and Jerry, or Dawn and Donna, were only too pleased by the opportunity to express their commitment in a legally binding and universally recognized way. And for those who felt unsure about their partner's level of commitment previously, such as Jesse or Eric of Massachusetts, the wedding was essential to assuaging these lingering fears and doubts.

In the end, the couples who married for romantic and personal reasons did so regardless of the ability to also seal their commitment via domestic partnership (in California) or commitment ceremony—or their having already done so. Some, such as Mindy and Julie or Michael and Ed, had explicitly avoided other forms of union that they felt would not hold the same emotional resonance as marriage. Others, such as Ari and Leslie or Mark and Neil, could say from experience that there was something distinct about legal marriage—its appeal transcended the instrumentality of law and was deeply meaningful on a personal level. Although couples in Massachusetts did not have the option of securing a comprehensive domestic partnership through the state, longtime couples such as Mike and Moe had nonetheless taken every step available to secure their lives together—including a formal wedding ceremony a few years prior—but still felt uniquely emotionally affected by their legal marriage.

At the same time, particularly in reference to couples like Nicola and Renee, it is important to recognize the distinction between one's initial *motivation* for marrying, and their later *experience* of marriage and its aftereffects. Indeed, some of the couples with the most profound emotional reaction to their nuptials were, by their own admission, not initially motivated by romance; in some cases, they were not motivated to marry at all and had to be convinced either by their partner or other friends or family. To be sure, there were those couples who were insistent that their reasons for marrying could only be for love; they distinguished quite sharply between instrumental or political goals and their own more personal motives. Mindy and Julie from San Francisco, for example, along with Neri and her spouse, or Jason and Richard in Massachusetts, were in fact quite adamant on this point: they did not want their marriages to be understood as anything other than an expression of love and commitment, and they remained unwavering in this conviction from the start.

More common were those couples whose motivations and interests in marriage evolved over time to the more personal and who were surprised to find themselves so emotionally invested. This meant that for several couples, such as Nan and Marie, Betsy and Barbara, or Andrew and Jim, the political had truly become personal. For others, such as Gilbert and Alex, the practical became more deeply personal, as Gilbert had initially been interested in marrying Alex primarily for financial reasons. Surprisingly consistent from coast to coast, across demographics and motivations, was that no matter how much or how little planning went into the marriage the couples were, as Mark put it, blindsided by the emotional poignancy of getting legally married. This surprise element might help explain why these couples did not tend toward the more jaded (and increasingly common in some sectors) view of marriage as an institution on the decline, both normatively and numerically—they simply didn't see the emotional resonance coming and therefore did not think it through rationally in relation to divorce rates and broader critiques of marriage. Whether this revelation is unique to same-sex couples is unknown; undoubtedly there are heterosexual couples who are emotionally taken off guard on their wedding day as well. Two important points of departure are worth noting, however: (1) the option to marry was so new to these same-sex couples that they had far less time to contemplate what marriage might mean to them, and (2) the degree to which, as a historically excluded minority, the ability to now marry tapped into other deep-seated feelings of the sort noted in the prior two chapters—a possibility suggested by Linton in California as well as Robyn in Massachusetts, among others.

The types of transformations suggested by these evolving reasons for marrying, and the unanticipated emotional reactions they evoked, implicate one of the more important questions to be answered by these couples: what are the effects of marriage? Some of these effects have already been addressed in prior chapters. A sense of legal security and a feeling of legitimation are perhaps more intuitively connected to the newfound ability to enter a legally regulated institution. Less obvious is the link between access to a legal institution and romance, relational harmony, or even self-esteem—all arguably things that can and have been achieved successfully outside of state-sanctioned marriage. How is it, then, that a couple like Jerry and Bob could be together for more than twenty years and find themselves so deeply transformed by, as Jason put it, "a piece of paper"? The answer lies, in part, in the rather bizarre fact of having made an intimate relationship the locus of so many rights and such revered civic status. The connection between their individual experiences and the structural realities of LGBT existence and marginalization was very apparent to some couples, such as Jake and Chico of Massachusetts, or Sherri and Dawn of California.

Scott, Anne Marie, and Carey all noted that getting married—or perhaps more aptly, the ability to get married—had boosted their self-esteem, helping to reverse the damage of years of internalized homophobia.

The more typically relationship-focused change also reported by couples after marriage was a greater sense of commitment and responsibility to the relationship. While straight couples might experience the same, in the case of same-sex couples, legal realities pre-2004 dictated that their pre-marriage life together was far longer than the average heterosexual couple's. This no doubt means, then, that by necessity, same-sex couples might have devised other ways of demonstrating their devotion to the relationship or of establishing a sense of permanence. Often, however, it simply left an unspoken, unrealized absence of a recognizable guarantee of commitment. Even when couples such as Aleda and Anne Marie or Mike and Moe thought they had achieved the height of commitment and devotion to one another —whether by ceremony or simply by words and deeds—they sometimes found themselves in the unexpected position of feeling more committed and, in the words of more than one couple, more "solid" because of the legal marriage. The sense of calm that emerge from this heightened emotional security was articulated in plain terms by Jesse and Eric, and is also evident in the comparatively less acrimonious marital relationships of Jason and Richard, or Ron and Dan.

These couples would not be the first nor the last to find themselves surprised by the emotional implications of a legal document or decision. Traditional assumptions of legal orthodoxy aside, the imprint of emotion is unmistakable in criminal law, family law, and other arenas. Thus, although I have previously designated emotional motivations for pursuing marriage as "outside the law," such rationales are hardly so, because, as Abrams and others aptly point out, disentangling the emotions from the law is not only unnecessary but perhaps futile as well. The surprisingly poignant emotional response of those accessing legal marriage for the first time, as well as the deeply felt sense of loss accompanying the removal of this right, suggests as much. The conclusion that law not only expresses emotions and can be driven by them, but also simultaneously channels and cultivates them, might well represent a new take on the old law and society axiom that "the law is all over"[12]— or, more colloquially, in a loose translation of the French balladeer Francis Cabrel, "No matter what you do, love is everywhere you look."

7

Conclusion

The Multiple Meanings of Marriage

In a real sense, there are three partners to every civil marriage: two willing spouses and an approving State.
   Civil marriage is at once a deeply personal commitment
to another human being and a highly public celebration of
the ideals of mutuality, companionship, intimacy, fidelity,
and family.
–*Goodridge v. Massachusetts* (2003)

When Phyllis Lyon and Del Martin donned their brightly colored wedding
pantsuits and stated the vows that would mark a milestone in American
history, few would have predicted that they would ever see that moment,
not least the two women themselves. As LGBT rights pioneers they had
already made history by defying convention and living outside of the
mainstream as feminist lesbian activists. Who would have thought that
one of their most well-remembered and documented moments, cement-
ing their status as icons for a younger generation, would be one in which
they entered what has long been thought of as the most conventional,
heteronormative, and anti-feminist institutions America has to offer?
Their reasons for doing so no doubt differ from those of the Goodridges
in Massachusetts, or Wes and Craig in San Diego, Dean and Garrett in
Cambridge, or even their one-time neighbors Pat and Terry in San Francisco. That different people marry for different reasons, whether gay or
straight, is beyond dispute, but it is still a fact that often remains glossed
over or ignored in legal doctrine, public discourse, and scholarly analyses.

Moreover, the fluidity of these motivations—the degree to which they overlap, intersect, and evolve—and what it reveals about these actors' relationship to new legal rights, is something that has rarely been explored.

Many now-classic texts in law and society have concluded that legality in its many forms permeates social institutions and everyday life in ways that are too varied and, in some instances, too subtle to fully enumerate. That this process is mutual, ongoing, and diversely experienced is also commonly taken for granted. Often there has been an emphasis on the "everyday," which could be as diffuse and undefined a subject as asking people about their "troubles." Few have been as episodically focused as to study a newly won right and its impact on the lives of the first to experience it, along with the unique experience to have gained this right in a game-changing historical moment, only to have it overturned by the state's highest court. Admittedly, this is a rare experience with the legal institution of marriage. The same-sex couples in this book and their varied experiences, emotions, and motivations give us valuable insight into the singularly powerful constitutive potential of new rights and one of the western world's most common and enduring, if evolving, legal institutions. Few legal events qualify as both a typical life-course milestone and also front-page news. That many of these weddings were both of these things allows a unique insight into how something as mainstream and taken for granted as legal marriage can profoundly affect one's relationship to legality, the state, and those in their life, showing us how law is constitutive of emotion in often unexpected ways. It also provides an uncommon perspective on rights consciousness and a natural experiment in the giving and taking of rights.

Likewise, scholars of legal consciousness have pointed out that it can take multiple—sometimes even contradictory—forms, and these forms of consciousness can overlap, even within one individual. For example, a person's reason for marrying may be entirely political to begin with, but the political action becomes so saturated with personal meaning in the process of getting married that it is difficult to separate the two. Likewise, a fundamentally private act can be imbued with such public significance that it becomes a civic moment as much as a personal one.

All of these motives—emotion, validation, activism, pragmatism— appear in the narratives of the couples in this book in ways that demonstrate this variability, fluidity, and often unexpectedness. As we have read, were it not for the need to navigate litigation and legislative processes to gain access to marriage, there would not be the expectation that *anyone* would frame their desire to marry as only a function of material and legal benefits. It was rarely the case, however, that such a pragmatic orientation dominated the conversation, or remained untethered to other motivations and orientations to legal marriage.

The same shifting of consciousness was observable in politically driven motives and narratives. Contrary to other studies of socially situated legal consciousness, there were no differences across demographic categories; those prioritizing resistant or political motivations came equally from across the social spectrum. They were not significantly more common in San Francisco than in Massachusetts, despite the differences in legal process and outcome. Some were committed to enacting civil disobedience, or making a gay rights statement, and that remained a driving force for them; others were admittedly entering the institution in order to radically transform it. However, by the time the actual wedding took place, very few remained driven solely by defiance. The stakes of same-sex marriage for the couples who seek it are deeply embedded in both the emotional and the symbolic: marriage became a source of validation, inclusion, and public affirmation for what is essentially a private act. Again, orientation to law as a source of validation was remarkably consistent across social strata—its importance as a motivation did not differ across gender, socioeconomic status, or domestic partner status. Only youth seemed to predict, at least initially, greater interest in the validating function of legal marriage. The symbolic resonance and sense of inclusivity that legal marriage engendered surprised the license applicants themselves—a remarkably consistent theme. Thus marriage became, akin to the right to vote, a marker of full citizenship and humanity.

Finally, couples expounded on what was at once the most obvious, and the most counterintuitive, of motivations to legally marry: that of love and romance, which had everything to do with marriage but

nothing to do with law. Here too, there was little variation across gender, class, or age. The persistence of this distinctly extralegal motivation
for marriage, even when other means were available to publicly mark
and celebrate the relationship, demonstrate the uniquely potent ability of law to express emotions, as well as channel and cultivate them.
Indeed, the evidence was extensive that suggested that even when
couples had chosen (or had been forced) to accomplish the emotional
facets of marriage—defining their relationship to one another, cement-
ing their commitment, expressing romance—in other ways, the difference was palpable, if again often unexpected. Taken together, though
they represent an eclectic range of orientations to marriage and legality, the themes of instrumentality, resistance, validation and emotional
fulfillment are intertwined and cross cutting. As with law and society
more generally, here the public and the personal mutually constitute
one another in sometimes unexpected ways: a relationship is solidified,
made more binding, while its members at the same feel, for the first
time, like fully realized civic persons. They are a tightly bound intimate
unit but also part of the integrated whole of citizenry. That legal marriage can satisfy all of these distinct yet integrated motivations speaks
to not only the diversity and fluidity of legal consciousness but also the
ubiquity and even hegemony of law itself.

Implications of Inclusion and Exclusion

In 2013 President Barack Obama's history-making public affirmation of
the right to same-sex marriage marked the long-awaited end to what the
president called an "evolution" in his thought process that had defined
his stance on the topic. Obama never denied his support for some form
of relationship recognition but felt that it should be called something
other than "marriage," a not uncommon stance in the early years of
marriage equality. This view seemed to at once discount and deify the
named status of marriage: it was not important enough for same-sex
couples to need it in order to be truly equal, but it was *so* important that
it must be preserved for "traditional" different-sex couples.

This "nominal separation," as law professor Courtney Megan Cahill points out, is neither new nor accidental but rather part of a long tradition of enforced silence and exclusion, or as she puts it, "the gay *linguistic* closet."[1] It harkens back to a time when homosexuality was simply, and nearly ubiquitously, referred to as "the crime unfit to be named." Purported supporters and opponents of gay rights who are willing to extend this silencing by calling same-sex unions something else—a version of "separate but equal," exclusion of same-sex couples from marriage—extend a sociolinguistic history unique to gays and lesbians as those "unnamed."

The harms and effects that flow from this exclusion are far from solely linguistic and epistemological, though. An overriding commonality can be found in the various chapters of this book and the experiences the interviewees retell: it is that marriage—*legal* marriage, with the name "marriage"—does make a difference in many ways and along a variety of dimensions. Sometimes the differences are quite subtle, and are themselves not even nameable or fully identifiable until after the fact. Common were the refrains that "it's just *different*," or "nothing changed, but *everything* changed." When surveyed after the annulment of their 2004 marriages in San Francisco, nearly one-quarter of those couples stated that nothing had in fact changed after they wed. But the fact that three-quarters of the recipients of these *annulled* licenses still felt changed by having received them is in itself telling. When looking at the experience in Massachusetts, the numbers are staggering: only 6 percent (three couples) felt unchanged by the experience of marrying, and those that did perceive a change spanned all lengths of relationship and demographic categories.

Aftereffects

When it is apparent to couples that something has changed, those effects vary widely, although they generally fall into one of four broad categories: (1) *personal* emotional changes in oneself or the relationship itself; (2) *social* changes in how others treat or orient to the couple; (3) *material* changes in the ability to access newly acquired financial or legal rights; and (4) *political* changes dealing with broader societal shifts they perceived, differing conceptions of justice, or perceptions of government. Deciphering the cause-effect relationship is also complicated because couples' reasons for marrying shifted over time. Some of the unanticipated effects of marriage might not be unique to same-sex couples; the unexpected difference a "piece of paper" makes to one's relationship might be nearly as common among heterosexual couples who cohabited prior to marriage. At the same time, some of these shifts might also be a function of the *newness* of this right. The couples in this book were, after all, among the first same-sex couples in the United States to receive marriage licenses.

The unique experience of those in San Francisco also gives us a rare opportunity to view the effects of having been *un*-married by the state. Invariably, these too were keenly and often unexpectedly felt on both a political and an emotional level. A large number of those surveyed claimed to have expected this result and were therefore inured to a certain degree against the upheaval they might have otherwise felt. The majority, however, still expressed disappointment and hurt, even when they understood the rationale. While the most common effects of getting married were personal and social in nature, the most common effects of getting one's marriage *overturned* largely resided at the intersection of the personal and the political. Couples expressed a profound sense of disenfranchisement, of civil *devaluation* and, eventually for some, a greater distrust in their government and the courts.

An interesting, if relatively unexplored digression from the experience of those who married in 2004 in San Francisco is to look at the number of couples who, after having their licenses revoked, did or did not marry again when given the opportunity in 2008, and what their reasons were. We have limited data with which to answer that question, as only half of the fifty couples interviewed in San Francisco responded to attempts at follow up in 2008. The pull of legal marriage was strong enough that two-thirds of these couples were willing to undergo the process again for a variety of reasons, from the instrumental concerns to being politicized by the experience of having their marriage annulled.

However, those that chose *not* to marry in 2008—as well as several who had hesitated but ultimately decided to do so—were nearly unanimous in their reason: they had lost their trust in the system. They did not want to risk another disappointment, and preferred to wait until the issue was further resolved, either by a hopeful defeat of Prop 8 or by federal recognition. Little can be generalized reliably from a total of five couples who responded that they had declined to marry in 2008. But adding this observation to the more widespread voices of disappointment and disenfranchisement in the interviews and surveys tells us something compelling about the power of recognition and the pitfalls of exclusion.

What does this portend for the future of same-sex marriage in America? Most likely very little in the short term, since the mechanism by which it has been banned in most states relies not on social scientific evidence and research, but rather on public sentiment. Although more successful as a strategy for gaining marriage rights, litigation often reduces the stakes of the debate to the utilitarian terms that are not necessarily at the heart of the issue for couples seeking marriage themselves. The most far-reaching decisions, such as *In re Marriage Cases* and *U.S. v. Windsor,* are those that have recognized and embraced the notion that the stakes of marriage go far beyond the particular rights associated with it financially and legally. But even they suffer from a limited account of *how* marriage matters for a wide swath of same-sex couples, who seek marriage for different reasons, and who may or may not have much in common with the named litigants in each of the landmark cases.

Increasingly, however, there are calls to broaden the discussion, to understand marriage not just as a package of rights and benefits, and not just as a romantic (or religious) bond, but as a civil status and marker of state sanction. The evidence in this book certainly suggests that this recognition is not only overdue but in need of further elaboration. Marriage can in fact be *all* of these things, and more—or it may, in some cases, be none of these but nevertheless carry unique meaning and have significant effects. Any attempt to reduce or essentialize the meaning of marriage and its consequences belies its complexity as a status and institution that bridges the emotional, the legal, the symbolic, and the political. Moreover, the stakes of legal marriage are not static; rather, they vary both across and within couples, and evolve over the course of time and experience—even within the short duration of the wedding itself. No less importantly, this also means that marriage must be a *choice* and not a mandate, since the diversity of attitudes toward marriage and its consequences among those who *do* seek it inevitably means that it will not be desirable to some. At the very least, because the experience of those who have wed shows us that marriage itself cannot be reduced to just a package of rights, it is not necessary that these rights be confined to only those who marry. In that sense, the queer anti-assimilationist arguments against same-sex marriage are not at odds with the recognition that the institution means many different things to many different people.

In broader application, the lessons of these initial experiences with same-sex marriage can be extended to other forms of legal inclusion and exclusion. One obvious parallel is to voting rights and felon or parolee disenfranchisement. In South Africa, for example, the first African nation and one of the first in the world to also legalize same-sex marriage—a 1999 decision ruled that even currently incarcerated felons must be given the right to vote, with language that echoes what many of the couples in this book expressed regarding the right to marriage: "[t]he vote of each and every citizen is a badge of dignity and personhood. Quite literally, it says everybody counts."[2] In both matters, moreover, the consequences are not limited to the symbolic. In the case of ex-felon disenfranchisement, studies report that their inability to vote adversely affects successful reintegration of the formerly incarcerated by discouraging and disincentivizing pro-social civic participation. Conversely, restoring the vote encourages participation in the community as full citizens, giving these individuals a stake in their community and thereby increasing their chances of remaining crime-free. While limiting marriage does not have the same impact on public safety, it nevertheless adversely affects in similar fashion the integration of the individual, or couple, into the broader social fabric.

In the realm of family law, although far less ubiquitous than laws banning same-sex marriage, prohibitions on same-sex parent adoptions or LGBT foster parents also serve multiple deleterious functions. First and foremost, they deprive children of a legal link, and in some cases, a relationship at all, with a loving parent or guardian. As has been noted by the American Academy of Pediatrics and others, this can be harmful to children both materially and emotionally. Conversely, the ability to formally adopt or serve as a foster parent or legal guardian has far-reaching effects for both LGBT parent and child. Such things as medical decision making and insurance benefits provide a sense of interpersonal and emotional security, and also a symbolic imprimatur of state sanction. The court's typical definition of rights does a disservice to families by not framing rights as relational rather than individualistic.[3] In other words, the law forces a set of competing interests where none exist by orienting to children and their parents or would-be parents as having distinct rights claims, rather than prioritizing the mutual right to a *relationship* between the two. This ignores the lived reality of families headed by same-sex parents—and *how* rights matter to them—in a way similar to the narrow conception of same-sex marriage rights that reduces them to simply a bundle of legal and financial benefits. The ability to conceive of rights and legality as multifaceted and multipurposed, in both contexts, enhances the ability to better reflect the experience and aspirations of those most affected by them.

Because this book focuses on the experience of legal same-sex marriage in the United States, we do not know whether its findings would generalize to other parts of the world. It is estimated that, as of 2010, 4 percent of the world's population lived in places where same-sex marriages are recognized.[4] Still other nations, including Australia, Colombia, Finland, Nepal, and Germany, have debated the issue, indicating that they may be poised to legalize same-sex marriage in the near future. Additionally, several European and Latin American countries have adopted laws akin to Vermont's civil unions, which bestow all or most of the rights of marriage but reserve the terminology for heterosexual couples. These include, for example, Great Britain, where the international pop star Elton John entered such a union with his longtime partner. Some early studies suggest that there may be significant differences in the symbolic and affective meaning attached to marriage in these other countries. For example, some researchers from the UK, where civil partnerships are treated by many as marriages, have pointed out that couples there are less likely to marry in the hopes of gaining wider acceptance or to do it publicly and also note that commitment ceremonies or other same-sex marital rituals are rare. This suggests that the symbolic functions of marriage, or at least its approximation in civil partnership, are not as emphasized as they are in the United States. At the same time, the few couples who have been interviewed after dissolving their partnership almost uniformly cited discomfort with the legal consequences, suggesting they, like their American counterparts, were not primarily in it for the legal rights—and that their experience of legal partnership evolved over time.[5]

If students of marriage across the disciplines can make any universal claim, it is that there are no universals. The same can be said of law—or perhaps more specifically, peoples' experience of law. Same-sex marriage is unique as an area of sociolegal inquiry because it is such a hot-button issue, one whose legal status remains in flux and which is so fundamentally stationed at the cross-section of public debate and private reality. Even among same-sex marriages, those described in this book may be unique among the approximately 100,000-plus legally recognized same-sex unions in the United States, because of the pioneering jurisdictions in which they occurred (and their tenuous legal status, as in San Francisco).[6] And yet the story they tell about legality, emotion, and the experience of marginalization extends beyond these couples and this particular topic. It is a story that speaks to the singularly powerful impact of legal recognition and the vast diversity of expectations and experience, even within a population often lumped together as one. It is a cautionary tale against simple, tidy assumptions about seemingly distinct forms of legal consciousness, or the stability of rights consciousness over the course of a single experience or short period of time. It speaks to the reach of law in a multitude of practical and public venues, but also into the most personal recesses of emotion. It is a story that is present wherever there is inclusion and exclusion and is at the root of the most unexpected of transformations, both public and private.

Survey Instrument

University of San Francisco Same-Sex Marriage Survey

1. At the time when you and your partner obtained a marriage license at San Francisco City Hall, how long had you been together:___ years, ___ months

2. Are you still together? Yes ___ No ___

3. Do you have children? Yes ___ No ___ If so, how many? ___
   Are your children from this relationship or a prior relationship? _____

4. What is your gender? Male ___ Female ___ Other ___

5. What is your age? ____

6. What is your partner's age? ____

7. What is your approximate household yearly income? _____

8. What is your profession? _____

9. What is your partner's profession? _____

10. What is your level of education? _____

11. What is your partner's level of education? _____

12. What is your race or ethnic background? _____

13. What is your partner's race or ethnic background? _____

14. What is your religion? _____

15. What is your partner's religion? _____

16. Where do you reside (city, state)? _____

17. Would you describe it as rural, urban, or suburban (circle one)?

18. On a scale of one to five how would you describe your community's tolerance toward the gay and lesbian community:

1 ——————— 2 ——————— 3 ——————— 4 ——————— 5
(Least Tolerant)   (Neutral)   (Most Tolerant)

19. What is your political affiliation? _____

20. How strongly do you feel about your party on a scale of one to five?

1 ——————— 2 ——————— 3 ——————— 4 ——————— 5
(Weakest)   (Neutral)   (Strongest)

21. Are you and your partner registered as domestic partners in the state of California? _____ In another state (and if so which)? _____
    For how long? _____
    Why or why not? _____

22. Please rate each of the following on a scale of one to five as they relate to your reasons for obtaining a marriage license at city hall:

   a. We had always wanted to get married and could now do it officially:

1 ——————— 2 ——————— 3 ——————— 4 ——————— 5
(Not Important)   (Neutral)   (Very Important)

        Comments: _____
        _____
        _____

   b. To provide security for our family and children:

1 ——————— 2 ——————— 3 ——————— 4 ——————— 5
(Not Important)   (Neutral)   (Very Important)

        Comments: _____
        _____
        _____

   c. Because only having domestic partnerships makes us feel like second-class citizens:

1 ——————— 2 ——————— 3 ——————— 4 ——————— 5
(Not Important)   (Neutral)   (Very Important)

Comments: _____

_____

_____

d. To take advantage of the tax and other financial and legal benefits of marriage:

1 ——————— 2 ——————— 3 ——————— 4 ——————— 5
(Not Important)   (Neutral)   (Very Important)

Comments: _____

_____

_____

e. To protest the government and/or president's conservative agenda:

1 ——————— 2 ——————— 3 ——————— 4 ——————— 5
(Not Important)   (Neutral)   (Very Important)

Comments: _____

_____

_____

f. To legitimize our status as a couple or family to ourselves, our families of origin, and/or our community:

1 ——————— 2 ——————— 3 ——————— 4 ——————— 5
(Not Important)   (Neutral)   (Very Important)

Comments: _____

_____

_____

g. On a whim:

1 ——————— 2 ——————— 3 ——————— 4 ——————— 5
(Not Important)   (Neutral)   (Very Important)

Comments: _____

_____

_____

h. To make a statement about gay rights:

1 ——————— 2 ——————— 3 ——————— 4 ——————— 5
(Not Important)   (Neutral)   (Very Important)

Comments: _____

_____

_____

i. For emotional/romantic reasons (Ex: to show my love for my partner)

1 ——————— 2 ——————— 3 ——————— 4 ——————— 5
(Not Important)   (Neutral)   (Very Important)

Comments: _____

_____

_____

j. To change the institution of marriage:

1 ——————— 2 ——————— 3 ——————— 4 ——————— 5
(Not Important)   (Neutral)   (Very Important)

Comments: _____

_____

_____

k. To be a part of history:

1 ——————— 2 ——————— 3 ——————— 4 ——————— 5
(Not Important)   (Neutral)   (Very Important)

Comments: _____

_____

_____

l. Other (please explain): _____

_____

1 ——————— 2 ——————— 3 ——————— 4 ——————— 5
(Not Important)   (Neutral)   (Very Important)

Comments: _____

_____

_____

23. Which of the above was the MOST important in your decision to marry?

_____

_____

_____

24. In your own words, please describe your motivation for getting married at City Hall: _____

_____

_____

_____

_____

25. Were you present for the August 13, 2004, California Supreme Court decision legally invalidating your marriage license? ____
   If not, did you watch on television or follow on the Internet that day? ____

26. In your own words, please describe your feelings and reaction to the August 13, 2004, Supreme Court's decision: _____

_____

_____

_____

_____

27. On a scale of one to five, how surprised were you by the August 2004 California Supreme Court's decision?

1 ——————— 2 ——————— 3 ——————— 4 ——————— 5
(Stunned)   (Neutral)   (Not Shocked)

28. Were/are you a named party in the current lawsuit by the city of San Francisco against the state of California (*Woo v. Lockyer, et al.*), decided on March 14, 2005? ____
   Were you in court to hear the verdict? ____
   Were you in any prior lawsuit regarding same sex marriage? ____
   In your own words, please describe your feelings and reaction to the March 14, 2005, Supreme Court decision: _____

_____

_____

_____

_____

29. If this case were successful at the appeals level, would you marry again? _____
    Why/why not? _____
    _____
    _____

30. Have you or will you have a commitment or wedding ceremony on your own,
    independent of obtaining a marriage license? _____When? _____
    Why/why not? _____
    _____
    _____

**Optional:

   If you are willing to be contacted for a face-to-face or phone interview regarding these issues, please provide your information below:

   Name(s): _____

   Phone: _____

   Email: _____

   Preferred mode of contact? _____

   Preferred day/time to call: _____

   Preferred day/time/location for interview: _____

   Would you prefer to be interviewed individually or as a couple? _____

   If you do not reside in the SF Bay area, would you be willing to be interviewed
   by phone? _____

*While there is no financial reward for agreeing to be interviewed, the researchers
will gladly reimburse you for parking, bridge, and/or public transit tolls if you are
required to travel to the interview.

THANK YOU FOR YOUR TIME!

Overview of Survey Findings

	Mean	Variance
Instrumental motivations		
To take advantage of financial/legal benefits of marriage	4.11	1.52
To provide security for our family and/or child(ren)	3.51	2.46
Oppositional motivations		
To protest government or president's conservative agenda	4.16	1.63
To make a statement about gay rights	4.35	1.11
To change the institution of marriage	3.49	2.30
Validating motivations		
Always wanted to get married and could now do it officially	3.98	1.61
Having only domestic partnership makes us feel like second-class citizens	4.16	1.44
Legitimize our status as a couple or family	4.06	1.75
Personal motivations		
For emotional/romantic reasons	4.42	1.19
To be a part of history	4.06	1.37
On a whim	2.01	1.78

Notes to the Preface

1. Here and throughout, interviewees' first names are used with their permission on record; those who did not give permission to use their names were given pseudonyms of their own choosing (and in rare instances, when they did not come up with their own, were assigned pseudonyms by the author).

Notes to Chapter 1

1. Jia-Rui Chong, "Lifelong Partners, Activists Wed at Last," *Los Angeles Times,* February 13, 2012, A29.

2. In the surveys, the unit of analysis is the couple; 1,467 surveys were returned, representing the input of more than 2,900 individuals (taking into account the few surveys in which one spouse had since passed away, or the couple was no longer together). Some individual demographic items, such as age and occupation, were asked of each spouse within the same survey instrument, which means that average age reported is based on over 2,900 participants.

3. Gary J. Gates, "Same-Sex Spouses and Unmarried Partners in the American Community Survey, 2008" (2009), Williams Institute on Sexual Orientation Law (Los Angeles: University of California Los Angeles), available at http://www.law. ucla.edu/williamsinstitute/pdf/ACS2008FullReport.pdf. See also Verta Taylor et al., "Culture and Mobilization: Tactical Repertoires, Same-Sex Weddings, and the Impact on Gay Activism," *American Sociological Review* 74 (2009): 865, which found that 57 percent of participants were women, 55 percent were between the ages of thirty-six and fifty, couples had been together on average twelve years, 88 percent were Caucasian, and most had a college degree.

4. While I was not able to find a conclusive figure of average years together before heterosexual couples marry, estimates range from two to four years.

5. This is largely consistent with Gates's 2008 study by the Williams Institute at UCLA, which found that 56.6 percent of same-sex spouses were female. See Gates, "Same-Sex Spouses and Unmarried Partners in the American Community Survey."

6. The percentages of couples identifying as white versus non-white are identical to those found in the study of 2004 marriage participants by Verta Taylor and colleagues. See Taylor et al., "Culture and Mobilization."

7. This proportion is slightly higher than the estimate that 30 to 50 percent of same-sex couples have completed commitment ceremonies. Michael S. Wald,

"Same-Sex Couple Marriage: A Family Policy Perspective," *Virginia Journal of Social Policy and Law* 9 (2001): 291.

8. *In re Marriage Cases*, 183 P.3d 384 (Cal. 2008).

9. Of the fifty couples who were initially interviewed in San Francisco, twenty-five responded to the request for follow-up. Of these, seventeen of the couples reported that they subsequently got (re)married after *In re Marriage Cases*; one couple had split up, and in two cases one of the partners had died. The remaining five had not gotten married at the time of the follow-up interview, as they wanted to wait for the result of the November 2008 election and the fate of Prop 8, which subsequently banned same-sex marriage by amendment to the California Constitution. Even though these couples (and perhaps others who did not respond to the follow-up) are no longer technically legally married, because the distinction of import to this analysis is whether the couple displayed a commitment and *desire* to marry and took actions to do so, they remain included in the study.

10. I did not find significant differences between those interviewed alone versus those interviewed together, with the exception that interviews with both members of the couple tended to last longer, and interviewees spent more time discussing how they had met and their relationship history.

11. All of the couples and individuals agreed to have their interviews recorded, whether on the phone or in person. The majority of couples also consented to have their first names used. Those few who did not were given the opportunity to choose their own pseudonyms.

12. Michael McCann, *Rights at Work: Pay Equity Reform and the Politics of Legal Mobilization* (Chicago: University of Chicago Press, 1994).

13. Benjamin Fleury-Steiner and Laura Beth Nielsen, "Introduction: A Constitutive Perspective of Rights," in *The New Civil Rights Research: A Constitutive Approach* (Aldershot, UK: Dartmouth/Ashgate Press, 2006), 4, citing in part Patricia Ewick and Susan Silbey, *The Common Place of Law: Stories from Everyday Life* (Chicago: University of Chicago Press, 1998), 43.

14. Michael McCann, *Rights at Work: Pay Equity Reform and the Politics of Legal Mobilization* (Chicago: University of Chicago Press, 1994), 283.

15. Ibid.

16. Kristin Bumiller, *The Civil Rights Society: The Social Construction of Victims* (Baltimore: Johns Hopkins University Press, 1988), 35.

17. Susan Silbey, "After Legal Consciousness," *Annual Review of Law and Social Science* 2 (2005): 323–68.

18. Kathleen Hull, "The Legal Subjectivities of Lesbian, Gay, Bisexual, and Transgender People," presented at "The Future of Law and Society" conference, Center for the Study of Law and Society, University of California at Berkeley (2011).

Notes to Chapter 2

1. 539 U.S. 558 (2003).

2. 798 N.E.2d 941 (Mass. 2003).

3. There are one or two documented prior cases of individual county clerks issuing marriage licenses to same-sex couples, but the San Francisco Winter of Love in 2004 was the first instance of such a directive being issued by the mayor and implemented uniformly by the entire municipality and its officials. See William Eskridge and Darren Spedale, *Gay Marriage: For Better or Worse? What We've Learned from the Evidence* (New York: Oxford University Press, 2006), 22–23.

4. See Daniel Pinello, *America's Struggle for Same-Sex Marriage* (Cambridge: Cambridge University Press, 2006).

5. *Lockyer v. City and County of San Francisco*, 95 P.3d 459 (Cal. 2004).

6. See Frederick Hertz and Emily Doskow, *Making it Legal: A Guide to Same-Sex Marriage, Domestic Partnerships and Civil Unions* (Berkeley, CA: Nolo Press, 2011).

7. See Gust A. Yep, Karen E. Lovaas, and John P. Elia, "A Critical Appraisal of Assimilationist and Radical Ideologies Underlying Same-Sex Marriage in LGBT Communities in the United States," *Journal of Homosexuality* 45, no. 1 (2003): 45, 53; Paula Ettelbrick, "Since When is Marriage a Path to Liberation?" *OUT/LOOK National Gay and Lesbian Quarterly* 8–12 (1989): 12.

8. Nancy Cott, *Public Vows: A History of Marriage and the Nation* (Cambridge: Harvard University Press, 2002).

9. Nancy Polikoff, *Beyond (Straight and Gay) Marriage: Valuing All Families under the Law* (Boston: Beacon Press, 2008).

10. Nancy Polikoff, *Beyond (Straight and Gay) Marriage: Valuing All Families under the Law* (Boston: Beacon Press, 2008).

11. 852 P.2d 44 (Haw. 1993).

12. Eskridge and Spedale, *Gay Marriage*, 229.

13. 28 U.S.C. § 1738C. Andrew Koppelman makes a legal argument to the contrary. His interpretation is that DOMA is not a direct violation of the Full Faith and Credit clause, but rather is redundant of it. He points to a provision in the Constitution that allows exceptions to the clause if the law in question violates the public policy of the state to which it is being brought. See Andrew Koppelman, *Same-sex, Different States: When Same-Sex Marriages Cross State Lines* (New Haven: Yale University Press, 2006).

14. Hearing on "S.598, The Respect for Marriage Act: Assessing the Impact of DOMA on American Families," Written Testimony from the Williams Institute, UCLA School of Law, July 20, 2011.

15. Wyoming has a version of this law that was enacted before the federal DOMA law was passed. Additionally, Maryland had passed a similar law prior to 1993 but has since amended its law to recognize same-sex marriages both within Maryland and from other states.

16. See James Dao, "Same-Sex Marriage Issue Key to Some GOP Races," *New York Times*, November 4, 2004, 4; For a critique of the view that same-sex marriage debates helped to decide the 2004 presidential election, see Greg Lewis, "Same-Sex Marriage and the 2004 Presidential Election," *Political Science and Politics* (April 2005): 195–97.

17. *Baker v. State*, 744 A.2d 864 (Vt. 1999).

18. Vt. Stat. Ann. tit. 15, § 1201 (2000).

19. See William Eskridge, *Equality Practice: Civil Unions and the Future of Gay Rights* (New York: Routledge, 2002).

20. At the time of the interviews for this book, only Massachusetts had legal same-sex marriage, and it was recognized in no states but Rhode Island and New York. Since then, the landscape has shifted somewhat in that those states that have legalized same-sex marriage generally do recognize as a matter of policy same-sex marriages performed elsewhere. Additionally a small number of other states have begun to pass legislation, which allows them to recognize same-sex marriages performed in other states even though same-sex couples cannot marry there. These include Illinois and New Mexico.

21. It should be noted that the analogy to racial segregation is not without controversy. Law professors Andrew Koppelman and William Eskridge draw attention to the limitations of this analogy in their respective books on same-sex marriage and civil unions. Koppelman, for example, finds that particular characteristics of the claims made in racist and anti-gay laws and rhetoric in some cases distinguish the two. See also Russell Robinson, "Marriage Equality and Post-Racialism" (unpublished manuscript, on file with author).

22. *Lockyer v. City and County of San Francisco*, 95 P.3d 459 (Cal. 2004).

23. Judge Kramer's trial court opinion was based instead on gender discrimination, which is held to strict scrutiny in California but only intermediate scrutiny under federal law.

24. This effort was distinguished from the earlier measure overturned in court in that Prop 22 was statutory and therefore subject to review by the state supreme court, whereas the constitution is not.

25. To add further complication, the 4,037 marriage licenses that had been issued by the Newsom administration in 2004 remain on file at City Hall, even though they do not have the force of law.

26. *Perry v. Schwarzenegger*, 268 F.R.D. 344 (N.D. Cal. 2010).

27. *Perry v. Brown*, 671 F.3d 1052, *2012 U.S. App. LEXIS 2328.

28. 289 Conn. 135, 957 A.2d 407.

29. 763 N.W.2d 862 (Iowa 2009).

30. In addition to Massachusetts, Connecticut, and Iowa, these include Vermont, New Hampshire, Washington, Maryland, New York, and California, which once again became the largest state to offer legal same-sex marriage as a result of the U.S. Supreme Court's decision in *Hollingsworth v. Perry* (2013).

31. *Gill v. Office of Personnel Management* and *Massachusetts v. United States Department of Health and Human Services* (consolidated); *Pedersen v. Officer of Personnel Management*; *Golinksi v. Office of Personnel Management*; and *U.S. v. Windsor*.

32. Eskridge and Spedale, *Gay Marriage*, 21.

33. Still, the implausibility of same-sex marriage has sometimes been taken as a given by its opponents. In the closing arguments of *Perry v. Schwarzenegger*, the federal

case challenging California's Prop 8, when the attorney for the Prop 8 proponents was asked what evidence he had that marriage is meant to regulate procreation between heterosexuals (and therefore not necessary for same-sex couples), his answer was, "You don't have to have evidence."

34. Again, the trope proves persistent. As late as 2010, Representative J. D. Hayworth (R-AZ), in arguing against same-sex marriage, stated that the *Goodridge v. Massachusetts* decision could be read to legalize the marriage of a man and a horse if such affection existed.

35. Kimberly Richman, review of *Unhitched: Love, Marriage, and Family Values from West Hollywood to Western China*, by Judith Stacey, *American Journal of Sociology* 117, no. 5 (2012): 1536. Ironically, however, as Stacey demonstrates, the very forces that *eradicated* polygamy in the United States—modernization, increased gender equality, and allowing government (rather than religion) to have a hand in defining marriage—are those that laid the groundwork for same-sex marriage. See Judith Stacey, *Unhitched: Love, Marriage, and Family Values from West Hollywood to Western China* (New York: New York University Press, 2012).

36. The exception was *Baehr v. Lewin*, the Hawaii case, in which the court accepted the gender discrimination argument. However, this decision was subsequently invalidated when Hawaii amended its constitution to outlaw same-sex marriage.

37. See Eskridge, *The Case for Same-Sex Marriage*; Suzanne Pharr, *Homophobia: A Weapon of Sexism* (Berkeley, CA: Chardon Press, 1997). For a more recent example of the mutual implications of homophobia and sexism in the family law context, see Clifford J. Rosky, "Like Father, Like Son: Homosexuality, Parenthood, and the Gender of Homophobia," *Yale Journal of Law and Feminism* 20 (2009): 257–350.

38. Susan R. Schmeiser, "Changing the Immutable," *Connecticut Law Review* 41 (2009): 1495–1520.

39. Cited in Shannon Minter, "The Great Divorce: The Separation of Equality and Democracy in Contemporary Marriage Jurisprudence," *Review of Law and Social Justice* 19, no. 1 (2010): 89–146.

40. Ibid., 115.

41. Ibid., 98.

42. See Julie Nice, "The Descent of Responsible Procreation: A Genealogy of an Ideology," *Loyola of Los Angeles Law Review* 45 (2012): 781.

43. Ibid.

44. Gary L. Gates and Abigail M. Cooke, "United States Census Snapshot 2010," Williams Institute.

45. See Lynn Wardle, "'Multiply and Replenish': Considering Same-Sex Marriage in Light of State Interests in Marital Procreation," *Harvard Journal of Law and Public Policy* 24 (2001): 771–814, 798.

46. Stanley Kurtz, "The End of Marriage in Scandinavia: The 'Conservative Case' for Same-Sex Marriage Collapses," *Weekly Standard* 9, no. 20, 2004, available at www.weeklystandard.com/print/Content/Public/Articles/000/000/003/660zypwj.asp.

47. According to scholars who have since critiqued Kurtz's work as well as most standards of social science research, he seems to conflate correlation with causation—assuming that two phenomena happening in the same decade are causally related. Lee Badgett points this out in *When Gay People Get Married: What Happens When Societies Legalize Same-Sex Marriage* (New York: New York University Press, 2009).

48. See Richard Green, Jane Barclay Mandel, Mary E. Hotvedt, James Gray, and Laurel Smith, "Lesbian Mothers and Their Children: A Comparison with Solo Parent Heterosexual Mothers and Their Children," *Archives of Sexual Behavior* 15, no. 2 (1986): 167–83; Charlotte Patterson, "Children of Lesbian and Gay Parents," *Current Directions in Psychological Science* 15, no. 5 (2006): 241–44.

49. Judith Stacey and Timothy J. Biblarz, "(How) Does the Sexual Orientation of Parents Matter?" *American Sociological Review* 66, no. 2 (2001): 159–83.

50. Polikoff, *Beyond (Straight and Gay) Marriage*, 120.

51. Stacey, *Unhitched*.

52. "Asia's Lonely Hearts: The Decline of Asian Marriage" *Economist*, August 20, 2011, 21–24.

53. Kathleen Hull, *Same-Sex Marriage: The Cultural Politics of Love and Law* (Cambridge: Cambridge University Press, 2006).

54. Ironically, the original version of the law contained a prohibition against same-sex couples adopting children. Unlike in the United States, where bans on same-sex marriage between consenting adults have been remarkably successful in the same space of time that prohibitions on LGBT parents' custody and adoption rights have steadily disappeared, many European countries have legalized same-sex unions long before permitting the right to raise children in these unions.

55. Eskridge and Spedale diminish the difference between these registered partnerships and actual same-sex marriage, pointing out that the couples they interviewed tended to refer to themselves as married and did not see much of a difference. I argue that this might be a product of the particular time and place of the research—the 1990s, when same-sex marriage was not yet a legal option in these countries, and Scandinavia, where marriage may carry the same cultural resonance in contemporary society as it does in the United States. Stanley Kurtz also implies that there is no relevant distinction between such partnerships (which he rightfully compares to Vermont-style civil unions) and same-sex marriage—an assumption contradicted by the findings in chapters 3 through 6.

56. Badgett, *When Gay People Get Married*, 113.

57. Esther D. Rothblum, Kimberly F. Balsam, and Sondra E. Solomon, "The Longest 'Legal' U.S. Same-Sex Couples Reflect on Their Relationships," *Journal of Social Issues* 67, no. 2 (2011): 302–15; Kimberly F. Balsam, Esther D. Rothblum, Theodore P. Beauchaine, and Sondra E. Solomon, "Three-Year Follow-Up of Same-Sex Couples Who Had Civil Unions in Vermont, Same-Sex Couples Not in Civil Unions, and Heterosexual Married Couples," *Developmental Psychology*, 44, no. 1 (2008): 102–16.

58. Comparing couples who had civil unions in Vermont with heterosexual married couples and same-sex couples who had *not* had a civil union (this study took place before same-sex marriage was legalized in Vermont or elsewhere), same-sex couples in civil unions did not differ significantly from same-sex couples who did not have them in any way except likelihood of breakup, which was higher for those not in civil unions (and also higher than those in a heterosexual marriage). The studies find significant differences in measures of relationship quality such as level of conflict, compatibility, and intimacy, but these were higher for same-sex couples—whether in a civil union or not—as compared to heterosexual married couples. The researchers hypothesize that the relative lack of effect of civil unions has to do with their limited tangible effects, especially in the context of cross-state and federal recognition, as well as the persistence of other forms of anti-gay bias (including, presumably, the continued exclusion from the word "marriage"). A subsequent article focusing on the qualitative data from this study presented competing claims from couples, with some stating that the civil union had significantly changed their lives, and some asserting that very little had changed. However, the greater likelihood of the relationship staying intact once the couple is registered in a civil union is telling of the power of legal binding. In a subsequent study, Rothblum and colleagues compared same-sex couples who were married in Massachusetts in the first year it was legal with those who were in civil unions in Vermont or domestic partnerships in California. Since this was not a longitudinal study but rather a one-time comparative snapshot, it was not able to find much about the lasting effects of these different forms of union. The most obvious variations they found were along gender lines, rather than relationship recognition lines—meaning that they found several demographic and attitudinal differences between male couples and female couples but relatively few between those who had married in Massachusetts and those who had entered into a civil union or domestic partnership in Vermont or California, respectively. This may be due in part, again, to the relative recency of the marriages—in other words, the study was conducted so soon after the legalization of same-sex marriage in Massachusetts that the parties may have had little time to assess any effects on their relationships. The authors themselves admit in regard to this, "this study is more about who chooses to have a legalized relationship and less about how being in a marriage, civil union, or domestic partnership changes a relationship."

Notes to Chapter 3

1. Martha L. Fineman *The Neutered Mother, the Sexual Family, and Other Twentieth Century Tragedies* (New York: Routledge, 1995). Some scholars, including Fineman and Nancy Polikoff, have argued that it makes little sense for these rights to be linked to marital couples, as opposed to other familial relations, biological or otherwise.

2. Jonathan Goldberg-Hiller *The Limits to Union: Same-Sex Marriage and the Politics of Civil Rights* (Michigan: University of Michigan Press, 2002): 60.

3. Ibid., 52.

4. Shannon Minter, "The Great Divorce," 89.

5. Ibid., 115.

6. The written comments following this item suggest that for many people this was the case—several stated that they rated the item low because they had no children. A significant number also explained that they rated it highly despite the absence of children because they nonetheless considered themselves a family. In any event, the additional measure of pragmatic motivations—the item that asked about being able to take advantage of the financial and legal benefits of marriage (without reference to family or children)—allowed an additional measure of reliability in assessing the relative importance of practical financial and legal concerns.

7. The correlation between female gender and high ratings for this item was significant at the .01 level in a two-tailed test.

8. "Bears" are a subgroup within the gay community who are attracted to and identify with men of a particular build and appearance, usually large or stocky, hypermasculine, and hairy.

9. Email communication, October 8, 2008.

10. Email communication, October 30, 2008.

11. Email communication, November 9, 2008.

12. Email communication from Shannon P. Minter, legal director of the National Center for Lesbian Rights, May 22, 2010.

Notes to Chapter 4

1. Taylor et al., "Culture and Mobilization," 876.

2. Some of the difference may be accounted for by the way the question was phrased in the survey. For example, asking whether political motivations were *among* a couple's reasons for marrying will yield a higher number than asking whether political reasons were their *primary* motivation.

3. Hull, *Same-Sex Marriage*, 199.

4. This same speech was cited by Mayor Gavin Newsom himself in his explanation of what motivated him to direct the county clerk to issue the marriage licenses.

5. Both women were named Jennifer and used "Jennifer" and "Jen" interchangeably. In order to distinguish the two and avoid using last times, I refer to one as Jennifer and one as Jen.

6. See Taylor et al., "Culture and Mobilization"; Katrina Kimport, "(Un)Intended Normativity: The Legal and Cultural Meanings of Marriage for Same-Sex Couples" (December 2, 2009) (unpublished manuscript on file with author).

Notes to Chapter 5

1. 671 F.3d 105.
2. Sally Merry, *Getting Justice and Getting Even: Legal Consciousness Among Working-Class Americans* (Chicago: The University of Chicago Press, 1990); Ewick and Silbey, *The Common Place of Law.*
3. Kimberly Richman, "In Times of Need: Abused Women's Sources of Support and Changes in Legal Consciousness." *Studies in Law, Politics, and Society* 22 (2001): 171–94.
4. Michael McCann, *Rights at Work.*
5. Hull, *Same-Sex Marriage*, 200.
6. By this time, Nancy and Leilani had already had a large wedding ceremony with family and friends, and had given birth to an infant daughter. Sadly, during a chance encounter in 2012 in San Francisco, Leilani informed me that the couple was in the midst of divorce and custody proceedings.

Notes to Chapter 6

1. Stacey, *Unhitched.*
2. Martha Nussbaum, *From Disgust to Humanity: Sexual Orientation and Constitutional Law* (New York: Oxford University Press, 2010).
3. Terry Maroney, "Law and Emotion: A Proposed Taxonomy of an Emerging Field," *Law and Human Behavior.* 30, no. 3 (2006): 119–42.
4. Ty Alper, "Watching Gay Marriage Opponents Evolve," *Huffington Post*, April 2, 2012.
5. Kathryn Abrams, "Barriers and Boundaries: Exploring Emotion in the Law of the Family," *Virginia Journal of Social Policy and the Law* 16, no 2 (2009): 301–21, quote on 304.
6. Cheshire Calhoun, "Making Up Emotional People," in Susan Bandes, ed., *The Passions of Law* (New York: New York University Press, 1999).
7. Kathryn Abrams and Hila Keren, "Law in the Cultivation of Hope," *California Law Review* 95, no. 2 (2007): 319–81.
8. Ibid., 380.
9. Thirty-two percent of responded cited these reasons as most important for them. The next most frequently cited type of reason for marrying were those dealing with validation and "official" status (cited by 26 percent of couples), followed by protest-based reasons (25 percent) and, finally, instrumental reasons (17 percent).
10. This woman completed the survey on her own, as her spouse had passed away just months before. She indicated that she and her partner had both felt motivated by the same romantic impulses.
11. Hull, *Same-Sex Marriage*, n. 35.
12. Austin Sarat, "The Law Is All Over": Power, Resistance, and the Legal Consciousness of the Welfare Poor," *Yale Journal of Law and the Humanities* 2 (1990): 343–80.

Notes to Chapter 7

1. Courtney Megan Cahill, "(Still) Not Fit to be Named: Moving Beyond Race to Explain Why 'Separate' Nomenclature for Gay and Straight Relationships Will Never Be Equal," *Georgetown Law Journal* 97, no. 50: (2009): 1155–60.

2. *August v. Electoral Commission* 1999 (3) SA 1 (CC) (South Africa): 3.

3. See Kimberly Richman, "(When) Are Rights Wrong?: Rights Discourses and Indeterminacy in Gay and Lesbian Parents' Custody Cases," *Law and Social Inquiry* 30, no. 1 (2005): 137–76.

4. These include the Netherlands, Belgium, Canada, Spain, South Africa, Norway, Sweden, Portugal, Argentina, Iceland, France, Brazil, New Zealand, Uruguay, and Denmark.

5. Rosemary Auchmuty, "Civil Partnership Dissolution: Expectations and Experiences," presented at the 2012 Annual Meeting of the Law and Society Association.

6. Significantly, a 2011 report found that 130,000 same-sex couples reported themselves as married in the 2010 census, outnumbering by about 30,000 the number that could possibly be married or partnered legally under state law.

INDEX